BOUQUET OF Miracles

ROSA MARIA SANTIAGO

BOUQUET OF MIRACLES

Rosa Maria Santiago © Copyright 2021
All rights reserved.

Published by Exodus Christian Book Publishing
ExodusChristianBookPublishing.com

All Scripture quotations, unless otherwise noted, are taken from the Holy Bible, King James Version (Public Domain).

ISBN: 9798450709864

Cover and Book Design by Kristine Cotterman,
Exodus Design Studio - ExodusDesign.com

Printed in the United States of America

Dedication

To my amazing children – My Three Miracles! And to my two beautiful granddaughters (and future grandchildren). Each of you is a miracle from God and the most precious gift a mother and grandmother could ask for. I love you all so very much.

Thank you for your love, support, understanding, patience, and hugs during the good and the difficult times, especially when you were growing up. Thank you for not judging me when I made mistakes or wasn't there for you when you needed me the most or for not being the perfect mom. Thank you for being my sunshine in the middle of our darkest storms.

Remember my story. Remember the miracles in our life. Most importantly, remember that when a door shuts in your face, and you are told that what you're trying to achieve is impossible – remember that for our Heavenly Father and His Son, Jesus Christ, nothing is impossible – all you need to do is have Faith, Trust, and Believe.

Table of Contents

Introduction

It is extremely hard for someone who is getting hit with one hardship after another to have faith and believe the hardship will pass. It is even harder to believe that the devastating hardship we are going through might actually give birth to a miracle. During a hardship, the desperation of not knowing how, when, and where we are going to find the solution to our problem takes over our mind, body, and spirit—especially when we have children. I know because I have been there many times and every time, no matter how much faith, trust, and belief I had in my Heavenly Father and His Son, Jesus Christ, my faith weakened, desperation and fear took over, and I crumbled.

My hardships did not come close to the hardships many people suffer, but to me, they were devastating enough to almost destroy me. They were so consistent that in the rare occasions that I wasn't experiencing one, I couldn't enjoy the moment because I felt something horrible was heading my way. It was like being in the eye of a storm, knowing that the worst was yet to come. There were times when my body, mind, and spirit felt lifeless, with no energy left to even pray. I would fall on my knees exhausted, wanting to give up. All that came out of my mouth was a weak, "God, please help me. I can't do this anymore."

The Bible says not to question God, but I'm human—I couldn't help it. I questioned because I couldn't understand why he allowed so many hardships in my life.

Why was I rejected when I was born? Why was I sexually, physically, and mentally abused throughout my innocent childhood? Why did I suffer so many disappointments, heartaches, and betrayals? Why was I knocked down physically, mentally, and spiritually more times than I could count? Why did depression, anxiety, panic attacks, phobias, and fear, possess me just when I thought my life was going to get easier?

Why? Why? Why? A question God probably hears thousands of times a day from people all over the world who get to a point where they just can't take anymore.

One night, when I drifted off to sleep after crying my eyes out, Jesus spoke to me.

"Life is not easy. You will face many hardships—some small—some devastating, but no matter how horrible a hardship feels, I promise that you will not be alone because I will be there beside you through it all.

Don't ask why hardships happen. If it's meant for you to know the reason, you can be sure that I will let you know; however, there are times when hardships need to happen for reasons that you will learn many years later—or maybe never.

I promise that you will not be hit with more hardships than you can handle. I also promise that the hardship will pass—on my time—not yours.

All you have to do is have faith, believe, and trust in me unconditionally—meaning that when you face a hardship and feel your strength and faith weakening, you have to believe—without a doubt—that I will rescue you. To put it simply, you have to believe that if someone pushes you off a cliff—I will catch you before you hit the ground."

Unconditional trust, belief, and faith in my Heavenly Father and His Son, Jesus Christ, did not happen overnight. It was planted, nourished, and throughout the years flourished into a loving personal relationship that cannot be compared to any other in my life.

The Bible says that God and Jesus are one, but in my personal relationship with them, I speak to each one individually.

My Heavenly Father is my protector and my counselor. He loves me but will hit me upside the head when I am heading in the wrong direction—just like any loving father would.

My Beloved Jesus is my confidant. He is the one I vent and cry to because when He was human, He faced temptation, bullying, pain, abuse, and so much torture that He can relate to our suffering and understands our weaknesses.

Believe me; there are no two beings on this universe that will love and protect you as our Heavenly Father and His Son, Jesus Christ, will.

When I was asked, "How do you do it?" I answered, "My faith keeps me going." I never said more than that because I really didn't think anyone would understand my personal relationship with God and His Son.

One day, while reading the Bible, every passage I read spoke of the importance of giving testimony of God's love.

I felt God was sending me a message, and the message was that He wanted me to give testimony of my personal relationship with Him, His love for me, my hardships, my faith, and the miracles He had blessed me with.

I closed the Bible and asked, "How?"

God didn't answer my question in one day; instead, it took many days of reading and catching bits and pieces of words I felt were meant for me until finally, I had the answer.

God reminded me of the Gift of Writing He had given me since I was in elementary school. He wanted my testimony to be written.

When God asked me to write about my relationship with Him and His Son, Jesus Christ, I thought it would be easy, but I was wrong—it was so hard that I spent thirty years (on and off) trying to put my story together and every time I tried, I just sat in front of a blank page. I couldn't find the words, so each time, I gave up.

Every time I gave up, God reminded me that I had not obeyed Him. Every time He reminded me, my heart ached because I knew I had failed Him. He wasn't asking me for money or something impossible to do. He had given me the Gift of Writing, and all He asked was for me to use my talent to share the power of His love in my life with the world.

While I struggled with my frustration of not being able to write my testimony, God sent me a message through one of my readings. It said, "If you have a story to tell and never tell it—it dies with you." These words were very deep because I did not want to die without giving God the only thing He had ever asked of me.

One day, while I was dozing off, I heard a voice tell me that I had already written my testimony.

Confused, I asked, "Where?"

The voice clearly said, "In the many journals you have written throughout the years."

I still get chills when I think of that night.

It took me almost a year to find all my journals, read them, and transfer them to a file on my computer.

Once that was done, I asked my Heavenly Father, "Is my testimony supposed to be a novel or a short story—a biography or a memoir?"

He didn't answer.

While waiting for an answer, I tried to use the events in my journals to form my story and testimony, but I couldn't. I became so frustrated that I decided to step away from my computer and pray for guidance.

Through different passages, readings, dreams, and even people, I continuously received messages telling me not to worry. When the time came to organize my story, the Holy Spirit would guide me.

Months later, a very cold and snowy winter forced me to practically hibernate indoors for weeks, making it the perfect time to take a shot at my writing. As soon as I typed the first sentence, the words just kept flowing, sentence after sentence, and paragraph after paragraph—I was on a roll.

There was no doubt in my mind the Holy Spirit was guiding me. Finally, my story and testimony of the many miracles my Heavenly Father, and His Son, Jesus Christ, had blessed me with— began to take form.

I can DO
ALL THINGS *through* CHRIST
who strengthens ME.
PHILIPPIANS 4:13 KJV

CHAPTER ONE
Emilia

*"Even if my father and mother abandon
me, the Lord will hold me close."*
(Psalm 27:10 KJV)

Most call me Rosita, but my real name is Rosa Maria, and my story begins before I was born, with my mother—Emilia.

In the 1930's it was customary for poor Puerto Rican parents to send their children to live with families who were wealthy. The children helped with house cleaning, laundry, cooking, babysitting, and farming in exchange for an education and a better way of life.

Emilia was born in that era. She lived with her parents and eleven siblings in a small village on the southeast coast of Puerto Rico. Their home was a one-room hut built from uneven old planks of wood, ceiling covered with plantain leaves, and floor covered with hay.

Emilia's father, Ramon, was an alcoholic. Her mother, Maria, a patient God-loving woman, whose main concern was to care for her children while dealing with her husband's drunken behavior.

A few towns from Ramon and Maria lived a tall, dark, slim, quiet man named Leonardo. He was not rich yet lived comfortably while earning a decent salary as the best head herdsman in the south.

Leonardo had a loving wife, a son to carry his name, a great job, a respectable reputation, a house, a car, and savings. There was only one thing missing in his life—a daughter.

One very hot and humid morning, while Leonardo and his men led the herd southeast, they stopped near a waterfall to rest.

Leonardo had just closed his eyes while resting on one of the huge rocks across from the waterfall when he heard laughter.

Startled, he looked up, spotting three children high on the rocks, preparing to dive into the foamy waters below.

One particular child caught his eye—a little girl. She couldn't have been more than four years old.

Leonardo watched mesmerized as the little girl extended her arms upward, closed her eyes while smiling up at the sky, and then dove into the water below where she disappeared.

When she reappeared, she swam like a mermaid, jumped out of the water, and ran up the rocks back to the spot where she repeated her angelic diving performance.

The little girl's giggles brought a smile to Leonardo's tired face as he watched her; the old desire of having a little girl overpowered him.

Without a second thought, Leonardo walked closer to where the children were swimming.

"Come here, child," he called out to the little girl. The child shyly swam towards Leonardo.

"What is your name?"

"Emilia," the little girl softly said as she stood before him, shivering.

Leonardo looked into Emilia's beautiful green eyes. She had very light skin—probably from Spaniard descendants. Her dark hair was long and straight with curly ends.

"Where do you live?"

Emilia pointed towards the path she had climbed earlier.

"Please take me to your father," Leonardo instructed.

Emilia put her small hand in Leonardo's hand and pulled him towards the path that led to her home.

When they reached her humble home, Emilia called out, "Papa! Papa! Someone is here to see you."

Ramon suspiciously walked towards Leonardo. As usual, he had been drinking.

"Emilia, go inside and put on some dry clothes before your mother gets back," he instructed as he shook Leonardo's extended hand.

The two men exchanged names and then walked away from the hut deep in conversation.

Leonardo came straight to the point, "Ramon, how would you feel about Emilia staying with my family a couple of weeks per month?"

"Go on," Ramon said, not showing any emotion.

"My wife and I have a son, but I feel she needs a little girl to do the things a mother and daughter usually do. Emilia would be a companion to my wife. In exchange, we will provide everything she needs—including a good education. She will be treated as part of the family and will be able to visit you regularly. What do you say, Ramon?"

A few years ago, when Ramon had heard that most of his neighbors had found wealthy families for their children, he had selfishly taken advantage of this type of arrangement with his older children. Although he did not show it in front of Leonardo, inside, he was scheming on how to get the most out of this opportunity.

"Leonardo, I have eleven children, of which seven are already part of similar arrangements. My wife made me promise I would not send the youngest four children away. Emilia is the third youngest—she is almost four years old. It would break my wife's heart..."

"I understand, Ramon. It was a pleasure meeting you," Leonardo interrupted as he prepared to shake Ramon's hand and walk away.

"I'm not finished," Ramon quickly said. "My wife is very fragile. If Emilia visits us, it would be emotionally draining for Maria to let go of her repeatedly."

Confused, Leonardo asked, "What are you saying?"

"I'm saying that the arrangement you propose will not work for me; however, I have one that might."

Suspiciously, Leonardo slowly said, "Go on."

"What if I give you Emilia permanently? Emilia will have the opportunity to be part of a prominent family. My wife and Emilia will not have to relive a heartbreaking separation every month, and you and your wife will have the little girl you always wanted—forever. Everyone wins."

"Let me get this straight. You would give your daughter away just like that?"

"Yes, I am willing to give my daughter away when it's for her own well-being and future; however, not just like that. I know my wife. I know she will be so grief-stricken that she will need bed rest for weeks. While she's in bed, I will have to care for her and my other children—which means I will not be able to work until she is back on her feet. How am I going to feed my family during such a difficult time?" Ramon asked sarcastically.

"Are you saying you want to sell me your daughter?" Leonardo asked in shock and disgust.

"Leonardo—I would never sell my daughter. I'm simply asking for a little money to tie my family over for a few weeks. After all, the only people that are benefiting are Emilia, you, and your wife."

Leonardo slowly sat on a fallen tree trunk. He stared at Ramon while wondering how a father could sell his daughter.

Part of him wanted nothing to do with Ramon's proposal, especially if it was going to hurt Emilia and her mother—yet another part felt this was a God-sent opportunity to have the daughter he had always wanted.

Leonardo was about to refuse Ramon's proposal when a horrible thought entered his mind, "What if Ramon sold Emilia to someone else—someone who was a pervert."

The thought quickly brought him to his feet as he firmly said, "It's a deal, Ramon."

Ramon hurried home before Maria returned from the market. Without saying a word, he lifted Emilia in his arms and quickly made his way back down the path that led to the stream where Leonardo sat on his horse waiting.

Without the slightest sign of remorse, Ramon handed Emilia to Leonardo.

Frightened and confused, Emilia whimpered, "I want Mommy."

"Go with him! He's going to give you a better life," Ramon sternly told her.

Emilia knew better than to disobey her father—shyly, she obeyed as Leonardo gently sat her in front of him on the saddle.

Emilia thought back to that morning. She could still hear her mother's soft voice singing while combing her hair. She could still feel the warmth of her mother's hug just before she left for the market promising to return soon.

"Mommy, where are you. Where is this man taking me?" she silently cried.

Emilia thought of the seven brothers and sisters that had left with her father and never returned.

"Maybe this nice man is taking me to see them," she thought.

Sensing Emilia's fear, Leonardo whispered, "Please do not be frightened, Emilia. I know this is all very confusing to you right now, but I promise that from this moment on, I will do everything in my power to make sure you are happy. Some day you will understand. I promise."

With tears in her eyes, Emilia glanced up at the waterfall where she had been playing and laughing with her two brothers just a few hours ago.

She spotted her father climbing the path that led to her home. "PAPA," she called out.

Ramon did not look back.

Exhausted, Emilia leaned her head back on Leonardo's chest and closed her tear-filled eyes.

On the ride home, Leonardo began to worry. Not only about the cold-blooded way Ramon had sold his daughter, but to how his wife would react to Emilia.

Suddenly, Leonardo's thoughts were interrupted when Emilia let out a broken sigh that melted his heart, disappearing all his worries. Full of joy and gratitude, he raised his eyes up to the sky and said, "Thank you, Lord, for giving me a miracle—the little girl I have always wanted."

Leonardo's wife, Rosa, was a small domineering woman who came from a huge family of prominent landowners. She was the oldest of seven siblings—and the only female.

Rosa was so close to her parents that when she married Leonardo, their wedding present was a house next to theirs, which Leonardo reluctantly accepted.

When Rosa heard her husband's footsteps, she rushed to the living room to greet him.

"Leonardo, why are you so late? Dinner is…" she stopped.

"Who is this?" she asked suspiciously.

"This is our daughter," Leonardo answered without batting an eye.

Rosa stood in the middle of the living room in shock. The thought of Leonardo cheating on her and having a child with another woman filled her heart with anger and resentment. She wanted to argue and ask for an explanation, but instead, she kept quiet.

The first two weeks in Emilia's new home were challenging. Rosa and her son were not thrilled with Emilia's presence. They barely spoke to her.

Emilia hardly ate or drank—most of the time, she sat with a blank stare.

One morning, after sipping warm milk, Emilia fainted. Leonardo rushed her to the nearest hospital, where she went into a coma for a few days. When she woke up, she had amnesia. She couldn't remember who she was, her parents, or where she came from.

In a way, the amnesia was a blessing because when Leonardo and Rosa brought Emilia home from the hospital, she automatically began calling them Papa and Mama—something Leonardo did not deny.

Emilia tried to keep herself busy while Leonardo worked, but when she tried to help around the house, Rosa sternly told her to go outside and play or go next door and help feed the farm animals. She found her mother's behavior odd and wondered why she was so cold and distant towards her yet so loving towards her brother.

Sometimes, Emilia experienced flashbacks from her past, which left her confused and sad because even though she did not recognize the faces, she felt she knew them.

When Emilia felt sad, a beautiful woman would appear to comfort her. She had a very soft voice and spoke in a warm and loving manner. When the lady sang, Emilia felt safe and loved.

Emilia's happiest moments were when Leonardo came home. As soon as she heard him open the front gate, she would be the first one to jump into his arms. After showering him with kisses, he would give her the usual gift of cookies.

Leonardo and Emilia were inseparable, which made Rosa very jealous. Her feelings of resentment towards Emilia were very strong.

How dare her husband bring a child he had with another woman home? How dare he expect her to raise this child as if she were hers?

One morning, while Rosa washed dishes, she felt a draft. Out of the corner of her eye, she spotted a shadow — as if someone had just walked by her into the dining room.

A strange feeling overpowered her. She wiped her hands and immediately walked into the dining room nervously, asking, "Is someone here?"

Rosa slowly walked across the dining room towards the archway that led into the living room.

When she entered the living room — she froze. Standing next to Leonardo's rocking chair was a beautiful young woman.

Chills ran through her body. This woman couldn't be real — she seemed almost transparent. Who was she? What did she want?

The woman answered Rosa's unspoken questions, "My name is Maria. I am Emilia's mother.

I am here to ask you to stop treating my daughter so harshly. She is not Leonardo's daughter. She is only an innocent victim.

My husband sold my daughter to Leonardo in exchange for beer money while I was at the market one morning. When I returned, Emilia was gone. My heart couldn't take the grief, so I died.

Ever since then, God has allowed me to comfort Emilia when she is sad by singing to her until she falls asleep—something you should be doing."

In a low whisper, Rosa slowly said, "I didn't know."

Maria walked closer to Rosa, continuing, "I know, that's why I'm here. I came to tell you the truth, hoping you could find it in your heart to accept and love Emilia. Please be kind to my daughter. Please be a mother to her."

Rosa's heart softened with every word Maria spoke. She sat quietly, with her head bowed, tears running down her cheeks. When she looked up, Maria was gone.

After what seemed like hours, Rosa returned to the kitchen to continue washing dishes. Her heart was full of peace and love. From that moment on, she loved and protected Emilia as her own.

When it was time to register Emilia in school, Leonardo was not able to because they did not have her birth certificate; therefore, he had no choice but to visit Ramon.

When Leonardo reached the old shed, he found it abandoned.

About half a mile from the shed, he came across a couple who knew Ramon and his family. Over coffee, the husband told Leonardo the heartbreaking story, "We've known Ramon and Maria since they married. We were the ones that suggested they find families that would give their children a better life. It worked for us, so we really thought it would work for them; unfortunately, it didn't. Ramon did not make the usual arrangement with the families he found; instead, he sold his children to wealthy families in exchange for drinking and gambling money. The last time I saw Maria was at the Market. She seemed very fragile and dazed. All she kept saying was that her children were all gone—even her babies. A few weeks later, she died. Shortly after, Ramon hung himself."

Leonardo slowly stood up. He thanked the nice couple for the coffee and the information and headed home.

On the way home, Leonardo had mixed emotions. Part of him felt bad about Ramon and Maria's death; another part felt relief because now nobody could take Emilia away from them.

As for Emilia's birth certificate, Leonardo hired a lawyer who was able to get a copy just in time for her to start school on schedule.

While Emilia lived happy and carefree—Rosa carried a guilt that could only be removed by telling Emilia the truth about her birth family. She had an overwhelming feeling this was what Maria wanted.

One Saturday morning, while Emilia helped feed the farm animals—Rosa approached Leonardo.

"We have to tell Emilia about her birth family!" Rosa firmly said as she added sugar to her coffee.

Leonardo banged his coffee cup on the kitchen table as he angrily raised his voice, "Why do you insist on disrupting Emilia's life? She's been through hell. She's happy. We'll tell her when she's older!"

Rosa was not giving up. "Instead of worrying about us disrupting Emilia's life, maybe you should start worrying about someone else disrupting it."

"What do you mean?" Leonardo asked.

"I mean that this town is full of family members and friends who know about Emilia's past. Eventually, someone will bring up the subject. Do you want her to hear a twisted version of the truth from one of them? Or would you rather she learns the truth from the people who love her the most? Besides, how long do you think you could hide her birth certificate from her? How long before she asks why we don't have the same last name?" Rosa's lips quivered as she spoke.

Leonardo sat silently starring at the spilled coffee on the table.

Rosa slowly got up and stood behind her husband. Lovingly she wrapped her arms around him while gently placing her chin on his head. Softly she whispered, "I don't want to hurt Emilia any more than you do, but she deserves to know the truth. It's our responsibility to make sure she is told in the least hurtful way."

Leonardo leaned back and rested his head on Rosa's chest. Sadly, he said, "You're right—we'll tell her tonight."

That night while Leonardo, Rosa, their son, and Emilia sat around the dining room table, drinking their usual hot chocolate—Leonardo told Emilia who she was and where she came from.

Emilia listened quietly with tears running down her cheeks.

Rosa and Leonardo glanced at each other worried. "Emilia, we love you—is there anything you want to say or ask us?" Leonardo asked, concerned.

Almost in a whisper, Emilia asked, "What did my mother look like?"

Leonardo was about to say he had never met her when Rosa interrupted, "She was just as beautiful as you are, dear. She had your skin color, eyes, and hair, and the softest voice."

Emilia's face lit up as she said, "The lady with the beautiful singing voice. That's my mother?"

"It's very possible, dear. You see, your mother was ill and probably suffered a lot, so God sent for her so that she would not suffer anymore. Mothers always sense when their children are sad, so when you were sad, your mother asked God to let her sing to you so you could feel better," Rosa lovingly said.

Leonardo was confused. He had no idea what they were talking about. He was about to ask Rosa when she put her hand over his, lifted her eyebrow, and shook her head. Leonardo somehow felt he should not ask any questions right then.

Emilia walked shyly to Leonardo, who pulled her up on his lap. She hugged him just like she had done so many times, then she whispered, "Thank you, Papa—I love you so much."

Emilia lived the type of life she would never have lived if she had not been sold to Leonardo. Aside from being showered with love and affection, Rosa and Leonardo made sure she had everything she needed, plus more.

By the time Emilia reached her senior year of high school, she had grown into a beautiful young lady with long dark wavy hair, green eyes, and a lovely singing voice.

Emilia carried herself with social grace and glamour that made her very popular among her classmates—especially the young men. Unfortunately, the boys respected Leonardo and were very afraid of him, making it almost impossible for Emilia to date or have a boyfriend.

Emilia loved her parents, but they were so overprotective of her that she felt like they were smothering her. She didn't even have privacy at school because Rosa's brother was a teacher there and constantly watched her. That's why she was super excited to complete her internship at the accounting office where her cousin Lisa worked. At last, a place where her parents couldn't supervise her.

At the accounting office, she met Omar, who was originally from Ponce, and who had just broken up with his fiancée Nora. He was the oldest of nine children, of which most were already professionals or attending college.

Without giving himself time to get over Nora, Omar became interested in Emilia. His looks and charm won Emilia's heart, and somehow between Emilia's constant begging and Lisa's good references on Omar—Leonardo gave in and allowed Omar to visit Emilia.

In those days, when a young man visited a young lady, they were not allowed to hold hands, hug, or kiss; instead, the couple would sit side by side while the girl's parents remained close by supervising them.

For Emilia and Omar, it was very hard to stay away from each other, especially when they constantly hugged and kissed at the office when they were alone.

One rainy Sunday afternoon, while Leonardo sat in the living room reading his newspaper, near the door that leads to the balcony where Emilia and Omar were—Omar gently pulled Emilia to him and kissed her passionately.

When Leonardo did not hear Emilia and Omar speak for a while, he became suspicious. He did not trust Omar's intentions, mostly because Omar was ten years older than Emilia. The silence was way too long for comfort, so he dropped his newspaper and walked out to the balcony, where he found Emilia and Omar completely lost in a passionate kiss.

When Emilia slowly opened her eyes and saw Leonardo, she jumped out of Omar's arms, not knowing what to do or what to say.

The look on Leonardo's face was full of rage as if he had caught his daughter having sex with a man—except, this wasn't sex—it was just a kiss.

Omar turned and faced Leonardo. With deep embarrassment, he nervously said, "Please forgive us; we meant no harm or disrespect to you. We are in love."

Leonardo looked directly into Omar's eyes as he firmly said, "You have six months to get married or else you will never see each other again." Then, he furiously walked back into the house, slamming the door behind him.

That was it! No conversation—No rational thinking—No arguing.

Emilia was in shock; this was not the Leonardo she knew. Leonardo was a rational man of few words. His family and friends valued his opinion. When he spoke, people listened mainly because they knew that if he spoke, it was because he had something important to say. This time, he wasn't being very rational.

Why didn't Emilia argue with Leonardo?

Well, for one thing, Emilia was young and actually thought she was in love. After all, Omar was her first passionate love. Besides being tall, dark, and handsome, he was mature with a prospering career as an accountant. She was totally infatuated by the affections he bestowed upon her. Marrying Omar would be a dream come true, so why question or argue with her father?

What about Omar? Why didn't he tell Emilia that he couldn't marry her because he was in love with someone else? Why was he standing in front of Leonardo shaking in his shoes instead of speaking up—obviously, because he was a coward!

It didn't take long for Leonardo's rage to disappear. He loved Emilia too much to stay angry. Emilia was his princess, and he was going to do everything he could to make sure she had the fairy tale wedding that she deserved—no matter what the cost.

The wedding ceremony was held at the Baptist church Omar attended, and the reception in the beautiful gardens of the church. Family, friends, and the most important people in town were invited.

Every detail was exquisite. The chapel and garden were decorated with lilies of the valley. The beautiful pond in the garden was filled with water lilies and goldfish. Surrounding the pond were round tables covered with white lace and ribbons.

Behind the chapel, just off the path leading to the garden, were two rooms. The larger room was set up with an exquisite buffet of the most expensive tropical foods; the smaller room was filled with presents piled high atop three long banquet tables.

The entire wedding party was elegantly dressed in white. The simple elegance of the bridesmaid's full satin ankle-length dresses, each holding flower baskets filled with lilies of the valley, could only be compared to a royal Spaniard wedding.

When Emilia appeared at the entrance of the chapel holding Leonardo's arm, she looked like a princess straight out of a fairy tale book, wearing a simple satin-laced gown and long lace-trimmed cathedral bridal veil covering her soft wavy dark hair.

After the ceremony, the happy couple, together with their wedding party, gathered at the front of the church to have their pictures taken.

While the newlyweds stood at the church steps waiting for the photographer to line up the bridesmaids and groomsmen for the photoshoot, three women appeared out of nowhere, snatching Emilia's bouquet from her hand while yelling horrible slurs.

When Leonardo heard the commotion, he ran towards the front of the church, with his son right behind him. They arrived in time to hear all three women chanting incoherently. All they understood was, "…you and your heirs will be cursed for all eternity."

When the women saw Leonardo coming towards them, they fled down the street waving Emilia's bouquet.

Everyone stood in shock—even the reverend, but no one was more stunned than poor Emilia, whose face had turned as pale as her dress.

When Leonardo reached Emilia, she fell limp into his arms and weakly asked, "Papa, who were those women?"

"I don't know, princess, but don't worry; we're not letting your wedding be ruined by three crazy women whom we don't even know. Come, let's go inside and rest before the reception begins," Leonardo said, as he and Rosa helped Emilia walk towards the gift room.

Emilia's brother and his wife were instructing the guests to go into the reception area when Lisa walked up to them. She seemed very upset.

"Lisa, where's Omar?" Emilia's brother asked.

"I don't know," Lisa nervously answered. "The last time I saw him, he was running after those women."

When Rosa opened the door to the gift room, she gasped at the horrific sight before her. The room was completely destroyed. The gifts were opened, smashed, torn, or shattered. The three banquet tables were flipped, and red paint had been splashed everywhere.

Emilia buried her face in Leonardo's chest, sobbing uncontrollably. Leonardo lifted her up and carried her back into the chapel.

Confused and outraged, he left Rosa with Emilia and stormed down the chapel stairs that led to the garden.

"Does anyone know who trashed the gift room and who the three women that verbally assaulted my daughter were?" Leonardo yelled.

Lisa stood nervously waiting for Omar's family to speak out. When no one did, she called out, "I know who the three women are, and so does Omar and his family. The woman that snatched the bouquet is Omar's ex-fiancée, Nora. The other two are her mother and sister."

Omar walked in when Lisa was speaking. He nervously walked up to Leonardo and said, "I'm sorry. I wish this hadn't happened. Nora and I broke our engagement weeks before I met Emilia. The other day she burst into my office demanding I marry her instead of Emilia. When I told her it was too late, she stormed out furious, saying I would regret it. I never thought she was capable of doing something like this."

The more Omar said, the more outraged Leonardo became. Just as he was about to launch himself on Omar, his son stopped him,

"Papa! Emilia has suffered enough today. If you assault her husband, she will be devastated. Please calm down."

Leonardo took a deep breath and turned to Omar and said, "Go to Emilia—comfort her—and let's move on to the reception."

Lisa ran up to Leonardo.

"Uncle Leonardo, those three women cannot be trusted. They are evil," Lisa said with concern in her voice.

Frustrated, Leonardo said, "The Bible says to be vigilant of your enemies. From this moment on, I will be vigilant of those women—and of Omar."

The first six months of Emilia and Omar's marriage were full of nightmares, mysterious occurrences, and much sadness.

Emilia tried very hard to be a good wife and make her husband happy. She kept the cottage immaculate and prepared scrumptious meals.

Unfortunately, Omar didn't notice any of her efforts because he was hardly home. Every night he came home late with the excuse that he was working late hours at the office.

Omar's behavior caused Emilia so much anxiety that she began having nightmares where she saw herself running barefoot in the dark, in her nightgown, with a kitchen knife in her hand, looking back as if someone were chasing her.

One night, she was awakened from one of her nightmares by Omar's heavy breathing. He had made love to her in her sleep.

Two months later, Emilia learned that she was pregnant. When she broke the news to Omar, he didn't bat an eye; instead, he told Emilia he wanted a divorce so that he could marry Nora. That same night he moved out.

The weeks after Omar moved out were extremely hard on Emilia. She hardly ate or spoke, which made Leonardo and Rosa worry about her and the pregnancy.

"I ran into one of Omar's co-workers at the market this morning," Rosa told Leonardo as she put away groceries. "She said Omar was not in his right mind and that he is in jeopardy of losing his job. He never speaks of Emilia or the baby. It's as if they didn't exist."

"Do you think the rumors are true?" Rosa asked Leonardo.

"To be honest—I don't care. My concern is for the safety of Emilia and our grandchild," Leonardo said. "Pack her things and move her back home—I don't want her alone in that house."

Emilia's health was deteriorating. When it got close to her giving birth, she was so fragile that Leonardo had to hire a mid-wife to stay with her until the baby was born.

Emilia's labor was long and difficult. She was so weak that she could barely push. She lost a lot of blood during labor, so as soon as the baby arrived, they were both rushed to the hospital, where they were hospitalized immediately.

A month later, Emilia and her baby girl were well enough to go home. When they arrived, her parent's house was full of relatives, friends, and more baby gifts than she needed.

Even though Omar had not visited his daughter at the hospital or even bother to donate blood in case she needed a transfusion, Emilia hoped he would know they were home.

One night, while Emilia rocked the baby to sleep, she softly said to her daughter, "Now that we are both stronger, there are a few things you and I need to do.

First, we have to take you to meet your father. I have a feeling once he takes a look at you, he is going to fall madly in love with you.

Secondly, we have to give you a name. How about Grisel? Do you like that name?"

When the baby heard the name Grisel, she made a funny face.

"Don't you like it? Why not—it's a beautiful name.

I'll tell you what. First thing in the morning, we'll go visit your father, and while we're there, we'll ask him if he likes it. Ok?"

The next morning, Emilia dressed her baby in a beautiful pink ruffled outfit with a matching bow. When Rosa asked where she was going, she simply said she was meeting some school friends in town to show off the baby.

As Emilia walked towards Omar's office, she began getting nervous. "What will I tell him?" she thought.

She wished Lisa would still be working with Omar, but she wasn't. She had moved to New York with her husband shortly after Emilia's wedding.

Omar, who happened to be looking out his office window, froze when he saw Emilia walking towards his office with her baby.

Emilia took deep breaths as she walked closer to Omar's office door. She could hear her heart pumping in her ear. "Calm down, Emilia—you have to do this for your daughter. You must be strong," she told herself sternly.

Emilia held her head high and proudly marched straight into Omar's office without knocking.

Omar's heart sank when he heard the door open and Emilia's soft voice say, "I am not here for me—I am here because it's only right that you meet your daughter."

Omar did not respond—he didn't even turn around to acknowledge their presence.

With tears in her eyes and a broken heart Emilia said, "Take a look at your daughter because this is the last time you'll ever see her."

Omar stared out of the window without saying a word.

Emilia felt as though a knife had pierced her heart. A stab of anger filled her very soul as she realized that her baby girl was being rejected by her father, just like she had been rejected by her own father.

"Coward," Emilia cried furiously, storming out of Omar's office holding her precious baby tightly in her arms.

With Leonardo's help, Emilia was able to get a quick divorce. She was free to go on with her life. Right after the divorce, Emilia's little girl was baptized. She was named Rosa Maria—after both of Emilia's mothers—and, lovingly called, Rosita.

Emilia dreaded living in the same town where Omar and his family lived. She wanted to move far away, but every time she mentioned it to her parents, they would bring up all the reasons why a young woman with a baby should not live alone.

One day they had a terrifying experience. Emilia had left Rosita in her crib for a few minutes while she went to the kitchen. When she returned, Rosita was gone.

Emilia screamed frantically as she looked all over the room, thinking that Rosita had fallen from the crib.

When Leonardo and Rosa heard the screams, they ran to Emilia's room, where they found Emilia crying frantically.

As they searched the house, Leonardo noticed that the living room door leading to the balcony was open. He ran towards the door, with Rosa and Emilia at his heels.

When he walked out to the balcony, he stopped.

An old woman with long gray stringy hair and raggedy torn clothes was holding Rosita.

Leonardo signaled for Rosa and Emilia to step back as he spoke softly to the woman, "Where are you taking my granddaughter?" he asked.

"This is not your granddaughter. This is my baby. She was missing, and I found her. I'm taking her home," the woman snarled.

While Leonardo tried to convince the old woman to give him the baby, Rosa slipped out the back door and ran to ask her brother for help.

Rosa's brother quietly made his way down the path that led right to the balcony stairs behind where the woman stood. When he came up behind the old woman and grabbed her, Leonardo was able to rescue Rosita.

They sent for the police, and the woman was taken away.

The frightening experience left Rosa with a bad feeling. She felt the old woman was sent to kidnap Rosita and that Nora was behind it. When she shared her concern with her family, they offered a solution; however, she wasn't sure if Leonardo would agree to it.

When Leonardo heard Rosa's plan, he was outraged.

"Have you lost your mind, Rosa?" Leonardo yelled. "New York City is across the ocean in another country. They don't even speak Spanish there. How is Emilia going to survive in a strange country, without knowing the language, and with a baby, when she's barely a child herself?"

Rosa tried to convince Leonardo by saying, "Leonardo, please listen to me. Most of my nieces and nephews have already migrated to New York City. Did you forget Lisa and her husband moved there shortly after Emilia's wedding? My brother says Lisa is doing fine. Her husband found a very good job and is providing for her and the children. He said Emilia and the baby could live with them until Emilia finds a job and an apartment. Emilia and Lisa have always been close—she won't be alone—she'll be with family."

"I, too, have worried and have been praying for a way to keep Emilia and the baby safe. This idea sounds crazy, but it could be the answer to my prayers," Leonardo said with sadness in his voice.

That night while they sat around the dining room table drinking their usual hot chocolate, Rosa presented the idea to Emilia.

"I love you both and will miss you terribly but moving far away from Omar and Nora is the best thing I can do for myself and my daughter. I've been praying for a way out, and I feel this is God's answer to my prayers," Emilia said.

Leonardo's heart was breaking, but he knew it was time to let Emilia and Rosita go—for their safety.

"I'll arrange everything," Leonardo said sadly. "Remember one thing, Emilia. Once you are in New York City, if you ever feel it's not where you want to be, all you have to do is come home. Do you understand?"

"Yes, Papa, I understand. Please don't worry—God will keep us safe!" Emilia said tearfully as she hugged them tightly.

I can DO
ALL THINGS *through* CHRIST
who strengthens ME.
PHILIPPIANS 4:13 KJV

CHAPTER TWO
Dark Childhood

*"Though I walk through the valley of the
shadow of death, I will fear no evil: for
thou art with me; thy rod and thy staff
they comfort me."*
(Psalm 23:4 KJV)

On a chilly October day in 1954, Emilia courageously left the comfort of her home and departed to a strange country, barely speaking the language, with no husband and her twenty-three-month-old daughter—me.

Lisa and her husband welcomed Emilia at the airport with loving hugs, but during the ride to their apartment, Emilia sensed a little tension in the air, which made her a little nervous.

"Lisa, you have no idea how much I appreciate you letting us stay with you. You don't have to worry about me staying long. If everything goes according to my plans, I should be moving into my own apartment in six months tops," Emilia said.

"Six months?" Lisa asked. "Aren't you being a little unrealistic, Emilia? It's going to take a few years just to secure a job that will pay for an apartment."

"No. My goal is six months," Emilia said as she took out a piece of paper from her pocketbook and handed it to Lisa. "See? It's the third item on the list of things I must accomplish during my first year in New York City."

"Emilia, did anyone explain the challenges you will be facing as a Puerto Rican living in New York?" Lisa's husband asked.

"Except for the big buildings, cold weather, and language—how different can it be from life in Puerto Rico?" Emilia answered.

"Ok, first, let me start by teaching you a little about what an immigrant faces when they arrive," Lisa's husband began. "No matter what country they come from, they face discrimination, economic exploitation, and racism."

"We're not immigrants; we're American Citizens," Emilia interrupted.

"It doesn't matter," Lisa's husband continued, "This year alone, close to 75,000 Puerto Ricans left the island and migrated to New York looking for work. Unfortunately, because of criminal acts committed against the United States Government by a group of Puerto Ricans that arrived before us, Puerto Ricans not only face what every immigrant face, but they also face the extra challenge of being viewed as anti-American. We are discriminated against so badly that many restaurants have signs that read 'No dogs or Puerto Ricans allowed.'"

"Ok, but if all those thousands of Puerto Ricans, including you and many of our family members, are making it here—so can I," Emilia said.

"Let me finish, Emilia," Lisa's husband impatiently interrupted. "You will face more challenges than we did. Because of your age, not having a husband, and having a baby, you will be falsely judged. This is going to sound harsh, but I'm being realistic.

You will be seen as a whore with a baby out of wedlock."

"I am not a whore! When I conceived my baby, I was a married woman. How dare you say this!" Emilia angrily said.

"Emilia, he is not saying you are a whore—he's saying American society will view you as one which will make it even harder for you to find a job and an apartment," Lisa said.

"Then I will prove American society wrong," Emilia said stubbornly.

Living with Lisa and her family did not turn out the way Emilia expected. Although she was thankful to have a place to stay, she was not happy—not because we were sleeping in the living room sofa bed and lacked privacy; but because she felt we were in the way.

The desire to have her own apartment motivated Emilia to search for work every single day; unfortunately, although she knew some English and had office skills, no one hired her.

One cold winter afternoon, after a long day of job searching, Emilia came home to find I was burning with fever. She rushed me to the hospital where I was hospitalized with German measles and quarantined for five days in an isolated room where Emilia could only see me through a small glass window.

I was a little over two years old when I was hospitalized. At that age, children tend to imitate what others do, so it wasn't surprising that I would play nurse with my cousins, imitating what the nurses did to me at the hospital.

One day, Lisa caught me trying to take my cousin's temperature rectally with my play thermometer. Lisa freaked out.

Later that day, after a freezing morning of job hunting, Emilia came home to find her suitcase packed at the door and me with my coat on.

"Your perverted child tried to molest my daughter!" Lisa's husband screamed as he threw me into my mother's arms. "You are no longer welcomed in our home—Get out!"

Lisa's husband pushed Emilia out to the hallway and shut the door without even giving her a chance to say a word.

Holding me close with one arm and her heavy suitcase with the other, Emilia slowly walked into the cold rainy afternoon. "What just happened?" she asked God, too exhausted and confused to cry.

Emilia needed to find shelter before dark, so she put aside her pride and called the only other person she knew that lived in Brooklyn—my father's brother, Uncle Daniel. She hated to turn to her ex-in-laws, but she was desperate.

After Uncle Daniel spoke to Emilia, he came for us. Over a cup of hot chocolate, Emilia told him what had happened earlier at Lisa's.

"Lisa and her husband handled this situation the wrong way," Daniel said. "Rosita is just a child, and children tend to imitate grownups. They had a right to be upset, but all they had to do was discuss it with you so that you could teach Rosita not to play nurse in the manner she did."

"They threw us out like animals," Emilia sobbed. "I didn't know what to do or who to turn to."

"Don't cry, Emilia. You made the right choice. I have an idea, just let me make a phone call, and I'll tell you about it," Uncle Daniel said and then stepped out for a few minutes.

When Daniel returned, he seemed very excited. "Ok, here's the plan," he announced. "I'm getting married in a few weeks. After the wedding, Sarah and I are going to Puerto Rico for a month. You and Rosita can stay here. In fact, we wouldn't mind if you lived with us until you find your own place."

"Thank you, Daniel. You're an angel sent from heaven," Emilia said softly with tears in her eyes.

Before Uncle Daniel and Sarah left for their honeymoon, they asked Sarah's sister, Martha, who lived down the street, to help Emilia find her way around the neighborhood. Martha was a very kind woman who loved to help her neighbors. Everyone loved and respected her. Daniel and Sarah left trusting that we were in good hands.

With Martha's help and guidance, we were able to settle into our new life. Emilia felt comfortable living in the friendly neighborhood and was seriously considering Uncle Daniel's offer of living with him until she found her own place.

When Emilia opened up to Martha about all she had been through since her father sold her, Martha couldn't help but feel the need to help make life easier for Emilia.

"Emilia, as you probably already noticed, I am respected in this neighborhood. I love children and take very good care of them. I have babysat every child on this street at one time or other, mostly because their mothers trust me.

If you allow me, I am willing to babysit Rosita while you look for work and continue to do so after you find a job.

I have done many favors for a lot of the landlords in this area. Once you find a job, I'm sure one of them will rent you an apartment so that you can stay in the neighborhood," Martha said.

"That sounds like a wonderful idea. Thank you so much," Emilia said as she hugged Martha tightly in excitement.

A few days before Uncle Daniel and Sarah returned from their honeymoon, Emilia found a job at a jewelry factory in Manhattan.

Things seemed to be falling into place for Emilia. She lived in a safe place surrounded by nice neighbors, earned a salary, and had a very nice lady taking care of me while she worked. Finally, she had found peace and normality in her life. Or had she?

Martha's kitchen smelled of Puerto Rican spices as she rushed to prepare dinner. It was one of those days when she just didn't have enough time on her hands.

Gratefully, her 18-year-old son had volunteered to put me down for a nap so that his mother could tend to her cooking.

In the back bedroom, the afternoon sun peeked through the white lace eyelet curtains casting dancing shapes on the wall.

I laid on the edge of the bed, as if in a trance, motionlessly staring at the colored marbles on the floor where I had been playing just a few minutes before.

"Mommy, where are you?" I thought.

"Help Me! Take me away, far, far away from this pain!" I pleaded silently.

A vision of the beautiful colored marbles inflating and coming to my rescue appeared before me. They picked me up and hid me among their sparkling colors while swirling and immersing into each other like waves, numbing the unbearable pain he was causing me.

While at work, Emilia was overpowered by a feeling that something had happened to me. Her desperation was so great that she asked to leave her job early.

An hour later, Emilia arrived. She rushed into Martha's apartment, finding her standing by the sink, washing dishes.

The sweet old lady immediately looked up and smiled at Emilia while cheerfully saying, "You're early! Rosita is in the backroom taking a nap."

Emilia, still sensing something was wrong, rushed through the living room that led to the back bedroom, never imagining what she was going to find.

The bedroom door was ajar. Emilia was about to enter when she noticed someone's feet dangling from the corner of the bed. Then, she heard sounds similar to the ones Omar made every time he climaxed.

Emilia pushed the door open and momentarily froze at the sight before her, for there on the bed laid her three-year-old daughter starring hypnotically at the floor, with her little dress pulled up to her waist.

Emilia's scream shattered the silence in the room. The animal sat up dazed, slowly realizing he had been caught.

Emilia threw herself on her knees next to the bed, shaking me as she tried to bring life to my hypnotic stare.

"Is she dead?" Emilia thought. "No, I can hear her breathing!"

Emilia's scream was heard for blocks. In a matter of minutes, the apartment was full of neighbors, including Uncle Daniel.

Uncle Daniel took my small limp body in his arms, pushing his way out of the apartment.

"What kind of animal rapes a defenseless three-year-old child?" Daniel muttered to Sarah as he drove us to the hospital.

I can still recall the horrible experience of being raped. I remember the room. I remember the beautiful colored marbles. Strangely, I can't remember his face, the hospital, the spectators, the trial, or the courtroom.

Nine months after the rape, my mother explained some of what had happened. She told me I had been in the hospital because a very bad man had hurt me, but not to worry because he was sent to jail for a very long time and would never hurt me again.

She told me we were going to visit my grandparents in Puerto Rico, but what she didn't tell me was that she planned to leave me in Puerto Rico until I was old enough to start school.

I vaguely remember the plane ride to Puerto Rico or saying goodbye to my mother, but I do remember my stay with my grandparents—especially my grandfather.

I remember running around barefoot in the fields and eating some really yummy meals and desserts.

I remember sitting on my grandfather's lap listening to stories of when Emilia was a little girl, working with him in the yard, sipping hot chocolate before bedtime, and lots of road trips—mostly, I remember feeling safe.

While I was living with my grandparents, I heard the names "God," "Jesus," "Mary," "Guardian Angels," and "Saints." I had never met them, but I felt they were very important people because my grandparents spoke of them many times.

Every evening after dinner, my grandparents sat together and spoke to God. They called it "praying." I would sit next to them, quietly waiting for God to appear.

When I asked my grandfather why I couldn't see God, he said we couldn't see God, but that he could see us and that he watched over us and protected us.

I was too young to understand, so I just took it for granted that there was an invisible person named God who everyone around me seemed to know.

Sundays were a very special day. We dressed in our finest clothes and went to visit God's house, which they called "church." After church, my grandfather took us on a country road trip, where we stopped to eat lunch and buy homemade bread and yummy desserts.

During the week, I was very busy. In the mornings, I helped my grandfather with yard work. In the afternoons, my cousin Christina and I helped my godfather feed the farm animals.

After dinner, I sat with my grandparents to say the Rosary, and then my grandmother and I would go next door where Christina and I sang our hearts out, imitating singers and watching television until 9 p.m.

Before bed, I played cards with my grandparents while drinking hot chocolate made with fresh warm cow's milk.

At bedtime, my grandparents tucked me in, and then from our beds, we prayed out loud before going to sleep.

My grandfather was the kindest and most loving person. I followed him everywhere. I don't know why everyone feared him because I certainly didn't. He hardly spoke to others, yet he spent hours telling me stories and teaching me things like mixing cement and building a shelf.

My grandmother was a very nice person too, but very different from my grandfather. She wasn't gracious like my mother. She smoked a cigar and sometimes used foul language—different from my grandfather, who was very educated and well-spoken.

My grandmother and my godfather (her brother) spoke of God but also mentioned witches, demons, and curses. Sometimes they said things that scared me. When I told my grandfather, he said not to be scared because God protected me. He also told me not to listen to them when they spoke such gibberish.

Two months before I turned five years old, my mother sent for me because it was time to start school. I was heartbroken because I didn't want to leave my grandparents. It was a tearful goodbye, but they comforted me by assuring me I would be visiting them every summer, spring, and winter school breaks.

Emilia had changed. I barely recognized her when she greeted me at the airport. Her hair was short and wavy. She was dressed like the elegant women on television sitcoms.

She treated me differently, too. She was less lovable and very critical. She kept remarking on how fat and dark I had gotten and how dirty my feet looked. She also said I looked more like my father and nothing like her, which coming from my mother was not a compliment.

Her remarks made me feel worthless, belittled, and like a tiny worm. At that moment, I wished I was back in Puerto Rico with my grandparents, far away from the strange woman who obviously thought very little of me.

My new home was in the Bedford Stuyvesant section of Brooklyn. We shared a small apartment with two of my aunts from my father's side and a cousin who was three years older than me.

Emilia worked long hours at a jewelry factory in Manhattan. My aunts also worked, so although my mother dreaded leaving me with a babysitter, she had no choice. Luckily for my mother, my cousins' babysitter was willing to care for me also.

The sitter was a sweet elderly lady who lived on the first floor of our building, who had an adult mentally delayed son in his forties living with her. She often left us alone with her son while she went to the store.

One afternoon, while the sitter was at the store, my cousin and I played a game with the sitter's son. The game consisted of running around the coffee table avoiding being grabbed. The first one grabbed lost.

Around and around, we went until the sitter's son grabbed my cousin, who laughed hysterically when he threw her over his shoulder, ran to the bedroom, and closed the door.

I waited patiently in the living room, wondering why they were taking so long. Just when I was about to go find out, the sitter's son appeared without my cousin. He said she was taking a nap and that we would continue playing without her.

Around the table, I ran laughing, trying to avoid being trapped between his legs.

When he grabbed me, he held me so close I could smell his breath. He caressed the back of my neck. I felt uncomfortable. I froze.

Fear overpowered me when he began touching me in places not to be seen or touched by anyone.

He picked me up and carried me into the bedroom where my cousin slept on one of the twin beds.

Suddenly, I wasn't in that room anymore. I felt like I had been carried far away—far away from the pain. All I saw was a rainbow and beautiful colors swirling around me.

When I awoke, I was alone in the bedroom, "Was it a dream,

or did it really happen?" I thought.

Suddenly, reality hit me when I sat up, and I felt the same pain I had felt when I was three years old.

Again, I had been hurt. Again, I couldn't scream. Again, there was no one there to help me. "Is this part of life?" I wondered.

I never told my mother what had happened, nor did I bring up the subject with my cousin. Instead, after school, I went directly to my apartment, where I did my homework and cleaned until my mother came home from work.

When my mother realized that staying in our apartment cut down on her time of having to help me with homework and cleaning, she said it was ok, as long as I let the sitter know when I was home from school and went to her if I needed anything.

Living with my cousin and aunts was fun. On weekends we went to the movies, restaurants, shopping, and family gatherings. During the summer, we went to the beach, amusement parks, and Bear Mountain.

The summer before I started third grade, my youngest aunt got married. A few weeks later, my other aunt and my cousin moved to an apartment a few blocks away.

Living alone with Mom was not what I had expected. The change from the happy chaos of an apartment full of females to finding myself alone most of the time was drastic.

Mom woke me up every morning at 6 a.m. before leaving for work. Then I dressed, had breakfast, and left for school alone. After school, I watched television, did my homework and chores until Mom came home at 7 p.m.

Elementary school was pretty normal, except for the sarcastic remarks from some of the other students who said I was a teacher's pet and a nerd.

I guess they called me a nerd because I had straight "A's," which I had because I spent most of my time studying and because if I brought home grades lower than an "A," my mom would punish me.

I was considered a teacher's pet because my teachers were very nice to me and always used me as an example of how a student should behave. I don't think they realized they were doing more harm than good; or how embarrassing it was for me.

Tanya was my one and only best friend. She lived down the block in a pretty brick house. Her mother was my piano teacher.

I loved going to Tanya's house because her mother, grandparents, and siblings were all very loving. They welcomed me into their home as if I were part of the family.

Some Sundays, Mom allowed me to go to church with Tanya and her family. I loved going to their church because their choir sang beautiful, uplifting songs that made me feel so happy. I was devastated when Tanya moved.

Spending the summers in Puerto Rico with my grandparents helped ease the pain of losing Tanya. It was my second home, and I loved being there because it was the only place where I felt safe.

When I was away visiting my grandparents, Mom met Lucas, who worked as a foreman at the jewelry factory where she worked. At first, Mom introduced him as a friend, but later I found out Lucas was more than a friend—he was her boyfriend.

Lucas visited us twice a week. On Thursday night, he slept over, and on Sunday, he took us out on the town in his red convertible, where we went to nice restaurants and expensive stores. He always bought us very nice clothes and lots of presents.

For the first two years of Mom's relationship with Lucas, I really liked him; mostly, because he made my mom happy. He acted like a dad, and I felt very comfortable around him.

What we didn't know was that Lucas was the Devil himself.

He fooled my mom into thinking he loved her and was a decent man so that she would trust him.

He used his power and money to make my mom depend on him by paying her bills, rent, and food. And he used his fake "father figure" act to win me over and make my mom think he loved me as his own.

Unfortunately, the love my mother felt for Lucas blinded her to the point that she did not see how evil Lucas was. He was a woman beater, drug dealer, adulterer, and child abuser.

He was not only using my mom to fulfill his animalistic desires, but he was also fattening up his prey before striking—and that prey was me.

By my ninth birthday, I had developed much faster than most nine-year-old girls and was very self-conscience about it. That's when I started noticing that Lucas stared at my body a lot, which made me feel very uncomfortable.

One Thursday night, I woke up to the sound of my mother crying and Lucas yelling, so I tiptoed to Mom's bedroom door to listen.

When I heard a noise like someone being slapped, I peeked through the keyhole. What I saw will haunt me forever, for I saw my mother naked, and Lucas hovered over her, slapping her and making wild animal sounds.

I was so frightened I hurried back to my bed and huddled under the covers, not knowing what to think.

Later that night, Lucas came into the living room and sat on the chair right across from the sofa bed where I slept. I faked being asleep while peeking to see what he was doing.

He lit a cigarette and sat looking at me for a long time while breathing very heavily like a hungry animal. It was the first time I feared him.

Sixth grade was bittersweet for me. It was the year I was fortunate enough to have the most loving and caring teacher, Mrs. Davis, who helped me shine as a student. It was also the year I faced peer pressure, bullying, and racist attacks, for the first time.

I had never had a problem with anyone in school because of my race or skin color, even though 95% of the students were African American—but, in sixth grade, everything changed.

Most sixth graders belonged to packs or gangs, and if you didn't belong, they made your life in school absolutely miserable by bullying, beating, harassing, or pressuring.

On top of being Hispanic and lighter skin-colored than most, I was a straight "A" student, which made it even worse for me because the gang members loved to bully nerds and kids of other races.

My scariest experience was one afternoon when Mrs. Davis pulled me aside to tell me she was dismissing me early because she had heard a gang member in my class tell another student that her gang was going to jump me when we came out of school. I was petrified and shaking as I ran all the way home.

In the midst of the bullying, peer pressure, and racism, I was able to keep my grades up, won third place in the UNESCO city-wide essay contest, and was appointed Valedictorian of my graduating class.

The more I shined as a student, the more my enemies persecuted me. The fear of being attacked by one of my classmates for being smart, Hispanic, light-skinned, and a teacher's pet, did not allow me to enjoy my accomplishments.

Persecution did not end at school. I was persecuted by men for being an innocent ten-year-old girl with the body of a sixteen-year-old. I was a temptation to men, even though I was not doing anything to provoke them.

At home, I was persecuted by my own mother, who abused me verbally, mentally, and physically, all because I looked like my father, instead of being slim and light-skinned with green eyes like her.

Mom repeatedly told me that she thought someone had switched me in the hospital after I was born. When she introduced me to someone, she would say, "This is my daughter. She's dark because she looks like her father, and she's overweight because she has gland problems."

Mom hated my appearance so much that she forced me to do adult exercises for hours. Every time I begged her to give me a break—she threatened to hit me. She wanted my nose to be straight like hers, so she put clothespins on my nose to make my nose straighter. She put me on a very strict diet, which didn't work because it made me so hungry I would eat boxes of donuts and cakes after school. Cakes, donuts, and cookies became my comfort food.

Mom constantly accused me of doing things that I hadn't done and punished me severely for them. One time she beat me with an umbrella so badly that my back was bleeding. Once, on Good Friday, she made me kneel for hours on a pile of uncooked rice while she listened to the Stations of the Cross on television. I don't remember why she was punishing me, but I certainly remember the pain on my knees.

I trembled when Mom came home because I knew that even if I hadn't done anything wrong, she would find a reason to yell or hit me. I was never good enough, or pretty enough, for her. She made me feel worthless. Yet, she loved me and provided for me—and I loved her.

Towards the end of sixth grade, Lucas paid for Mom to go to beautician school some nights after work. When my mom told Lucas she didn't want to leave me home alone until midnight; he promised he would stop by and check on me so she wouldn't worry.

I feared Lucas and didn't want to be alone with him. How was I going to avoid him now? I couldn't. He was smart. He would find a way to trap his prey, and he wasn't going to waste any time doing so.

The first night my mother started school, he let himself into the apartment with the key Mom had given him. I didn't expect him and was taking a bath with the bathroom door open.

He startled me when he came into the bathroom and sat on the toilet seat. He conversed as if being there while I bathed was the most natural thing in the world.

When he sat on the edge of the tub and started to dry me, I froze. I was too scared to say anything that would make him angry, so I stayed quiet.

He wrapped a towel around me, lifted me up, and took me to my mother's bed, where he continued to dry my shivering body.

I will not detail what he did next, except to say that it was the first night of many years of sexual abuse.

Why didn't I tell my mother? Because she was always in pain and crying. Many nights she locked herself in her room and didn't even come out to see how I was. I felt she was going through a lot, so I didn't want to burden her with all I was going through—besides, she probably wouldn't have believed me anyway.

My first year in junior high school was very different from elementary school. From the beginning, it was very clear to me that the best way to survive seventh grade was to avoid being a nerd or standing out in any way that would create problems for me.

I stopped shinning as an "A" student and became an average student with passing grades.

I stopped dressing conservatively and began using makeup, wearing shorter skirts, and styling my long hair.

The new person I had become did not get bullied, pressured, threatened, harassed, or sexually assaulted in school or on the streets. It wasn't who I wanted to be—but it kept me safe.

I met my first boyfriend in seventh grade. Jason was tall, sweet, and the most decent boy I had ever met. He treated me respectfully without expecting sexual favors in return.

His twin brothers, on the other hand, were totally opposite from Jason; and very mischievous.

One day, I made a huge mistake. I let the twins stay in my apartment with their girlfriends while I was at school.

All day long, I had this weird feeling, so I left school early and went home. When I entered the apartment, there were boys and girls half naked making out everywhere.

What happened next was like a scene from a movie. Seconds after my arrival, someone yelled, "Truant cops are outside."

Kids pushed by me running out of the apartment—some going out the window and down the fire escape stairs.

In the middle of the chaos, my mother walked in. I tried to explain to her that the only thing I had done wrong was to give my key to one of the twins and that I was not part of whatever was going on.

My mother did not believe a word I said. Not even after the twins confessed. Not even when I begged her to check my attendance at school for that day. Two weeks later, I was on a plane to Puerto Rico.

Mom thought sending me to Puerto Rico was a punishment, but for me, it was the greatest thing that could have happened to me because with my grandparents, I was safe from sexual abuse, beatings, bullying, peer pressure, stress, and drama. I was relaxed, free, and happy.

Unfortunately, staying with my grandparents was not permanent. As soon as I completed eighth grade, my mother sent for me.

I didn't want to go back to New York. I didn't want to face Lucas again, and I was terrified of what high school would be like.

When I arrived home, I received a big surprise. Mom had switched rooms with me. She was sleeping in the living room, and I had my own room, which she had decorated beautifully.

My room looked like a princess' room with white French provincial furniture and a canopy bed. I finally had privacy and a door

I could lock if Lucas came back and tried anything.

"Thank you, Mom. I love it," I said as I hugged her tightly.

"Well, you're almost fifteen. It's about time you had your room," she said with a smile.

That's when I noticed how different she looked from the last time I had seen her. She looked very tired and was dressed simply. The high society air and glamour she had, was gone.

"Is something wrong, Mom?" I asked.

"Yes, but just temporarily," she began. "I don't work at the factory with Lucas anymore. I found a new job, but they are laying people off, and I'm afraid I might be next."

"Don't worry, I'm sure Lucas will help you if you lose your job," I said.

"Lucas isn't helping me financially as much as he used to. He barely comes around. I don't know what I'll do if I lose my job," she sobbed.

"We can always go back to Puerto Rico," I said hopefully.

She didn't answer me, but I could tell she didn't like what I had suggested.

My first year of high school was full of new and exciting events.

I started ninth grade at Prospect Heights High School, which was an all-girl school. I guess Mom thought it would be easier for me to keep out of trouble if I wasn't around boys.

I was worried about Mom being laid off, so I found a part-time job, after school, at a small fabric store a few blocks from home. I worked every day after school until closing time and occasionally on Saturdays.

Out of nowhere, two of Mom's eleven siblings, who lived in New York, arrived at our doorstep announcing they had been searching for her. I was a little skeptical about whether these people were really related to my mom, but she was so happy to reunite with her flesh and blood that when I questioned her, she simply assured me they were, so I believed her.

In total, I met eleven cousins who visited us constantly. The best part was that Lucas wasn't too happy with my mom's family being around all the time, so he distanced himself even more.

I finished my first year of high school with average grades. Mom wasn't too happy, but I really didn't care because I would rather be a normal student than bullied for being a nerd.

Mom's behavior towards me changed a little. She still accused me of things I hadn't done and criticized me constantly, but at least she wasn't physically abusing me as much as before.

My Sweet Sixteenth birthday was a Cinderella experience, and I owe it all to my mother, who surprisingly turned out to be my Fairy Godmother for the day.

I don't know how Mom did it, but she managed to rent, cater, and decorate a small room in a banquet hall and take care of every little detail, including preparing for the event, sewing my gown, plus sewing most of my cousin's gowns.

The day began with a full bridal-type experience at the beauty salon consisting of makeup, hairstyle, manicure, and pedicure.

We returned home to find the apartment full of cousins busy getting ready to leave for the banquet hall—laughter and chatter filled the room. As soon as the girls left, Mom hurried to help me dress.

With tears in her eyes, she did some final touches to my hair and makeup before allowing me to look in the mirror. Then, she told me to close my eyes and not open them until she said so.

When I opened my eyes, I saw the reflection of a beautiful princess with a shiny tiara on a head full of soft curls, dressed in a baby blue princess-style gown with a soft sparkling bodice and satin skirt, and plastic high heeled slippers that looked like glass slippers. My Fairy Godmother had turned me into a princess.

Every moment of my Sweet Sixteen birthday was like a fairy tale dream come true. Every detail was perfect. I was Cinderella for one whole night—and I owed it all to my mom.

The excitement of my first year of high school, the joy of having friends and cousins to have fun with, and the beautiful memories of my birthday came crashing down two months after my birthday.

One night, my boss asked me to stay after closing to help him balance the books. I was busy adding receipts when he grabbed me from behind and dragged me to a couch he kept in the office—he then beat me and raped me.

This time there were no colored marbles or escaping into a fantasy world. This time, I felt every painful moment. I felt my insides ripping. I tasted blood on my lips.

I did not see this coming. My boss always treated me with kindness and respect. I trusted him.

When I came home that night, Mom was beside herself when she saw my bruises. I didn't tell her what happened; instead, I said I had been mugged walking home from work that night. She believed me and didn't argue when I told her I was quitting my job because it was too dangerous to keep walking alone at night.

Alone in my room that night, I analyzed my life.

I had been hurt by every man in my life, except for my grand-father. My father rejected me when I was born, and men had sexually abused me since I was three years old. I came to a decision. If I was going to be sexually abused by men for tempting them when I wasn't, why not really flirt and tempt them?

My mother physically and verbally abused me. She beat me for things I had not done and said things to me that made me feel ugly and worthless. Again I thought, if I was going to be accused and beat for something I didn't do, then why not do the things I was being accused of?

Why be good? Why believe that an invisible guardian angel was watching over me and would sweep me up and take me to a beautiful fantasy world every time I was hurt?

That night all the anger and negative emotions I had hidden inside for so long possessed every fiber of my mind and body. That night I started walking a very dark path.

I stopped being good and turned into the temptress and bad daughter I was accused of being.

I cut class to hang out at the park with my friends. I flirted with older men, tempted them, and went as far as going to hotel rooms with them.

I didn't have sex. Sex did not turn me on or make me happy. What made me happy was being held, caressed, and told I was beautiful and that they loved me.

I wanted badly for one of those men to turn into a Prince Charming that would love and protect me forever, but all they wanted was sex, and when I didn't give it to them, they became angry and abandoned me.

I was playing with fire. Tempting and not giving a man what he wanted was very dangerous. I was lucky that one of those men did not become angry enough to beat me or, worse, kill me.

Towards the end of my sophomore year in high school, Mom and I moved to a three-bedroom apartment in a very nice two-family house on the other side of Brooklyn.

The new neighborhood was full of young people my age from all ethnic backgrounds, who welcomed me into their circle without judging me or caring about my race or skin color. We all had loads of good clean fun playing streetball, biking, and dancing in the street.

This new life was exactly what I needed to help me turn away from my dark ways and live a normal teenage life.

By the time I started my junior year in high school, I was working a part-time job as a Girl Friday at a lawyer's office, and I had a boyfriend. His name was Angelo, who was a Private First Class in the US Air Force. Angelo treated me with respect. He said he loved me and even told my mother that someday he was going to marry me.

Things were looking good for Mom too. She made friends with the neighborhood mothers and got together with them often. The owner of the two-family house we lived in liked Mom so much that he pretty much let her do whatever she wanted in his house, including gardening and barbequing in the backyard.

It was time to leave my past behind and focus on my future, so I set goals. I would graduate high school, go to college, and then be a famous writer. I would marry Angelo, who planned to buy us a cottage house with a white picket fence where I would be a stay-at-home mom who took care of our three kids while writing tons of books.

I was going to live the American dream that my mom never had a chance to live. I was in heaven!

During my senior year of high school, my world tumbled. The Air Force transferred Angelo to Spain. I was crushed. And even though we spoke on the phone constantly, and he sent me loving letters reminding me of our future together, they just weren't enough for me.

I had an addiction to love, attention, and caresses, and now that Angelo was far away, I needed to fill my craving for love some other way. So, I turned to one of my other passions—dancing.

I loved to dance and was very good at it, but dancing in my room in front of a mirror just wasn't enough.

One day, my friend Amanda, who was over eighteen and went club dancing a lot, invited me to go dancing with her and her boyfriend. When I told her that my mom would never give me permission to go to a club, she said, "Don't tell her we're going to a club. Tell her you're going to a party at my apartment and then sleeping over."

Mom believed my lie, not just once, but many times, probably because she had a very busy life with her new boyfriend (the owner of the house) and all her neighborhood friends.

I became addicted to club dancing. It was exciting, fun, and totally innocent—until I met Peter, who was about twenty years older than me.

Peter was Amanda's boyfriend's friend. When I first met him, he said he was single. He seemed decent, and my friend backed it up by saying her boyfriend had never mentioned anything bad about him.

Peter was a great dancer, and I loved dancing with him. Amanda said we danced like we had been dancing together all our lives. He was such a gentleman, and when we danced, he made me feel so special.

One night, while sleeping over at Amanda's, I shared my guilt of hiding club dancing and Peter from my mom and Angelo.

"Don't feel bad, Rosita," Amanda began. "Look at it this way. Dancing is fulfilling your craving for attention and passion. Peter and dancing are stopping you from fulfilling these urges in a way that could lead to you cheating on Angelo. You're not hurting anyone, so why stop?"

Dancing had become an addiction, just like the need for love, attention, and caresses. And, like any addiction, the craving was so strong that I had to satisfy it.

Dancing with Peter made me feel so good that when he confessed he loved me and wanted to spend the rest of his life with me, I did not discourage him by telling him that I was not in love with him. I was afraid that if I did, he would not be my dance partner anymore.

When I was on the dance floor, I turned into a totally different person. When I danced, the music and I became one, as if we were making love.

I didn't realize that while I considered my dancing art and a form of expression—the men who watched me thought I was teasing them. In their eyes, my dancing was a temptation.

My actions had consequences. Lying to my mother to go dancing with an older man had consequences. Not telling Angelo about going dancing had consequences. Tempting men with provocative dancing, although not intentional, had consequences. And the consequences—were all bad.

After months of clubbing, my mother discovered the truth behind my sleepovers at Amanda's and forbade me to see Amanda again. I rebelled by running away with Peter and sending Angelo a "Dear John" letter, without thinking of the pain I was inflicting on the people I loved; or what the consequences of my actions would be.

Peter rented a room in his friend's apartment. It was supposed to be for us to live together, but instead, he only stayed over a couple of times a week. When I asked him why he didn't sleep over every day, he said he would eventually.

On weekends, Peter took me to clubs and bars, but not with my friend Amanda; instead, he took me to strange clubs full of nasty men. When these men asked me to dance, I had to because he would beat me when I got home if I didn't.

One day Amanda came over to warn me about Peter. She said her boyfriend had told her that Peter was married and had five kids, and lived with his wife.

"Be careful, Rosita; I found out Peter pimps young girls, which is probably what he is planning to do with you if he hasn't already," Amanda said. "He puts a certain drug in their drink so that they do what he says."

"You have to get away from this man before it's too late," Amanda sobbed.

One night while clubbing, a drunk, perverted man who Peter had ordered me to dance with got fresh with me. I pushed him away and ran out the club's back door to a dark alley that led to a side street. I ran as fast as I could until I found a taxi.

A few minutes after I arrived at the apartment, Peter stormed in and beat me until I passed out. The next morning, I called my mother, who came and took me home.

Mom wanted to press charges against Peter, but I was so afraid of retaliation that she finally agreed not to.

Whatever Peter did to me had terrible consequences to my health because shortly after I came home, my menstrual period disappeared for months.

At first, Mom thought I was pregnant, so she took me to the doctor, where tests proved that I wasn't.

Many more tests were done until I ended up being hospitalized at a research hospital because they couldn't figure out what was causing my period to stop.

Blood was drawn constantly until they couldn't find my veins. I was placed on machines that turned me upside down and went around and around.

After two weeks of pure torture, I pleaded with Mom to take me out of the hospital. She spoke to the doctors, who agreed, with the condition that I continue getting blood work done daily for two more weeks.

The final diagnosis was that I would never be able to have children.

I was a mess, so I quit school in my senior year of high school to try to pick up the broken pieces and get back on my feet again.

I wanted to be alone, so Mom spoke to the owner of the house we lived in, who agreed to rent me the basement apartment.

I was depressed. I stayed in the apartment. I didn't socialize, and I slept most of the time.

One day, one of my neighbors came to visit. He said he thought I was under some type of spell and that he had a book that would help me get rid of anything bad that was holding me down.

As soon as I started reading the book, weird things began happening.

Every night I had a weird dream where I heard voices and saw black shadows rising through the living room floor and then surrounding my bed.

This recurring dream freaked me out so much that I rolled the living room rug to see what was on the floor one day. I was shocked to see a trap door nailed shut in the same spot where the black figures appeared in my dreams.

I became so frightened of being alone that I let my two dogs and their puppies in at night. Many nights they would wake me growling and barking as if someone were in the room. Obviously, something was causing them to bark—and whatever it was—was invisible.

My isolating myself worried my mom, so she went to a spiritual fortune teller to see if some light could be shed on what was happening to me.

The person told my mom that an evil snake was living in the basement. When she told me, I said, "I'm the only person living in this basement."

Mom didn't answer me; instead, she gave me a really weird look.

Was she implying that I was evil?

I kept reading the book, hoping to get rid of whatever was haunting me. My mistake was that I was reading the wrong book. I should have been reading the Bible—not a white witchcraft book.

One night, the dream felt very real. Black figures surrounded my bed chanting, while an animal-like figure had its way with my body while I was suspended in the air.

My mother's bedroom was directly over mine. When she asked me the following day if I had fallen asleep with the TV on, I began to suspect that what I thought was a dream — was real.

That's when I prayed. I asked God for forgiveness and pleaded for him to protect me.

God, who was watching over me the whole time and waiting patiently for me to come to him, listened to my prayers, grabbed my hand, and pulled me up from Satan's evil grasp.

A few days later, I moved back to my old room, in my mother's apartment.

There is no doubt in my mind that during my weakness and vulnerability, I had become easy prey, and if I hadn't prayed and gotten out of that basement apartment — Satan would have taken my soul.

I can DO
ALL THINGS *through* CHRIST
who strengthens ME.
PHILIPPIANS 4:13 KJV

CHAPTER THREE
The Mustard Seed

*"Faith is the substance of things hoped
for, the evidence of things not seen."*
(Hebrew 11:1 KJV)

On my eighteenth birthday, I made a resolution to leave my past behind and focus on getting a degree in writing so that I could pursue my dream of becoming an author.

I wanted to start college right away, but since I had dropped out of high school, I had to put college on hold until I was able to take the General Education Diploma exam. In the meantime, I searched for a job so that I could save money for college.

I was lucky. As soon as I started job hunting, I was hired as an order clerk at a Brooklyn jewelry factory. The first step was accomplished. Now, I just needed to focus on my goals and not let anything or anyone get in the way of reaching my dream.

I was on the right path until I met Manuel, the head foreman in the jewelry factory's production department, and who played a huge part in the unexpected turn that took me far away from the road that led to my dreams.

Manuel was different from other men, maybe because he was twenty-one years older than me and very old school in his ways.

He was polite and very attentive. He treated me with respect and consideration—something I wasn't used to.

Manuel and I became good friends. We shared our stories over lunch and walked together to the train station every evening.

Besides working at the factory, on weekends, Manuel was the lead guitar player of a well-known Hispanic band that played in different areas of New York, New Jersey, and Pennsylvania. He had played on several Spanish radio and television stations and even recorded an album. He was very well known among famous musicians.

Manuel had separated from his wife after catching her in bed with his best friend. He had four children (two boys and two girls) who lived with his wife. He shared that his wife was not a fit mother and that he wished he could get custody of his children before something happened to them, especially the girls (ages three and nine).

I thought of Manuel's situation with his wife and his children constantly. I pictured those little girls being abused just like I had been abused during my childhood. I wanted to help him keep his children safe, so when he told me that he hadn't filed for divorce because to get custody of the children, he needed to have a stable home and babysitter, I immediately came up with a plan; but first, I needed to run it by Emilia.

After telling Emilia Manuel's story, I asked if she would ask the owner of the house to rent him the basement apartment and if she would babysit his kids while he worked. I assured her it would only be temporary until his divorce was final and he had custody of the children.

Emilia wasn't thrilled about babysitting four kids, but the extra money would come in very handy, so she agreed.

During the six-month custody battle, Manuel was allowed to bring three of his kids home on weekends—adorable, three-year-old Jamie—nine-year-old Julie, who was understandably overprotective towards her little sister and very suspicious of me—and seven-year-old Junior, who was a handful. We spent every weekend going on outings, bike riding, shopping, the circus, street fairs, and just having fun.

Manuel got his divorce and full custody of his four children, mostly because his wife never showed up in court just like she never showed up for the divorce hearing, and because Manuel proved to the judge that he had provided the children with a safe home and a reliable babysitter.

As soon as the children moved in permanently, our worlds were turned upside down. Being around them daily was totally different from when they came to visit us on weekends.

When Emilia mentioned that the kids were a handful and that she might not be able to take care of them, I realized the seriousness of their behavior.

Julie and Junior were totally out of control. Junior did not want to live with his father, so he constantly cut school. Julie took a dump in Emilia's bathroom once and then wrote all over her bathroom wall and shower curtain with poop—she definitely needed psychiatric help. Jamie was the only one who behaved.

The kids were a huge challenge, but I was sure that with love, affection, and guidance, they would turn into regular kids instead of little monsters.

Manuel and I went from being very good friends to being engaged. It was a weird relationship. We weren't in love, but we did care and respect each other very much. We kissed and were affectionate towards each other, but sex had never come up in our conversations, which was fine with me.

I believe that his love towards me was more gratitude for helping him with his children, and mine was just being happy that I could be part of the process of keeping his children safe from abuse.

Emilia was beside herself when I told her I was engaged. "This marriage is not going to work," she argued. "Not only is he twenty-one years older than you, but you are going to become an instant mother to four very hard-to-handle children."

The more Emilia argued about my marrying Manuel, the more I became convinced that it was the right step. Aside from being rebellious, stubborn, and a know-it-all, I thought I was a superwoman with the capacity to save the world single-handedly.

I was convinced that God had put these children in my life to make up for not being able to have children of my own, and I was convinced that it was my job to keep them safe. I was also convinced that God had put Manuel in my life to protect me and provide for me without being forced to have sex with him unless I wanted to. I was so convinced of all this that I went full speed ahead with wedding preparations.

My wedding day was far from normal. The chaos began when I dropped the bride's champagne glass.

As I looked at the shattered pieces on the floor, one of my bridesmaids gasped, "This is bad luck. You must replace your glass right away."

So, instead of relaxing and getting ready for my big day, I ended up taking two buses to the bridal shop to replace my champagne glass.

When I got off the bus, I crossed the street so fast that I didn't see a pothole and fell on my right knee. It hurt, but I was in such a hurry that I continued without giving the fall a second thought.

At the bridal shop, I noticed my pants were bloodstained. By the time I got home, I was in extreme pain and limping.

Emilia was very upset, not only because I was late, but because the caterer delivered the food too early and the order was all wrong. When she saw my bloodstained pants and noticed my limp, she started yelling at me as if everything that was going wrong was my fault.

I was exhausted, hungry, and in pain. At that point, all I really wanted was to eat and sleep; unfortunately, neither was going to happen because I still had to shower, get my hair, nails, and makeup done, get dressed, and have photos taken with my mother and bridesmaids—all before three o'clock.

When I came out of the shower, I heard women talking all at once and kids screaming and crying. "How was I going to get any privacy with so many people around? Why were they even here; weren't they supposed to be at the church?" I vented silently.

I ran across the hall to Emilia's room, forgetting to lock the door. While I was trying to get my hair done, a parade of relatives, kids, and even the photographer barged into the bedroom.

The photographer kept complaining that he had to be at the church in an hour, and I still wasn't ready to be photographed.

Jamie kept clinging to me, refusing to let anyone near her.

Emilia stormed in and announced that she couldn't handle one more thing going wrong and that I should help her.

No privacy! I had to dress with people coming in and out of the room. My pantyhose ripped. My manicure, makeup, and hair weren't even close to what a bride should look like.

Photos were being taken while I was breaking up children's fights and wiping Jamie's tears. I was starving. And I was going to be late for my own wedding.

The church was just a few blocks away, yet the ride seemed like an eternity. I closed my eyes and tried to relax, but instead, a battle began in my head.

"This is not just a "one-day" thing—this is for the rest of your life," I heard a voice say.

"Once you say "yes," you'll be married to a man twenty-one years older than you and the step-mother to his four children," another voice said.

"What about college, your career, and your dreams of becoming a writer?" the first voice said.

"You're right. I can't do this," I said out loud to the voices in my head. "Emilia was right—this is too much for me. That's it; I'm not getting married."

When I arrived in front of the church, the best man opened the car door and extended his hand, waiting to help me out. I really wanted to close the door and tell the driver to take me back home, but instead, I found myself going through the motions of walking up the church steps and taking my place behind the wedding party.

The wedding procession began. First, the mothers were escorted to their seats. Next, the bridesmaids and groomsmen took their place on both sides of the altar. Behind them were the flower girls and the ring bearer. Now, it was my turn.

As I limped slowly down the aisle, I kept looking at the statue of Jesus on the cross behind the priest. I was about to turn around and run when I heard a voice say, "The doctors said you could never have a baby. God has sent you these children to love and care for. This is your opportunity to be a mother. Don't turn your back on them."

I stopped! My insides began to tremble. The room began to spin. I prayed, "Please, God, help me. I don't know what to do. Please send me a sign."

Then, I felt someone tucking at my dress and heard a low whisper, "Mommy, I'm hungry." It was Jamie—a very tired and hungry child who wanted my attention.

Immediately, my body stopped trembling, and the room stopped spinning. I looked into Jamie's tearful eyes and smiled.

Her face lit up when I pulled out a small bag of crackers I had shoved in my bridal purse and handed them to her. She was now a happy camper.

The sign could not be any clearer, these children needed me, and I was not going to turn my back on them.

I took a deep breath, took Jamie's small hand in mine, and together we walked up the aisle where I took my place next to my future husband.

Vows of promising to love, honor, obey and take care of each other until death do us part were exchanged. To those vows, I added one more in silent prayer, "Dear God, I promise that no matter what happens in my marriage, I will be a mother to these children until the youngest one turns eighteen years old—that's a promise that I will not break."

During the reception, all I kept thinking about was our trip to the Poconos, not because I was dreaming of a romantic honeymoon with my husband, but because I was exhausted and couldn't wait to get some much-needed rest.

Halfway to the Poconos, we stopped to call home. Emilia informed us that Jamie was not feeling well and that all she did was cry and ask for me. So, we turned around and headed back home, where my life as a wife and mother of three children began.

Married life turned out to be harder than I expected. Manuel was hardly home. He left for work earlier than I did and returned late at night, and on weekends, he was out of town playing with his band.

He never took part in the responsibility of raising his children and keeping our home and finances in order—he left me in charge of that. It felt like I didn't have a husband—which I really didn't mind because my main focus was to be a terrific mother and keep the children safe.

A few months after the wedding, two reasons forced me to quit my job and become a stay-at-home mom. Emilia could not handle the children anymore, and Junior was totally out of control and in need of constant supervision.

Junior's behavior was diabolic. He cut school and ran away from home constantly. He demonstrated how much he hated me by tearing me out of family photos and putting an "X" across my face on my wedding portrait.

He stared at me in an evil way. I was so afraid of what he might do that I wouldn't go to sleep until I was sure that he had fallen asleep. He needed some serious therapy. He made my life a living hell.

I was convinced that Junior's evil ways had to do with the weekend visits with his mother and brother, but I couldn't prove it.

During one of those visits, a tragedy occurred. While Junior, his brother, mother, and her boyfriend, were sunbathing on the roof of the five-floor building where they lived, she lost her footing and fell to the sidewalk, where she died immediately. The boys witnessed the incident, which totally traumatized them both.

After the funeral, Junior's brother moved in with us permanently. It was hard enough dealing with Junior when his mom was alive—after her death, it was worse.

Living with his little brother was not easy either because I had not met him until he moved in. He was shy, quiet, and polite; however, he gave me a bad vibe. I felt like he was a quiet volcano about to erupt.

Junior's constant bad behavior forced Manuel to take him to Puerto Rico. His plan was to stay with Junior for a few weeks until he adjusted to living with his grandmother, and then he would return.

Three weeks turned into three months, and Manuel had not returned. On the rare occasions that we spoke, he did not give us any indication of when he planned to return.

Due to his lack of communication with his boss, Manuel was officially terminated from his job with much regret.

The little money that I had saved was disappearing. Soon I would not have money to pay bills or buy food. To top things off, my mom, who had remarried, moved to another part of town.

Things were getting really bad. If I didn't do something right away to better our economic situation, the children and I would be forced to move in with Emilia and her new husband.

After unsuccessfully trying to reach Manuel, I became so desperate that I made what I thought was the right decision at that time. I asked Mom for a loan, sold what I could, and bought tickets to Puerto Rico.

We said goodbye to Emilia on New Year's Eve 1977, without the faintest idea of what I would do when I arrived in Puerto Rico. All I knew was that Manuel was my husband, and these were his kids. It was his responsibility to provide for us and protect us, and I was going to Puerto Rico to remind him of that.

The children and I walked into my mother-in-law's house a few minutes before midnight. The house was full of people. The kids clung to me while we searched for their father among the strangers who stared at us, wondering who we were.

We found Manuel in the kitchen laughing and drinking as if he didn't have a care in the world. When he saw us, his face went from shocking surprise to anger. He was not happy to see us.

"What are you doing here?" he snapped.

At that moment, I could not help but wonder why I hadn't sent the children to Puerto Rico and stayed in New York with Emilia. After all, they were not my children—they were his.

Then, I heard a familiar voice in my head say, "This is not about Manuel neglecting his children and not keeping the vows he made to you. This is about the promise you made to God on your wedding day to care for these children until the youngest turns eighteen."

I walked up to Manuel and looked straight into his eyes, and without caring about the room full of strangers staring at me, I said, "What are we doing here, you ask? Where else do you expect us to go after you abandoned us without an explanation? I am your wife. These are your children. It is your responsibility to take care of us."

La Parguera was a fishing village surrounded by beaches, rivers, and a phosphorescent bay. Many called it paradise, and I would have too if I didn't feel like I was trapped in a living nightmare that I would never wake up from.

My mother-in-law resented my living in her home, and I honestly do not blame her. I would have too, if I had eleven relatives already living in my home and had to give up my bedroom to accommodate four more people that arrived unannounced and without a clue as to when they were leaving.

Manuel also resented our arrival. He had gotten used to hanging out by the corner store, drinking all day and playing his guitar for a bunch of unemployed drunks, and partying with women at night, without the responsibility of taking care of children and a wife.

To make things worse, everyone in the village was related to Manuel's family or his ex-wife's family—all under the impression that I was the cause of Manuel's divorce and his wife's death.

I tried to fit in, but it was so hard because although I was a country girl at heart, I was also a city girl who spoke her mind. I just couldn't understand why the village women had an old-fashioned mindset where women had no say in anything and were only good for raising children, cooking, cleaning, and fulfilling their husband's needs, even when they were exhausted or sick.

After two years of living in La Parguera, we were stuck in a rut that only I saw. The kids adjusted just fine. They didn't seem to mind sleeping in a room with five people and waiting in line every morning for sixteen people to finish in the bathroom.

Junior, who had been staying at his aunt's house, somehow ended back in New York City living with his mother's boyfriend. Weird, isn't it? He was the reason why we ended up in Puerto Rico, and now he was back in New York City. I wasn't complaining. I won't deny that Junior's absence brought some peace to my life.

Manuel remained unemployed and hanging out with the drunks. If it weren't for my mom sending me money every month, we would have starved. Things were very distant between Manuel and me. Sometimes I didn't see him for days. He wasn't there for his children or me. It's like we didn't exist.

I felt like everything was falling apart. I felt tired, confused, and trapped. A big part of me wanted to abandon everyone and go back to New York, but every time I set my mind to leave, I heard that inner voice say, "You can't go. You made a promise on your wedding day. You cannot break that promise."

That's when I desperately prayed, "God, help me. I don't know what to do. I want to keep the promise I made to you, but everything is so wrong. Do I stay, or do I go? Please send me a sign."

My cousin Christina, who I hadn't seen for years, called announcing that she and my godfather would be visiting me the following weekend.

Finally, I was going to spend time with members of my family instead of the villagers who treated me like an intruder and acted like I had the plague.

Christina and my godfather's visit was what I needed to lift my spirits. We spent the day touring the beautiful sites of the fishing village and reminiscing about our childhood days.

When I hugged Christina goodbye, she whispered, "There's a long holiday weekend coming next month. Why don't you come to Ponce and spend it with us? I don't know why, but I have a feeling that getting away from everyone here and spending some quiet time is exactly what you need."

I was so thrilled with her invitation that I quickly said yes without even asking Manuel if it was ok.

When I told Manuel about my plans to visit Christina without him or the kids, he became very upset. He said I couldn't go, unless I took the kids with me. I really wanted to go alone so that I could get away from everyone and spend some quality time with my family, but I had no choice but to obey him.

The trip to Ponce was not only a happy walk down memory lane, but it was God's answer to my prayers. It was full of emotions and discoveries—and it was the weekend I was introduced to two beings that ended up giving me what no person in this world was capable of.

Our first day in Ponce was overwhelmingly busy. Christina gave us a complete tour of all the historic places of the town that I was born in and where I partially grew up.

At the end of the day, we were exhausted and famished, so we headed back to Christina's house, where my godfather had prepared a scrumptious banquet for us to feast on.

Dinner was delicious. The meal was made up of all my childhood favorites and cooked by my godfather, who I considered the best cook in the world. He really should have been a chef instead of a Spanish professor.

After dinner, I stood by the kitchen door and literally went back in time. Nothing had changed. The enormous backyard was exactly like I remembered it, with ducks swimming in the pond, chickens, roosters, and geese walking, lined up behind each other. And, straight across—the gate that led to my grandparent's house.

Tears ran down my cheeks as a vision of my grandfather standing behind the gate calling me to set the table for dinner, clearly appeared before me.

"I miss my grandparents so much. I wish they were still alive," I said to Christina, who was sitting at the kitchen table quietly observing me.

When the kids had gone to bed, and my godfather had retreated to his bedroom, Christina and I sat for hours in the living room talking and laughing about the mischievous things we did in our childhood.

At one point, when we both seemed to be wrapped up in our own thoughts, Christina looked up at me and asked, "Do you have a personal relationship with God and Jesus?"

"What do you mean by a personal relationship?"

"I mean—do you believe in God and Jesus, and if so—what kind of relationship do you have with them?"

I thought about her question for a few seconds and then answered, "My grandparents taught me very early in life that there is a God who created us and loves us very much, and that we should pray to him, especially when we need protection.

The few times that I attended church, I learned about the Ten Commandments and how important it was not to break them, but I didn't commit myself to a specific religion because, in every church that I've visited throughout the years, I found something that I didn't agree with.

I couldn't understand why some people called themselves children of God yet went to church to criticize or look down on the less fortunate. Or why they broke a commandment, confessed, and then broke it again, thinking that it was ok because they would be forgiven the next time they confessed.

I don't belong to a church, nor do I seek God constantly—yet, for reasons that I cannot explain—when things are going wrong, and I feel that I can't take it anymore—I ask God for help and strength."

Christina leaned back on her rocking chair and said, "Rosita, I used to feel like you do. I believed God existed because everyone said so, but I didn't feel Him.

I cried out to him. I prayed. I vented. But I didn't feel what I wanted to feel from Him. I wanted to feel his arms around me, comforting me. I wanted to hear Him say it was going to be alright. I wanted desperately to feel His love—but I didn't.

Then, one day someone spoke to me about God in a way that I had never heard before. Every word that person spoke made me crave more and more of God. Each word nourished the mustard seed that had been planted in my heart."

Into the wee hours of the morning, Christina shared her past life, tribulations, and what her personal relationship with God and Jesus meant to her.

Her story was intriguing. It sounded like a fairy tale with its usual good and evil characters fighting over a young girl's heart. And even though many parts were confusing, I hung on to every word she spoke.

I was in awe at this personal relationship she had with someone she could not see.

I mean, I believed in God and prayed to Him even though I had never seen Him, but this relationship she had with God and Jesus was not the same—she spoke about them as if they were best friends who hung out together all day. They seemed to be her everything.

After listening to Christina's testimony, I hungered for the type of relationship she had with God and Jesus.

I had so many questions, especially one, "How do you do it? How are you able to live a Christian life when my godfather, the man who has raised you as his own, is clearly an atheist who professes to be a Catholic?"

"That's a struggle I have to deal with every single day. He hates my relationship with God and Jesus and that I belong to the Methodist Church instead of the Catholic Church. He curses my Faith every day," Christina said with sadness.

"How can you stand the tension between you two?" I asked.

"I pray. Every day I put him in God's hands, and just like Jesus asked God on the cross—I too ask, "Forgive them for they know not what they do."

My trip came to an end, but my experience stayed with me for the rest of my life. As we said our goodbyes, Christina gave me a gift of the King James Version of the Bible, which she said was easier to understand.

We parted, promising that we would visit each other regularly. In a loving embrace, she said, "Walking with Jesus is not easy, but I promise you, if you truly believe and have faith, He will be by your side every second of the day, and if you read His Word, you can survive anything."

When I returned to the fishing village, I felt refreshed. Nothing had changed around me, but something had definitely changed inside me.

You see, the Bible wasn't the only gift Christina had given me; she had also given me the gift of a tiny seed of faith that she planted when she shared her testimony. Christians call this seed a "Mustard Seed."

The seed was planted, but that didn't mean that I had miraculously become a devoted believer of God and Jesus with indestructible faith overnight. It simply meant that the seed was planted, but like any seed, it would die if I didn't nourish it.

I did not want the seed to die. I wanted it to grow and be strong; so, I began to nourish it by reading God's Word every day, and if I didn't understand a passage, I would write it down so that I could go over it with Christina when we visited.

The simple task of reading God's Word and praying to Him every day made the tiny seed of faith grow in my heart.

I walked and spoke to God and Jesus, as I would to a best friend. I spent every moment with them. They became the most important beings in my life. I could finally say that I had a personal relationship with God and His Son, Jesus Christ.

One day, without even knowing why, I laid the Bible on my lap, closed my eyes, and flipped the pages until I felt I should stop. Then, I put my finger on the page, opened my eyes, and read the passage under my finger.

The passage read, "You can do anything through Jesus Christ who strengthens you."

When I read this, I felt as if someone had given me a warm, loving hug. I felt safe and protected. I felt Jesus' arms around me.

The feeling was so amazing that I just had to try it again, except that this time I prayed first, and then I asked God a question.

The words in the passage left me in awe because the Scripture answered the question I had just asked.

When I told Christina about my experience, she said God speaks to each of His children in different ways, and in my case, He spoke through words in the Bible.

I was so excited to know that God and Jesus could actually speak to me that I was beside myself until Christina very seriously said, "This gift that God has given you is not to be taken lightly. It is a powerful gift, but you need to keep strong in your faith and relationship with Jesus so that you don't misunderstand His words."

I felt like a little girl being reprimanded, but I did understand what Christina meant.

I had read in the Bible that Satan loved to trick God's children into believing that something came from God, instead of him, in order to cause us to sin. So, I understood how important it was to keep my faith strong, especially during an attack.

I also understood that having Jesus in my life did not mean that I was never going to experience hardships; however, if I kept my faith strong and believed that there was a reason for every diffi-culty—no matter how challenging a hardship seemed, God would not give me more than I could handle.

I did not abandon my husband and his children; instead, I stayed and prayed for strength to face and deal with the challenges of my marriage, which had gotten worse since I had returned from Ponce.

One-night, Manuel stumbled in drunk. When I served his dinner, he flung the plate against the wall shattering it to pieces while calling me by his ex-wife's name and saying that I was worse than a prostitute.

The yelling woke his mother up, who expressed her disgust with his behavior when she tearfully turned to me and said, "I don't know why you put up with him."

As I wiped the food stains off the wall, the thought of going back to New York began nagging at me again. I kept hearing a voice in my head say, "Manuel does not care about you. His children don't need you now that they live close to their family. Clearly, no one wants you here. So, why stay?"

Sobbing uncontrollably, I ran to my room and fell to my knees in front of my bed. I desperately prayed, "God, help me—I can't take it anymore. What do I do? Please send me a sign, or better yet, just take me."

Kneeling on the floor with my forehead resting on my folded hands, I fell asleep.

While asleep, I went in and out of dreams, with each dream replaying a part of my past.

I don't know if what happened next was part of the dream or an out-of-body experience. All I know is that when I opened my eyes, odorless gray smoke had filled the room and was circling around me.

Across the room, a patch of fog cleared, forming a bright cloud that slowly turned into a figure which I strongly felt was Jesus.

Jesus floated towards me with his arms extended and then took me in his arms. I felt warm, safe, and loved. I don't remember what was said. All I remember is that He held me until I fell asleep.

When I woke up, I was at peace. I felt confident that at the right moment, God and Jesus would guide me in the right direction—if I continued strong in my faith.

A few months after my dream, my health started deteriorating. Not surprising with all the stress I was under.

For months, I would get cramps, but my period would not come. The doctors in New York had said that I could never have children, so I knew I wasn't pregnant. Besides, Manuel hadn't touched me for years.

When the cramps became unbearable, I feared something serious was wrong, so I went to the town doctor for a check-up, who, in turn, referred me to Mayaguez Medical Center, which was a long commute away.

After many tests, the general GYN confirmed what the doctors in New York had already told me about not being able to have children. He also said that the only way to end the severe cramps was to have a hysterectomy.

When the doctor left the examining room, a feeling of deep sadness took over me because even though I knew for years that I couldn't have children, I hadn't lost hope; and, to have a hysterectomy would make it final.

I was still sitting on the examining table, lost in thought, when I felt my doctor's hand on my shoulder. He said, "Rosita, I want you to meet Dr. Guerrero. He is one of our GYN Specialists."

When Dr. Guerrero held my hand in both of his and gently

said, "Hello," I felt like I had known him all my life. His jolly eyes, dark hair, and beard reminded me of a young Santa Claus.

"Rosita, your doctor has brought your case to my attention, and I have gone over it very carefully. I know he presented the option of a hysterectomy; however, before you make a decision, I want to tell you of another option," he said with a soft English accent.

"My specialty is infertility, which I studied and successfully treated while working in Europe. I am now the head of the infertility department that will be administering this treatment in Puerto Rico, and you, my dear, are a perfect candidate.

I want you to know that even though this treatment has had a high percentage of success in Europe, I cannot guarantee that it will work on you; but, it is something to consider before having a hysterectomy," he softly said, and then continued, "You don't have to make a decision now, but the sooner you make it—the sooner we can start."

"Can I have a few minutes alone, please?" I asked. He nodded and walked quietly out of the room.

As I sat on the examining table, I prayed for guidance. Immediately, I felt warmth enfold my whole body, and I just knew that Jesus was sitting right next to me.

Then, a story that Christina had once told me came to mind. After many weeks of rain, the area where a very religious man lived, flooded. When the man's house began flooding, he took his family to the roof because he strongly believed that God would save them. As they prayed, a man in a rowboat came and asked them to jump in. The religious man answered, "No thank you, we're waiting for God to save us." A few hours later, a man in a motorboat came by and pleaded with them to jump in; again, the religious man declined. Just as the water was reaching their necks, a helicopter flew down, threw a rope, and signaled for them to grab on; and again, the religious man declined. The waters continued rising, and the man and his family drowned. When the man reached the gates of heaven, he asked God, "Why didn't you save us?" God replied, "I sent you two boats and a helicopter, and you refused all three, and now you ask me why I didn't safe you?"

Voices started debating inside my head. One voice said, "Doctors, not only in New York but here, diagnosed that you could not have children. This doctor just wants to use you as a guinea pig for his own research."

A softer voice said, "With God, all things are possible. Your faith can move mountains—Your faith can destroy obstacles—all you need to do is Believe! God just sent you a boat. Are you going to get on, or are you going to drown?"

When Dr. Guerrero returned, he asked, "Why are you smiling?"

"Because you are an angel sent to me from God, and we're about to go on an incredible ride together," I answered.

"Good, but remember, there are no guarantees," he said.

"I know people call this step "against all odds," but I call it "Faith and believing in the power of Jesus."

Dr. Guerrero took my hands between his and smiled. It was the beginning of an incredible journey guided by God and Jesus.

The infertility treatment was long, complicated, and divided into different stages, and the tests were very uncomfortable and painful.

During the first stage, I had to take medication to regulate my menstrual cycle; then, during the second stage, another medication was added to force my ovaries to produce more eggs. Both medications were taken at different times of the month and had to be carefully monitored.

Aside from the medication, I was instructed to keep a temperature chart to help me know when I was ovulating. Keeping track of my medication, menstrual cycle, and the ovulating chart was annoying but well worth it if it meant that I might have a baby.

Some probably thought that it was a bad idea for us to have a baby without a job and our own place to live, but I figured that if it was in God's plan, He would show me the way to provide for my baby.

Manuel's drinking got worse. Each morning, before getting out of bed, he took a drink from a whiskey bottle that he kept under the bed. His personality had totally changed. We hardly spoke.

When I was in the third and final stage of the infertility treatment, I began getting worried. How was I going to get pregnant if Manuel and I didn't have sex?

As soon as the question came to my mind, I remembered something I had read in the Bible where it said not to question, so I left my worries in God's hands.

What I hadn't realized was that all during the infertility treatment, God was breaking some of the barriers that had kept Manuel from being interested in me sexually.

Part of the infertility treatment included monthly visits to a nutritionist who put me on a diet and exercise plan that did wonders for my health. I lost weight, looked and felt great, and looked younger. Without me knowing, Manuel was already noticing me.

One night, while everyone in the household attended a relative's birthday party and I laid in bed reading, Manuel surprised me with a serenade outside my window. When I opened the back door to see what was happening, Manuel took me in his arms and kissed me passionately.

All I can say is that the next half hour was what I should have experienced on my wedding night.

A few weeks after having sex with Manuel, I began feeling as if I had the flu. I was horribly sick and throwing up all the time. The smell of beans made me nauseous, and I craved salty foods.

When my mother-in-law suggested that I could be pregnant, I immediately went to the local lab to get a pregnancy test. I was disappointed when the test results came back negative.

Dr. Guerrero had warned me that if I thought I was pregnant, I was not to take the pill that stabilized my menstrual period until I had a pregnancy test because if I was pregnant, the pill would kill the baby.

On the morning that I was supposed to take my medication, I felt extremely uneasy.

I kept debating with myself, "I still feel sick, but it can't be the flu because the flu doesn't last this long. Everyone is telling me that I have all the symptoms of being pregnant, but the pregnancy test was negative. I have to take my medication today, but what if I am pregnant and I kill the baby?"

I was so confused that I decided to do what I always did when I didn't know what to do—I prayed and put the whole situation in God's hands.

I was so edgy that, without knowing why, I grabbed my Bible, a glass of water, my pills and went for a walk down by the pier in front of the plaza.

I sat on a cement bench overlooking the beautiful waters of the bay. Except for a few boat owners cleaning their boats, there was hardly anyone around.

I looked at my watch—it was 7:30 am.

The sky was clear, with just a few small clouds moving slowly towards their destination. The morning breeze caressed my face while blowing my hair against it.

This was my favorite place to sit whenever I had a problem or felt uneasy. I would just sit and pray. After praying, I always felt Jesus' arms holding me close.

I knew that the answer to whether I was pregnant or whether I should take the pill was in the Bible, but instead of using my Bible, I closed my eyes and silently prayed and asked God for a sign.

I opened my eyes and looked toward the seagulls flying over the bay, searching for their morning meal. I waited for a sign. Minutes passed, and nothing happened.

I placed the pills and the glass of water on the bench beside me. I prayed and once again asked God for a sign, except that this time, I opened the Bible and laid it on my lap, without touching it, and waited.

Suddenly, the wind started flipping the pages back and forth until they stopped.

I closed my eyes and placed my index finger on a random spot on the page.

My heart was pounding. I waited a few seconds, and then I

slowly looked down and read, "...and shall bring forth a son... (Matthew 1:23 KJV)."

I was shaking because I knew, without a doubt, that I was pregnant. I placed my hands over my stomach, and full of happiness, I looked up at the sky and said, "Thank you, Father."

Without a second thought, I flung the pills and the glass of water into the bay and ran home full of excitement and joy.

The next morning, I went to see Dr. Guerrero. I was so excited that I hardly breathed as I told him the whole story.

I thought he would think I had gone crazy, but instead, he calmly said, "Urine pregnancy tests can be wrong sometimes, especially if you're only a few weeks pregnant. There's a blood pregnancy test that just arrived that I want you to take. If you are pregnant, we'll know in a few hours."

"Ok, I'll take the test, but trust me—I know I'm pregnant," I said stubbornly.

A few hours later, Dr. Guerrero walked into the waiting room with a big smile.

His arms went up in the air as he loudly announced, "We did it—we're three weeks pregnant!"

The nurses burst out laughing when one said, "Doctor, anyone listening would think it's your baby."

On my way home, all I could think about was the spiritual experience I had at the pier and what the experience meant.

God had actually spoken to me through the Bible. If it hadn't been for His words, I would have taken those pills and would have killed my baby.

God had spoken to me—who had been tainted with sexual and mental abuse since childhood—who had not lived the life of a devoted believer—and who was a sinner.

Not only did God speak to me, but I listened and acted according to what He said because I believed with all my heart that what He was telling me was the truth. If I had not believed, I would have killed my baby.

I was in awe, not only because I had my first personal experience with God but also because the baby I was carrying was a miracle.

My son, Alexander, was born October 5, 1981, weighing 7 lbs. 9 ounces and perfect in every way. The delivery and birth went smoothly; however, a few weeks after he was born, his health began deteriorating.

After every feeding, Alexander would vomit what little milk he drank, which caused him to lose weight very rapidly.

When we took him to the hospital, a team of pediatricians observed him for 24 hours and then presented us with a few diagnoses.

First, they said I was feeding and burping him incorrectly, causing his stomach to fill with gas and then vomit; however, they had to discard that diagnosis when he still vomited after the nurses fed and burped him.

Next, they said that he might be allergic to the milk formula, so they tried four different formulas—but he still vomited.

The blood tests, the urine tests, and the x-rays all came back normal, which baffled the pediatric team, so they asked us for permission to do a spinal tap, which they said had to be done immediately because if my son continued losing weight at the rate he was—he would be dead within a week.

Manuel agreed to the spinal tap right away, but something inside me kept telling me not to, so I told the doctors that I was going to pray for guidance and that I would return in an hour with my decision.

They all looked at me like I was crazy.

"You pray all the time. Why are you wasting time praying when we should consent to the spinal tap right away," Manuel whispered angrily.

Instead of responding to him, I closed my eyes, bowed my head, and silently began a deep conversation with God, "Heavenly Father, you know what's happening to my baby, and you alone know if the spinal tap is necessary to save his life. I only have an hour to make this decision, so please send me a sign that will help me know what to do. Please save my baby."

I sat quietly for an hour, waiting and praying for a sign, but it didn't come. "Why wasn't God answering me," I wondered. "Was it because I didn't have my Bible with me?"

While we walked back to the room, I kept praying silently, "God, please tell me what to do before I give them my decision."

I walked up to the head pediatrician, looked him straight in the eyes, and said, "I have one last question. Can you save my baby?"

"We will try everything we can to save him, but you need to understand that this is a very rare case—there are no guarantees," the doctor answered.

Then, for one split second, I caught the doctor looking at his colleagues in a way that told me that they didn't think my son was going to make it.

That exchange of looks between them was the sign that I had asked for.

If my son was going to die, he was not going to die in a hospital with tubes attached to a machine—he was going to die at home—in my loving arms.

When I told Manuel my decision, he thought I was crazy; but was too tired to argue with me.

That afternoon we signed papers releasing the doctors of all responsibility and took our son home.

That night, Alexander's cries were more like non-stop shrieks that pierced into my heart and soul.

The night seemed endless. For hours I rocked him in my arms and paced back and forth, trying to calm him.

Manuel couldn't take the crying, so he did what he usually did when things got tough—he went out.

I was so exhausted that I began wondering if I had made a mistake by bringing Alexander home, but then I remembered something Christina once told me.

She said no matter how strong our faith was, there were going to be times when we would not be sure if the decision we made was in accordance with God's plan. She said if I ever felt this way, to pray for guidance and leave everything in God's hands—so, that's what I did.

Very early the next morning, Emilia called from New York. I was so exhausted that I couldn't understand what she was saying, so I passed the phone to my mother-in-law.

Both grandmothers spoke for a few minutes, and then my mother-in-law handed me the phone while she took the baby from my arms.

Emilia said, "Follow your mother-in-law's instructions." Then, she hung up.

While putting a pot of water on the stove, my mother-in-law said, "Your mother and I both feel that the baby swallowed something during birth, and it's still in his stomach, which is why he keeps vomiting every time he drinks."

Then, she stepped out into the yard and returned with a handful of leaves, which she rinsed and placed in boiling water.

"In the olden days, many babies were born with this condition; especially, if they were born at home," she continued, "The remedy is a tea made from this plant—which we're lucky enough to have in the yard."

"Now, you must follow my instructions very carefully," she said. "Once the tea boils, let it cool down. Take one ounce of tea and dilute it with one ounce of water; then, pour it into the baby's bottle. Give the baby about an ounce, every two hours, until he vomits whatever is stuck in his stomach."

The love in my mother-in-law's eyes as she cradled my baby while giving him the first ounce of tea; and the way Emilia spoke to me on the phone made me realize that God had used these two women in his plan to save my baby.

After a couple of feedings of tea, my baby finally stopped crying and fell asleep on my chest—and so did I.

About an hour later, a startling sound woke me up. Alexander was wiggling and making very strange noises.

"Oh my God, he's choking," I cried.

My mother-in-law, who had fallen asleep beside us, quickly lifted him up.

I was about to grab him from her when he vomited what looked like slimy pieces of liver.

I thought he was dying. All I could do was sob and pray as I watched his tiny body jerk with every vomit.

My mother-in-law was not freaking out like me. Instead, she was rubbing his back calmly, saying, "That's a good boy. Vomit all that bad stuff that is making you so sick."

As soon as Alexander stopped vomiting, he relaxed, so I changed him and then left him with his grandmother while I took a quick shower.

When I returned to my room, my mother-in-law handed me a baby bottle filled with two ounces of milk.

I frantically said, "No, not the formula—he's only going to throw up again."

"This is not formula," she calmly said. "This is what your mother fed you when you were a baby. She said to start him off with one ounce of diluted evaporated milk until he can drink four ounces. She also said that if you argue, to call her."

I smiled—then said, "I'm not going to argue with two angels sent by God to save my baby."

Six months later, Alexander was drinking eight ounces of diluted evaporated milk mixed with baby cereal and eating two servings of baby food, veggies, and fruits a day.

Some might call this outcome a coincidence—I call it a miracle.

One morning, on our way back from Alexander's immunization appointment, Manuel seemed lost in thought.

When I asked him what was wrong, he quietly said, "While

you were scheduling Alexander's next appointment, his pediatrician called me into her office. She said the yellowing in my eyes could be hepatitis or liver problem resulting from excess drinking, and if I wanted to see my baby grow—I had to stop drinking."

I didn't say anything, but in my mind, I was thanking God for using the pediatrician to wake Manuel up.

The conversation Manuel had with Alexander's pediatrician impacted him so much that he stopped drinking cold turkey that same day. Glory be to God—three miracles in one year.

Manuel and I were getting along much better since he stopped drinking. And, after the green tea experience I shared with Manuel's mother, she and I were getting along much better too.

However, although things were better, I felt we really needed our own place to live. It just wasn't normal to live in the crowded conditions we lived in; besides, it was unhealthy for a baby.

One night, I received a warning in a dream—I was warned that my baby was in danger.

When I shared my concerns with Manuel, he didn't seem to care—it was like he never wanted to leave his mother's house.

The fear for my baby increased so much that one day I asked God for guidance; then, I closed my eyes, opened the Bible, and placed my finger on a page.

The passage I had placed my finger on read, "Take your child and leave…" God's words confirmed the fear that I had about my baby being in danger.

When God spoke—I listened. When God told me to do something—I did it. I didn't know where I was going, but I had faith that God would guide me.

I called Emilia right away, and without explaining why, I asked her if I could live with her. I was shocked when she said I couldn't because she was having trouble with her husband and was seriously thinking about leaving him and returning to Puerto Rico.

The day after my conversation with Emilia, I received a phone call from my godfather who said, "I spoke to your mother, and I have a feeling that you both need a place to stay, so I asked Emilia's brother if I could rent his parent's old house to you both. He said you could live there for as long as you want as long as you don't burn it down."

That evening, when I told Manuel that we were moving to Ponce and that Emilia would probably be joining us there, he became very upset.

He said, "I'm not going to take my children out of school and leave my hometown to go to a strange place."

To that, I answered, "Fine—stay—but I'm going."

With disbelief in his eyes, he asked, "Why are you doing this?"

With my head held high and with confidence, I answered, "Because God told me to."

Secretly, I was hoping that Manuel and the kids would not move to Ponce with us. I really wanted this move to be a new beginning for me and the baby; however, God had his own plan because a week later, we were all heading to our new home in Ponce.

I can DO
ALL THINGS *through* CHRIST
who strengthens ME.
PHILIPPIANS 4:13 KJV

CHAPTER FOUR
God Moves Mountains

"With God all things are possible."
(Matthew 19:26 KJV)

My grandparent's secluded country home surrounded by fruit trees, vegetable plants, and farm animals was home and the only place where I felt safe. But, for Manuel and his kids, who were used to the excitement and noise of the fishing village—it was a huge change.

When I entered the house, I became emotional. Every piece of furniture was exactly where it was when I was a child, and even though my grandparents were long gone, I could feel their presence and love in every room I walked through.

I sat on my grandfather's mahogany rocking chair, leaned back, closed my eyes, and prayed, "Thank you, God, for bringing us to safety. Thank you for granting us the miracle of finding a place of our own. Now, all we need is for Manuel to find a job so that we can survive here."

God answered my prayer of surviving, but not as I had expected. I was approved for food stamps. My mother sent us money, and Christina gave me a loan. Plus, my godfather brought us a casserole every day. I was very grateful, but it wasn't enough to cover our expenses. We needed for Manuel to find a job.

In a big city like Ponce, with so many job openings, Manuel could have landed a job easily, but he didn't, because he didn't bother to look for one—all he did was pluck away on his guitar all day long.

I was so frustrated that, even though Manuel did not approve, I began looking for work. Unfortunately, I was not hired because even though I had plenty of secretarial experience, I did not have a high school diploma.

Manuel's lack of energy and depressive whining was contagious. He was drowning, and he was taking me down with him. I felt that my faith was weakening, even though I still walked with Jesus and prayed to my Heavenly Father every day.

I prayed, but I wasn't getting any answers, so instead of trying to find a solution to our financial problems, I allowed myself to believe that God's plan was for me to continue accepting money and food from my family. I became so comfortable with accepting charity that I expected it, even though, deep down inside, I felt it wasn't right.

I did not want to lose my faith. I did not want to lose the personal relationship I had with my Heavenly Father and His Son, Jesus Christ.

When I spoke to Christina about how I felt, she said that when she felt as I did, she surrounded herself with people and things that brought her closer to God—so I began doing the same.

First, I attended Christina's church, where I actually felt the presence of Jesus and felt the Holy Spirit energize me—something I had never felt when I visited other churches in the past.

In addition to going to church, Christina and I began meeting every Tuesday night to have what we called—time with Jesus—to pray, share our spiritual experiences, ask for guidance, and lay our problems and questions at God's feet.

All that I was doing began to strengthen my faith and bring me closer to my Heavenly Father and His Son, Jesus Christ—something that Satan was not happy with.

You see, Satan's main purpose is to win our soul. To accomplish this, he studies us very carefully from the moment we are born to learn our vulnerabilities, fears, and weaknesses. Then, he waits patiently for the right moment to use what he learned about us to attack by manipulating, fooling, and terrorizing until he destroys us.

It was during one of our Tuesday prayer meetings that I had an experience that I will never forget.

I was in the middle of reading a passage from the Bible when suddenly I felt hands tightening around my throat.

I couldn't speak and was having trouble breathing.

Fear took over me because I didn't know what was happening to me.

"What's wrong, Rosita?" I heard Christina ask.

I couldn't answer! I was gasping for air.

Then I heard Christina praying in a strong, loud voice while placing her hand on my head.

As she prayed, the hands loosened their grip around my neck.

And then, I saw it—a dark human-shaped shadow floating away from me.

Christina was in tears as she asked, "Are you ok?"

Trembling, I described every detail of my experience.

Christina then shared something with me that stayed with me forever: "I have been living with this dark shadow in the house since I was a little girl. I feel that it is very evil—it might even be Satan himself. One night I woke up feeling something heavy on top of me—it was the shadow. Ever since I found Jesus, though it still lurks, God protects me from it. It appeared to you because your faith is getting stronger. It wants to distract you from your faith and win your soul. Don't let it. Every time you feel its presence, say in a loud voice—"In the name of Jesus Christ of Nazareth, I command you to leave." Keep repeating these words until you feel it leave. Don't be afraid of it. I promise God will protect you. Remember, the stronger your faith becomes—the more Satan will attack. Do not fear it because it feeds on fear."

Evil exists, and I had just witnessed it for the second time in my life. Believe me when I say that no one is exempt from Satan's attacks—not even the strongest body or mind.

It was dark and windy when I left Christina's house that night. Halfway up the path that led to my balcony, I heard a strange sound.

I stopped.

"Maybe it was the wind?" I thought as I looked around me.

Every bush seemed to have a human form as it swayed to the breeze. I felt uneasy, so I hurried home.

I entered the house, closed the door behind me quickly, and just stood facing the door while I tried to get a grip on my nerves.

Manuel sat plucking away at his guitar when I came into the living room.

He looked up, and when his eyes met mine—I froze.

The eyes that were staring back at me were not his. These eyes were red, full of fire and evil. His smile was wicked. This was not Manuel.

I shivered as I quickly escaped to my room and shut the door.

After checking on Alexander, who was sleeping peacefully in his crib next to our bed, I sat cross-legged on my bed, swaying back and forth while I clutched my Bible to my chest.

Fear began taking control. I was trembling.

Then, the evil hands began choking me again.

I was so overpowered with fear that I couldn't even pray.

The fear was horrible.

I never want to experience that again.

I was so terrified that I couldn't fight.

I heard a voice say, "Come to my side, or your baby will suffer the consequences." I was about to give up my faith and let Satan take me when a feeling of drowning overpowered me.

I had to save my son, and God was the only one that could help me.

Like a lion protecting her cubs, I yelled out with all my might, "In the name of Jesus Christ of Nazareth—I command you to leave."

Then, exhausted, I leaned forward face down on the bed and fell asleep.

When I woke up, evil was gone, and everything was calm.

Satan knew the right weapon to use against me—fear—fear of him hurting my son. He also knew the right moment to terrorize me, hoping that my fear of being attacked by him would be greater than my devotion to God.

It almost worked because battling Satan's attack was the hardest and most exhausting thing I had ever done. Without God's help, I would never have survived.

No matter how strong you are, you cannot physically destroy evil by punching, shooting, or stabbing it, because it is invisible. The only beings that have the power to rescue you from evil are our Heavenly Father and His Son, Jesus Christ. They have the power to grab your hand and pull you out of the worst evil situation you can imagine.

With the Grace of God, I had survived two of Satan's attacks in one night, and probably not the last. More reason to walk with my Heavenly Father and His Son, Jesus Christ, in order to stand strong against evil.

My Heavenly Father saved me from Satan; so, why didn't he save me from the hardships that I was facing? The answer was simple. He had to allow certain hardships in my life in order for me to learn from them.

He knew that I was capable of getting out of financial difficulty, but the only way that I was going to do so was by Him taking away the help that was enabling me.

All at once, I was hit with bad news.

My mother called to tell me that she was facing her own financial difficulties and would not be able to send me the monthly allowance that helped pay for our rent and utility bills.

My godfather stopped sending the usual daily casserole, which had been a blessing for us.

In desperation, I asked Christina for another loan and was shocked when she declined.

"Rosita, I'm not lending you any more money. You and your husband are two healthy people who need to get off your butts and find a way to provide for your kids. I'm not a bank. God sent me to plant a mustard seed, guide you, and teach you about His Word—nothing more. He did not send me to be your crutch," Christina said with tears in her eyes.

Then, she turned and walked away, leaving me standing speechless on my front porch.

A few days later, two of Manuel's old musician friends unexpectedly came to visit him. I was so happy to see them because I felt that their visit might rekindle the passion that Manuel once had for playing in a band. I hoped that they had come to offer him work.

While I was in the kitchen preparing coffee, I tried to listen to the conversation but couldn't because the men were speaking too low.

When I returned to the living room, I was surprised to find Manuel slumped on the chair, looking at the floor, and the men gone.

"Where are your friends? What's wrong? Did you get bad news?" I asked while setting the heavy tray on the coffee table.

Seconds turned into minutes before Manuel finally spoke.

He slowly said, "I used to play with those two men when I lived in New Jersey.

They moved to Puerto Rico a few years ago and have been playing their music at different hotels and clubs until recently when they lost their lead guitar player.

They heard that I was living in the fishing village and were very eager to get in touch with me, so they visited my mother, who gave them our address."

I listened, my heart racing with excitement. I visualized him back in the music business, earning enough money to provide for his family. I smiled with anticipation, eagerly waiting for the good news.

Manuel continued, "They came to offer me a position as their lead guitar player. They said they have enough contracts with hotels in San Juan to cover every weekend for the next two years. When I told them I didn't have a car to travel back and forth to San Juan, they said it wouldn't be a problem because they could pick me up on Fridays and bring me back on Mondays, and I could stay with them during the weekend. They said they were making good money, and if I joined the group, they anticipate making even more."

"Oh my God, that's wonderful. So, when are you starting?" I asked excitedly. "We must find your good shirts and suits and get them cleaned right away."

Manuel bluntly blurted out, "I did not accept their offer."

"What do you mean you did not accept their offer? Are you insane? What possible excuse could you have for not accepting their offer? You didn't even have to go out and look for this—it fell on your lap," I cried in disbelief.

He looked at me like I was his worst enemy and angrily said, "I didn't accept because I cannot leave you alone."

"For God's sakes, I won't be alone—I have the kids. And, my cousin and godfather are right next door," I cried out.

"I don't mean alone in that way," he quietly said. "I mean that if I go off every weekend, eventually you will find someone else."

"Are you serious?" I cried. "We're down to the last two cans of milk and hardly any food or money. God just sent us a way out of our situation, and you declined because of jealousy?"

Then I heard a voice say, "Remember, God will not let you drown—He will not give you more than you can handle."

I sat right in front of Manuel, looked deep into his eyes, and sternly said, "You just refused the only opportunity that you have had in six years to provide for your family.

From this point on—with—or without your consent—I will do everything in my power to provide for my baby and me."

I strongly added, "You can sink if you want, but I'm grabbing on to my Heavenly Father's hand because I have faith that He will not let me drown." Then, I walked into our bedroom and slammed the door behind me.

Alone in my room, I prayed like I hadn't done for a long time. While I prayed, God opened my eyes to many things I had not seen.

I realized that a lot of the financial hardships we faced were not all Manuel's fault. I, too, was to blame by allowing myself to become comfortable in a situation that He did not want me to be in; and worse, to actually expect others to bail me out.

I asked God to forgive me, and I thanked Him for letting me see my faults. I asked Him for guidance. I opened the Bible, flipped through the pages, and placed my finger on a page. The passage under my finger read, "I can do all things through Christ who strengthens me (Philippians 4:13 KJV)."

God knew that I needed to feed my family and pay my household bills. I felt confident that He would show me how to get the money for each; so, I closed the Bible, smiled, and prayed for a plan.

As I waited patiently for God to answer my prayers, an idea came. I remembered that I had brought a lot of things from New York that I hadn't used while living in Puerto Rico. Why not sell them?

The idea was brilliant, and I was living in the perfect place to do this because Puerto Rico was known for people selling just about anything on the sidewalks and even by the highways.

After a few days of cleaning out the items that were stored in boxes and putting price tags on them, I was ready to start selling.

Every morning, I walked to a different part of town, with my baby and sometimes with the girls, to sell the items.

By the end of the second week, I had made enough money from the sales to feed my family for a month and pay household bills. All thanks to God!

When the next month approached, I began to worry. I searched all over to see if there was anything else that I could sell, but all I found was my watch, which was worth about $100. "Maybe I can get half," I thought.

I walked around aimlessly until I ended up in a middle-class residential area about a forty-five-minute walk from home.

I was nervous and frightened to knock on strangers' doors, but my determination to come home with milk for my son was stronger than my fear.

After a few hours of walking up and down streets and

knocking on doors without any luck, I began to feel tired and hungry.

The last street left was a dead end. One side was lined with the back of the houses I had already knocked on, and the other side an old dirt road leading to a field.

I sat on a fallen tree trunk to rest my blistered feet and began to sob. "What do I do now, Father?" I prayed.

Suddenly, I heard a noise. I followed the sound until I reached the back of one of the houses where a lady, dressed as a maid, was putting clothes in a washing machine.

"May I help you?" She asked, startled when she saw me standing by the fence.

"I'm sorry. I didn't mean to startle you," I said as she cautiously walked towards me.

I don't know what came over me. I didn't know this woman; yet, I poured out my heart and soul to her as I explained that I needed to buy milk and food for my baby and I didn't know what else to do but to sell the last valuable item that I possessed which was my watch.

She seemed touched, as she sadly told me that she felt sorry for my dilemma, but all she had was five dollars.

"Right now, five dollars is like a million," I softly said.

"Wait here," she said and went into the house.

She returned with a tall glass of lemonade and sweet bread and handed it to me. I was so thirsty and hungry that I gobbled it down.

"I'll pray for you," she said as she handed me a five-dollar bill.

"May God reward you double for being so kind," I answered.

From where I was, I had to walk another 20 minutes to reach the nearest supermarket. I had blisters on my feet and barely could walk, but it didn't matter. I had come this far—I wasn't about to give up.

God had sent me an angel and the miracle of a huge sale at the supermarket. With five dollars, I bought milk, rice, and a few canned meats.

The walk back home was slow and painful but full of gratitude and happiness. We had enough food for a few days—maybe a week if I made enough rice. A week was enough time for me to think of another plan.

When I walked in, Manuel was sitting in his usual spot, plucking away on his guitar. He didn't even look up when I said, "Lunch will be ready soon."

While I cooked, I thought back to the person I was, compared to the person I had become.

I thought of all we had been through and the lessons I had learned—one being—humility. And the other was that I had the capability to deal with any situation with God and Jesus, who strengthened me.

One morning, while spending alone time with my Heavenly Father, I asked him to help me find a job. God answered my prayer, but not as I had expected, because instead of pointing me towards work, his message was, "You need to get your high school diploma."

"The idea makes sense," I thought. "But I need a job now."

Nevertheless, I knew better than to argue with my Heavenly

Father; so, the next day, I went to Christina for guidance on how to get my high school diploma.

Christina smiled and said, "Now, this is the Rosita I know. God is right. Getting your diploma gives you a better chance of getting a job. The process takes time, but don't forget that if it's in God's plan, you will find a way to provide for your family while you work on it. I'll bring you all the information you need to start the process."

Two weeks later, I registered in a six-month G.E.D. Preparation class at the local library.

To help with the financial situation until I found a job, God sent me the idea of going back to the streets to sell items.

I had noticed that in Puerto Rico, dolls were very popular. I loved to sew, so why not sell dolls dressed in princess dresses created by me?

At first, I wasn't sure if my idea would sell, but I went for it anyway, not only because I felt God sent me the idea; but because it sounded like a lot of fun.

I invested a small amount of my food money in buying a dozen plastic dolls, remnant pieces of material, thread, lace, buttons, doll stands, and glue.

I designed and created a beautiful gown, with a matching sun-hat, for each doll.

When I placed the dolls on their stand on my kitchen table, I gasped. They looked absolutely beautiful. Then, I packed six dolls carefully, and off to town I went.

It took courage to go to the busiest part of town, where regular vendors already had a spot. With my chin raised high, I held up a doll and joined the chorus of vendors, "Hurry—hurry—only five dollars."

At first, the food vendors gave me bad looks; but after a while, when they realized that I was not competition, they actually helped me by sending their customers my way.

I was on a roll. Within three hours, I had sold the six dolls and had customers ordering for the following week.

By the end of the second week, I had so many orders that I stopped selling in the streets and worked from home.

I studied for my GED exam and continued making and selling my dolls, which were a hot item for birthdays, weddings, and decorations. I was earning more than enough money to support us.

Manuel was not happy with me selling dolls and people coming to the house to order dolls, but every time he told me to stop selling them, I said, "I will—when you start providing for this family."

The power of God is amazing. He was waiting for me to get off my butt, and start doing something, instead of waiting for Manuel or someone else to solve the situation.

Six months later, I was holding my General Education Diploma in my hand. I was surprised to see that I had gotten a pretty high score on all the subjects except Spanish.

"What is your next step?" Christina asked while handing me a slice of cake she had bought to celebrate my accomplishment.

"I'm going to college to get a degree so that I can find a really good job," I answered with a smile.

The next day I visited the recruiting office at a university that had recently been built walking distance from home. I was told that I needed to pass the college entry exam, pay a five-hundred-dollar registration fee, and have enough financial aid or money to cover four years of college.

I felt like a huge mountain had fallen in front of me because I didn't have any of the three requirements.

However, my faith was strong enough to know that if college was the path God wanted me to follow, He would move this mountain—no matter how huge it seemed.

If the earth trembled every time God sent me a sign, I would have felt a huge earthquake on that day because my eyes came upon a tiny ad on one of the pages of a woman's magazine that read, "Contest for mothers over thirty who want to attend college."

I was in awe as I read the instructions. According to the ad, all I had to do was send in my personal information with a short essay explaining why I wanted to go to college and why I could not afford to.

The three top winners would receive a grant if they met all the requirements. "How great are Thou? Thank you, Jesus!" I prayed, filled with joy.

There was one slight problem. All contest participants had to be registered at an accredited university or college before entering. The deadline was in four months.

"How was I going to pass a college entrance exam and pay the registration fee before the deadline? It's almost impossible," I thought.

Well, one thing I had learned was that "impossible" was not in God's vocabulary. He had made it very clear that when a mountain did not move despite my efforts, if I believed and had faith, and it was in His plans—He would move it for me.

That's exactly what God did. He moved every obstacle that stood in the way of going to college. I passed the college entrance exam. My mother sent me the registration money. And financial aid was approved.

Before the contest deadline, I was registered at the Inter American University of Puerto Rico - Ponce, where I would start classes in two months.

God's miracle did not stop there.

A few weeks before starting classes, I was notified that I was one of the contest winners. The prize was a grant that covered whatever financial aid did not cover, plus room and board, books, and all expenses, for the length of time it took for me to obtain a degree—as long as my grades did not go below a three-point average.

On top of all this wonderful news, I was informed that my household expenses were covered under "room and board" because it was considered "off-campus" boarding. I would get a five hundred dollar check every quarter for expenses to use as I pleased.

Glory to God in the Highest! How could I not believe in God's miracles?

University life was not easy. It was quite stressful and challenging, and, for me, it was extra challenging because my Spanish was rusty, and most of the classes were in Spanish.

I juggled between day and night classes, which ended at 10 p.m., and I struggled to find the time to study and work on my assignments, which I had to do when everyone was sleeping and on an old fashion typewriter.

Nonetheless, I didn't let the minor frustrations get to me—I just kept plowing through with God's help.

Manuel hated that I was in school and knew that if he didn't take care of Alexander, it would be impossible for me to continue. So, in anticipation of the possibility of him refusing to do so, I enrolled Alexander in a nursery program across the road from the university.

Daycare for Alexander was covered, but I was still at Manuel's mercy to babysit during my night classes—and he knew it and constantly reminded me, which caused me a lot of stress I didn't need.

One day, at the beginning of my summer semester, I came home to find Manuel packed. He said he was returning to the states to find work. Just like that, without warning.

I'll never forget what he said when he walked out, "I guess now you have no choice but to quit school and stay home where you belong."

Alexander's nursery school was closed during the summer; so, I took a few days off from school to search for a babysitter, but they were too expensive and were not covered by my grant.

I wasn't going to give up, so I armed myself with God's courage, took a chance, and walked into class with Alexander—even though it was against school policy to bring a child to class.

God worked His usual miracle because each professor looked the other way as if Alexander were invisible.

My classmates loved Alexander (especially the girls). They helped hide him every time an administrator came near the class. And they kept him busy coloring or reading.

I believe my professors and classmates were angels sent by God so that I could complete my summer classes.

The fall semester was not going to be a problem because Alexander was scheduled to start pre-school at the same time. Since it was within walking distance to the university, I scheduled my classes at hours that allowed me to take him to school and pick him up.

I didn't need Manuel, but God must have wanted him back in my life because when he found out that I had continued school without his help, he had no reason to stay away. He returned home a few weeks after school started.

One Sunday, I had quite an experience during church service. I was praying and trying to hide my tears from Alexander when I looked up and saw a glowing white figure standing at the altar.

I knew in my heart that it was Jesus. He stretched His arms outward, looked straight at me, and smiled. I felt as if He had taken me into his arms, shielding me from all harm.

When my weekend school assignments became tougher, I stopped going to church so that I could complete them on time and replaced Sunday service with an hour of "alone time" with my Heavenly Father.

During my Sunday time with Jesus, I began to feel that God wanted me to give testimony of my faith; so, I wrote my testimony and asked Christina to give it to the pastor at her church.

When Christina returned, she told me that the pastor felt that my testimony should be shared publicly. I wasn't sure what that meant, so I left it in God's hands.

My second year of college was even harder than the first. Not only because I was struggling with my marriage, kids, and school;

but because I wasn't feeling well.

I was suffering severe stomach and back pain. My stomach couldn't hold anything in. I prayed for strength, but I was feeling so sick that I decided to see a doctor.

At first, the doctor diagnosed me with some type of gastric condition, which he felt was generated from stress. Then, after an emergency visit to his office with stomach pain and dehydration, he sent me to the lab to get a series of gastrointestinal exams, including fourteen abdominal x-rays.

The day that I went for my test results, I received shocking news. "You're not sick—you're pregnant," the doctor said.

"That can't be, doctor. I haven't missed a menstrual period. Besides, my husband and I have only had sex once in the last couple of years, and he used a condom. I can't be pregnant," I answered, puzzled.

"In rare occasions, some women will get their period while being pregnant," he explained. "The x-rays show that you are pregnant, but just so that you have no doubts, let's do a pregnancy test."

While I waited patiently for the pregnancy test results, I thought, "I can't be pregnant—unless—Manuel tricked me and didn't use a condom on the night that he unexpectedly forced himself on me."

The pregnancy test was positive. In fact, I was close to three months pregnant.

I was dumbfounded as I walked home in a daze.

When I told Manuel the news, he looked at me like I was making it all up.

"You can't be pregnant with my child—I haven't touched you," he said in a loud voice.

"What about the night you forced yourself on me? Did you forget that night?" I asked angrily.

His expression turned into one of a child caught doing something wrong, and then he walked out of the room without saying a word.

Manuel's silence confirmed what I suspected—he had not used a condom.

I wondered, "Did he intentionally want to get me pregnant so that I quit school?"

Whether Manuel intended to get me pregnant or not didn't matter because deep down inside, I felt that the baby was a gift from God.

I was happy that there was nothing physically wrong with me, and I was happy that I was having a baby.

Now, I had one more reason to keep working towards my degree—my children.

During my second visit to the gynecologist, I received distressing news. I was informed that because fourteen gastrointestinal x-rays had been taken during the first trimester of my pregnancy, there was a 99% chance that my baby would be born brain-damaged or without a body part.

"Your case has been reviewed by the heads of our gynecology and pediatrics department, and they both have concluded that your pregnancy should be terminated as soon as possible," the gynecologist coldly said.

"Are you serious? There's nothing wrong with my baby," I said loudly. "Besides, I'm on my fifth month. Isn't it dangerous to terminate a pregnancy at five months?"

"We can terminate a pregnancy at any time if we have medical evidence that the child will not be born normal enough to function. If you don't agree to terminate your pregnancy, we will need for you to sign papers stating that we are not responsible for anything that happens to the baby or you during birth or after. Think about it, but don't take too long to decide," the doctor said with no emotions.

Instead of disclosing what I had just learned, I kept it from Manuel until I had time to pray and ask for God's guidance. I needed God to tell me what to do—and I needed the answer now.

The next day I went to school as usual. I was very quiet in religion class, something that was unusual because ever since I started the class, all I did was debate with the professor, who happened to be a Baptist minister.

Concerned, my professor approached me at the end of the class. "Are you ok?" he asked. "You were abnormally quiet today."

"No, I'm not ok," I murmured.

"Do you want to talk?" he asked.

"No, I can't—not here," I said in tears.

He handed me his card and said, "Call me."

That night I told Manuel what the gynecologist had said.

"You're terminating this pregnancy. We don't need to bring a sick baby into this world to suffer," he said in anger.

I prayed so hard that night that I could hear myself praying even in my sleep.

Instead of going to school the next morning, I went to see my religion professor at his church.

I poured my heart out to him. I told him that I didn't want to make a decision without getting a sign from God on what to do and that I was worried because no matter how much I prayed, I had not gotten an answer.

My professor suggested that I be patient. He said God answers all our prayers but in His time—not ours.

"That's just it," I cried. "The doctors want me to decide by next week. What if God doesn't answer me by then, and I make the wrong decision?" I sobbed.

"Pray and trust that He will answer you. You said He's never abandoned you. You said that even when you thought you were drowning, He pulled you up just in time. Why have doubts now?" he gently asked.

I don't know if I was hallucinating or if the tears in my eyes were playing tricks on my vision because when I looked up, his handsome, kind face looked like the face I had seen in my dreams—Jesus' face.

We prayed together, and then he began telling me about his past life and how he ended up being a pastor.

Although I nodded once in a while, I really wasn't focusing on what he was saying until I heard him say, "…this was the only Baptist church in Ponce back then."

"Wait—did you just say that this was the only Baptist church?" I asked.

"Yes, my father was the pastor then. Weren't you listening?" he asked with a frown.

"I'm sorry, I was—well, some of it—but it's just that my parents were married in a Baptist church here in Ponce back in the fifties. That means that your father married them in this church. Isn't it coincidental that we met and that I'm here? I asked, fascinated.

"God works in mysterious ways," he sighed. We prayed again, and I left, feeling much calmer.

When I got home, I asked Manuel why he wanted to kill our baby.

"I don't want to kill it. I just feel that it's not fair to bring a baby into this world to suffer. What if it needs special medical attention? We won't be able to give it the attention it needs when we can barely afford to support ourselves. I couldn't bear watching my child suffer that way," he hoarsely said.

That night, I heard a voice in my dream say, "Your baby will be born normal."

When I woke up, I was calm and at peace.

After drying my tears, I touched my stomach, smiled, and said, "You're going to be ok."

After telling Manuel my dream and my decision, he asked, "Are you sure?"

"Yes, I am absolutely sure that this is the right decision," I answered.

On the day of our appointment with the gynecologist, we both signed the forms releasing the doctors and the hospital of all responsibilities.

As we got up to leave, the doctor said in an angry tone, "I hope you both know what you are doing."

We walked out, hand in hand, without giving him an answer.

My due date was supposed to be in the middle of June, yet it was the beginning of the second week in July, and I still hadn't given birth. Several trips to the emergency room with severe contractions that turned out to be false labor pains had me very stressed. Although worried, I put all my energy into my schoolwork, managing to finish my second year of college before the baby was born, something that would not have happened if I would have given birth in June.

On my last trip to the emergency room, my godfather instructed me to sit down and not move until he returned. When he returned, he was accompanied by a young doctor who he introduced as an old student of his who was now head of one of the medical departments.

In less than ten minutes, I was being rushed to a pre-delivery room, where a team of doctors and nurses were waiting.

They hooked me up to two monitors and attached rubber cables everywhere, including my birth canal.

The doctor that had admitted me came in and was kind enough to explain what was happening.

"We are monitoring you and the baby to make sure both your vitals are ok before we induce labor. A few minutes after inducement, your water will break, and you will begin to feel labor contractions," he said in a kind voice.

After my water broke, I was left alone with the beeping sound of the monitors. I prayed and asked God to let my baby be ok.

While I stared at the numbers on one of the monitors, I noticed the numbers descending very rapidly; then, an alarm went off.

At first, I thought it was a fire alarm, but it wasn't—it was one of the monitors.

Seconds later, the room was full of nurses and doctors. I wasn't sure what was happening. I heard one of the doctors say that my baby's heartbeat was slowing down rapidly.

Another doctor yelled, "Take her to the delivery room immediately. We need to deliver this baby right now before we lose it."

Labor was painful but fast. I heard someone say it was a girl, and after that, they were whispering amongst themselves, so I really couldn't hear anything else.

"Is she ok?" I asked.

No one answered.

"Why isn't she crying?" I asked frantically while I tried to sit up.

No one answered.

Then, I heard my baby cry. "Thank God, she's alive," I sobbed.

Then, instead of placing the baby on my stomach, like they did with Alexander, they rushed her out of the room without any explanations.

"Wait—why are you taking her away?" I desperately yelled. "What's wrong? Why isn't anyone telling me anything?"

"Calm down, you'll see her in due time," one of the nurses said as they worked on my afterbirth and stitches.

I was so exhausted that when I was wheeled into my room and helped onto my bed, I fell asleep right away.

The next morning, I was awakened by a nurse who insisted

that I shower and wash my hair.

When I got off the bed, I felt weak and lightheaded as I tried to stand on my own.

My bed was soaked with blood, and blood was dripping down my legs. I complained, but the nurse said it was normal.

When I returned from the shower, I was shivering uncontrollably. Minutes later, a woman doctor came in, did a vaginal exam, and then told me that I was discharged and could go home.

"How can I be discharged?" I asked loudly. "I gave birth less than six hours ago. I'm bleeding, and I feel weak. I haven't even seen my baby. Nobody has told me anything about my baby."

"You can see your baby when your family comes to pick you up. They've been called, and they should be arriving soon," she said coldly and walked out.

When my godfather walked in, I frantically told him what happened.

"Calm down," he said. "As soon as Manuel comes with your discharge papers, we will insist on a meeting with the baby's doctor."

After my discharge, we were directed to the pediatric ward, where a pediatrician informed us that my baby girl had suffered trauma during birth.

"Due to some concerns, we need to keep the baby in the hospital for a week or so," the doctor began, "She was born with a condition called Newborn Jaundice, which is treatable. We began treating her with phototherapy, which works in most cases, but if it doesn't, then she'll need a blood transfusion. Also, because her birth was overdue, we need to make sure she didn't swallow any fluids."

"My poor baby—she's been through so much," I said sadly. "Aside from all you told us, is she ok? I mean, was she born with all her body parts?"

"When her heartbeat descended so rapidly after inducing, the doctors did not have a chance to notice that she was "face-first," instead of "head-first," which caused her eyes to be poked during the examination. Her eyes are a little swollen, but they should be ok in a few days. As for disfigurements, one of her upper earlobes is slightly different from the other, but aside from that, she has all her body parts and is perfectly normal," he said, smiling.

"Thank you, God, for giving me another miracle baby," I whispered.

The nurse escorted us to a dark room and instructed us to look through a small window. On the other side of the window were around a dozen babies in their individual cribs, all under some type of spotlight and wearing sunglasses.

"Is that her?" I heard Manuel ask from behind me.

"No, that's not her," I said as my eyes searched the room until I spotted her near the back wall. I smiled as the nurse signaled to her. There she was with a funny, weird hat and paper sunglasses under a huge lamp.

"You are late young lady—do not make it a habit," I told her, laughing.

When I got home, I slept on and off for a few days. At one point, I remember Alexander hugging me tight and sobbing, "I'm so sorry, Mommy. I wished my baby sister would not come home, but I changed my mind—I want her to get well and come home soon so that I can take care of her."

One week later, my baby girl was home. Thank God she did not need a blood transfusion—all she needed were five days of phototherapy to stabilize her blood level.

Emilia and her husband arrived on the same day the baby was discharged. They insisted on baptizing her before they left, so we did.

I wanted to name her Leilani, but Manuel did not like it, so we decided on Rebecca—short and sweet.

Rebecca's first three months of life were spent in and out of the emergency room. She kept getting frequent colds and high fevers. She was constantly coughing and throwing up. Luckily, she did not have any trouble drinking her milk. Aside from her colds, she seemed pretty healthy.

One night, I woke up feeling someone shaking me. Strange noises were coming from where the baby slept. When I got to her, I found her lying with her face in her own vomit. I quickly picked her up, cleared her nostrils, and rushed her to the hospital.

The doctor said that if I hadn't woken up when I did, she could have drowned in her own fluid.

I have no doubt in my heart that Jesus woke me up that night.

A few months after I gave birth, my stomach began bothering me again. Twice, I was taken to the emergency room with severe chest and back pains, but all they did was send me home with a follow-up appointment.

On the second follow-up appointment, a regular doctor diagnosed me with hepatitis.

Everyone in the household was vaccinated, and I was placed on home quarantine, medication, and injections. I couldn't leave the house—no one could come near me or touch anything that I touched—I couldn't even hold Rebecca or Alexander.

The treatment should have made me feel better, but it didn't—I was actually feeling worse. When my urine turned dark red and my stool turned beige, I was sure something terrible was wrong with me, so I went to see a gastrointestinal specialist who ruled out hepatitis right away and scheduled a series of tests, which took weeks to complete.

In the meantime, I returned to school, hoping to be able to catch up with all the work I had missed.

God definitely showered me with incredible strength during that time because keeping up with school, taking care of Rebecca and Alexander, going back and forth to the doctor and lab, and taking care of the household—while being in constant pain—was something that I would not have endured without God's help.

After various gastrointestinal tests, the specialist finally had a diagnosis.

"You have gallstones, which usually is not considered a risk; however, because your condition was not treated on time, your gallbladder filled with so many gallstones that they passed on to your liver. This is a very severe condition. If you don't have an operation right away—you could die," the specialist informed me very seriously.

I felt like a mountain had just fallen on me and crushed me, leaving me weak and hopeless.

At home, alone in my room with my Heavenly Father, I did what any human being would do in my situation. I cried, screamed, vented, blamed, and asked over and over again—why?

After crying my eyes out, I felt so bad for yelling at God that I fell on my knees and prayed for forgiveness.

"My faith is weak, and I just don't have any energy left to fight the battles that keep being thrown at me. Please don't let me drown," I pleaded. "Please carry this cross for me or give me the strength to carry it myself." Exhausted, I fell asleep.

When I woke up, my spirit and mind felt energized enough to make a decision. Although I was in my third year of college, I was going to get my associate degree before the operation, and then when I was well again, I would get my bachelor's degree.

My graduation ceremony took place on a cool, windy day in May 1988. The pain in my back, chest, and stomach was so severe that when it was time for me to walk up the aisle to the stage where the graduates were receiving their diploma, I barely made it.

With every step I took, I felt a sharp pain shooting from my back to my chest, as if someone were stabbing me. I prayed and prayed. I pictured God, Jesus, and angels holding me on both sides—helping me with every step I took. By the time I reached the steps going up to the stage, I felt like I was floating.

As I extended my hand to reach for my diploma, the pain stopped long enough for me to enjoy the rest of my day as a Magna Cum Laude graduate with honors.

After graduation, my original plans were to accept a position the university had offered me working with transfer students and then rent a nice house and start fresh. Unfortunately, I had no choice but to put my plans on hold until after I recovered from the surgery I had to have because of my illness.

A few days before my surgery was scheduled, Manuel took a trip to New Jersey, leaving me without someone to take care of the kids while I had surgery and recovered.

I prayed, asking for guidance. God answered in a passage from the Bible that spoke of traveling far away. I was confused. Why would God want me to travel, and where to? The message did not make sense, so I asked for a sign.

The sign came the next morning when my mother called asking if I would consider returning to New York for the operation so that she could take care of the kids until I recovered.

I didn't want to leave Puerto Rico, but I accepted the offer because I had no doubt that New York was where God wanted us to go. Would I return to Puerto Rico? Only God knew.

I can DO
ALL THINGS *through* CHRIST
who strengthens ME.

PHILIPPIANS 4:13 KJV

CHAPTER FIVE
Betrayal

*"For by grace you have been saved
through faith. And this is not your own
doing; it is the gift of God."*
(Ephesians 2:8 KJV)

My babies and I arrived in New York on June 30, 1988. The needed surgery was way overdue. The pain was so bad that I spent most of the day in bed, moaning and praying that it would stop. It was a blessing to be staying with my mother and her husband, who took care of the kids and tried to make things as comfortable as possible for me.

After two months of dealing with the Medicaid process, new doctors, and new tests, I was finally operated on in September. It was touch and go for a while in the operating room because aside from removing my gallbladder, which was infested with gallstones, they had to cut a small piece of my liver where some of the stones had migrated.

A few days before being discharged, I received unexpected news. While I was in the hospital, Manuel had arrived with his three kids, and since they didn't have a place to stay, my parents let them stay in the apartment they had rented for me in the same building where they live.

"I told you I was returning to Puerto Rico after I recover, so why did you rent an apartment for us?" I asked Emilia.

"The doctor said it would take six months for you to recover. I rented the apartment with a one-year lease so that you can recover totally before you go back, and we also registered Alexander in school," Emilia answered.

I wasn't happy, but I didn't argue because it made sense; besides, I had to trust that God had His reasons.

"Ok, I'll keep the apartment for a year, but as soon as Alexander finishes school in June, I'm returning to Puerto Rico," I said.

The first three months of recovery were very hard for me; mostly, because I had no choice but to do what everyone else told me to do, and I had to let them make decisions for me—which I hated. I was also frustrated that Manuel and his kids were living with us, but since I didn't see much of them during the day, I figured I could deal with it until I was back on my feet again.

I felt deep down inside that my marriage was over—it had been for a long time. The only thing that had kept me with Manuel was the promise I had made on our wedding day, and that promise no longer existed because Jamie had turned eighteen shortly before I left Puerto Rico.

One lazy cold afternoon, in the middle of January 1989, while Alexander and Rebecca were napping, my life's journey took me down an unexpected path.

I was reading the newspaper, and for reasons that I did not know, I found myself reading the employment ads.

A small help-wanted ad for a receptionist popped right out of the page. The name of the company was "Guardian Home." The name of the company intrigued me, and so did the details of the ad.

The position was a night shift position. If I worked at night, I could be home during the day to drop off and pick up Alexander from school and take care of Rebecca. And, if Manuel was willing, he could take care of the kids while I worked at night.

The job also had another plus; it was a twenty-minute walk from my apartment. "Was God trying to tell me something?" I wondered.

"No! This makes no sense," I scolded myself, "especially when I still have two more months of recovery left."

I slammed the newspaper down as I thought to myself, "Not to worry, when the time comes, I will find the perfect job—in Puerto Rico."

I prayed and then tried to take a nap—but couldn't. The ad was haunting me. Then, my eyes opened widely as a thought came to mind, "Why not cut the ad out anyway? In fact, why not go for an interview, and if I'm hired, I could work until I leave?"

"That's it!" I cried out with excitement while I reached for the phone.

The day before the interview, I was extremely nervous. I didn't run anything by Manuel, but I did tell my mom, who reluctantly agreed to watch the kids so that I could go to the interview.

Dressed in the only professional outfit I owned; and holding a binder with all my certificates, awards, and diploma—I left for the interview.

The first part of the interview was with the director's assistant. She asked me some basic questions, made copies of my documents, and gave me a typing test.

The second part of the interview was with the director, who asked me many questions, which I answered honestly. And, who ended the interview by telling me that someone would call me with a decision.

The following morning, I received a phone call from the director's assistant. She said she and the director had been very impressed with my interview; however, they felt that I was overqualified for the receptionist position.

"I understand," I said, a little disappointed.

"No, I don't think you understand," the assistant said. "You're overqualified for the receptionist position, but you do qualify for a daytime administrative secretary position that will be opening soon."

I couldn't believe what I was hearing, and without even thinking, I asked, "May I get back to you on this?"

"Of course; since it's Friday, why don't you think it over and call us Monday morning," she said very nicely.

"Why was I so excited about this position if I planned to return to Puerto Rico at the end of June," I wondered.

There was no doubt in my mind that, for whatever reason, God had sent me this opportunity. Maybe He wanted me to work and gain experience before I returned to Puerto Rico.

The first step was to speak to my mom because if she refused to babysit—I couldn't accept the offer.

"You cannot go to work until you complete the six-month recovery. If you go to work before then, you are taking a huge risk with your health," she argued.

"Mom, listen. I will be sitting down typing most of the day, and

I promise that if I feel the job is jeopardizing my health, I will quit right away," I said.

After a few minutes, she agreed.

The next step was to speak to Manuel, who agreed. Why wouldn't he? After all, it meant extra money to pay the bills that he couldn't afford on the minimum wage job he had found.

When I called the Human Resources Department on Monday to accept the offer, I was surprised to hear my title and who I would be reporting to. I would be the Administrative Secretary to the Director of Human Resources—the same lady that had interviewed me.

Returning to New York was an adjustment for all of us. Even though I had lived in New York most of my life, coming back after living in a different culture for eleven years was difficult.

It was even more difficult for Alexander because Puerto Rico was his home. Even though I had taught him English, adjusting to school and the New York environment was very stressful for him, which was causing him to have constant Asthma attacks.

The new climate wasn't agreeing with Rebecca. She continually had bronchitis and was even hospitalized with pneumonia.

I was having difficulty with Manuel's youngest daughter, who was hanging out with the wrong crowd and taking drugs. I was afraid of her being around my children, so I asked her to seek help or move out. She opted to move out, and shortly after, her sister and brother did also.

Manuel and I argued a lot. I would say that our marriage was not a marriage. We slept in separate rooms, barely spoke, and when we did—it ended with a quarrel. At least once a week, he threatened to file for divorce.

One day, his irrational behavior went a bit too far.

I was reading quietly when suddenly he yanked the book out of my hands, ripped it to pieces, and threw it in the garbage. "I don't want you wasting your time reading books or writing things in that notebook of yours. Your job is to clean, cook, and take care of the kids and me," he shouted.

"Are you saying that I can't read or write? Are you insane? You have no right to forbid me to do anything," I hollered back. "You're my husband in name only. You cannot tell me what to do," I yelled as I slammed the bedroom door in his face.

My job at Guardian Home had its bittersweet moments. I loved my job, but Manuel was making it very hard for me to work in peace. He was so jealous of my job and my co-workers that he constantly called me, and if I didn't pick up, he would get furious. He even changed his work schedule so that he could walk me home after work every day.

When I was hired, I was informed that every spring, the company held a huge fundraiser at one of the most prestigious hotels in New York City. It was part of my job responsibilities to help my co-workers on the evening of the event, which ended at midnight.

I had told Manuel of the event from the start, yet, on the morning of the event, he called me at work and forbade me to go. When I spoke to my supervisor about my dilemma, she was nice enough to invite him; however, when I told him, he refused. I ended our conversation by firmly telling him that I was not going to lose my job over his ridiculous jealousy.

On the night of the event, I was so busy greeting guests, distributing name tags, handing out corsages and boutonnières, and directing guests to different areas of the ballroom, that it wasn't until after 10 p.m. that I was able to call home to check on the kids.

When Manuel answered the phone, he was very cold. He even insulted me by saying, "Why don't you stay with whomever you are with at that hotel?"

I could not believe his attitude, and I really didn't feel like arguing with him, so I asked to speak to Alexander.

"Is it true that you are at a hotel with another man and are not coming home?" Alexander sobbed.

I was shocked. What kind of a man would do this?

I was trying to calm Alexander down by explaining what a fundraiser was and what type of work I was doing when Manuel snatched the phone from him and hung up.

I was still holding the phone and sobbing when I heard one of my co-workers ask if I was all right. She was very sympathetic when I told her about my phone call.

At the end of the night, we were all given a beautiful bouquet of flowers in appreciation for our hard work. I innocently took the flowers home.

When I walked into the apartment, Manuel was sitting in the kitchen plucking away on his guitar. I walked past him without saying a word.

When I placed the flowers on the kitchen table, Manuel angrily shouted, "You have the nerve to bring home the flowers he gave you."

I ignored his idiotic remark as I sat down and began taking off my shoes.

Then, he lost it. He started calling me horrible names and saying that I had cheated on him. He said I was no better than his ex-wife.

I got up—walked to the kitchen sink—and started washing dishes—without saying a word.

Manuel kept yelling, but I wasn't listening; instead, I was praying and asking God to make him stop.

When I heard the word "divorce," I slowly turned and asked, "What did you say?"

"I said I'm getting a divorce, and I'm keeping the kids," he huffed.

I angrily walked right up to him—stared coldly into his eyes—and said, "No, YOU are not getting a divorce—I am. As for the kids, I will get custody because I have not done anything wrong. I kept my promise of taking care of YOUR children until the youngest one became eighteen. Did you keep your promise of supporting and providing for this family? No—you didn't."

I turned and walked out of the kitchen, leaving him stunned.

The next afternoon, I filed for divorce.

After reviewing my case, the lawyers informed me that my divorce was not a complicated one and that they didn't see any reason why I should not be granted the divorce and full custody of the children. They said that the process would take at least six months, but, in the meantime, their advice was for me to file for a legal separation, which I did, and which was granted within a few weeks.

It hurt deeply to be wrongfully accused of something I had not done because no matter how many hardships our marriage faced, or how Manuel behaved towards me, I had been a loyal and faithful wife up to the time we became legally separated—after that, in God's eyes—I wasn't.

I had met someone at work a few months before filing for divorce. His name was Nicholas, a mysterious, tall, dark, handsome man with an elegant mustache and captivating smile who resembled a 1930's movie star.

Nicholas was good-looking, but I can assure you—we were just co-workers who spent many lunch hours sharing our stories. Nicholas vented about his ex-significant other and the three daughters he had with her. And, I vented about my marriage, my hopes and dreams, and my children.

When my separation from Manuel became official, Nicholas invited the kids and me to watch him play baseball at our neighborhood park. I'm not a sports person, but I thought it would be a good chance for me and the kids to do something different, especially since they were having such a hard time with the separation; plus, it would be good for Alexander because he loved baseball.

The kids had a great time at the game, especially Alexander, who was allowed to hang out with the baseball players. After the game, we stayed at the park, eating hot dogs and watching the kids play. I hadn't seen the kids this happy in a long time—and so was I.

When Manuel found out that I had a "male" friend and that the kids had met him, he became very angry. He even had the nerve to ask me if he was the man I had slept with on the night of the fundraiser.

Instead of defending myself by saying that Nicholas and I were just friends, I responded to Manuel's accusations by reminding him that we were legally separated and that in our separation agreement, it stated we were free to see whoever we wanted.

The kids enjoyed watching Nicholas play so much that we

ended up going to many of his games. During one of them, Nicholas mentioned how he missed his daughters and how he wished they could see him play, so I told him about my father—ending the story by saying, "No matter what happened between you and their mother, the girls are not at fault. Trust me when I say that being rejected by my father messed me up for a long time. I wouldn't wish that on any child."

I must have hit a nerve because, after our conversation, Nicholas began visiting his daughters, going to their school events, and finally bringing them to his games.

One day, while we were having lunch, Nicholas mentioned that he hadn't seen a movie in a long time.

"I haven't seen a movie that isn't about animals or cartoon characters in ages," I chuckled.

"Why don't we see one together?" he asked.

"I would love to go, but I can't ask my mom to babysit after work hours—she's doing enough for me already," I answered.

"Would you consider taking a few hours off from work instead?" he asked with a big grin. "There's this movie about Lambada dancing that I've been dying to see."

"I love movies about dancing," I said while thinking about it. "Ok, sounds great," I said excitedly.

Our movie date started as any movie date between two good friends. We were like two school kids, eating popcorn and joking around as we eagerly waited for the movie to begin.

The movie was so romantic, passionate, sensual, and seductive that it aroused us in ways that neither one of us had been in a long time.

When our knees touched, I felt a tingle.

When he put his arm around my shoulder and gently pulled me closer—I felt like I couldn't breathe.

When he turned my face towards his and passionately kissed me—my whole body went on fire.

We had entered the movie theater as friends. But, when we came out, we both knew we were much more than that.

After the unforgettable movie date, Nicholas, and I, could not get enough of each other. It was hard for us because, at work, we couldn't let anyone know we were a couple. The only moments of privacy that we had were the ones spent on the phone every night before going to bed.

During one of our midnight conversations, Nicholas suggested that we take our relationship to a sexual level.

I was hesitant—not because I didn't want to, but because even though I was legally separated, my divorce wasn't final yet, and I wasn't sure if, in God's eyes, I would be breaking a commandment by having sex before the divorce.

I should have put my dilemma in God's hands and waited for his answer—just like I did with everything else in my life. But I didn't! Instead, I convinced myself that being intimate with Nicholas was ok because I was legally separated.

A few days later, we both took half a day off from work and spent a blissful afternoon in each other's arms at a Bed and Breakfast near Prospect Park.

Six weeks later, I found out that I was pregnant.

The news of my pregnancy was so overwhelming that I couldn't think straight. All I wanted was to go to sleep and never wake up.

I wanted to pray, but a part of me felt like I had broken one of the Ten Commandments, and God wanted nothing to do with me.

"You haven't sinned," my inner voice said. "The separation agreement clearly states that both you and Manuel are free to see other people while you wait for the divorce to be final."

"If that's true, then why do I feel like I've let God down?" I said to myself.

The battle in my head was too much to bear, so I called my co-worker, who had become a close friend.

"Rosita, you need to make a list of the pros and cons of your situation and your options. Then, you must dig deep into your heart and soul and ask yourself which option is the one that you will feel most comfortable with," Laura said after I told her the news and how I was feeling.

After hours of thinking, I angrily said to myself, "What am I doing? Why am I making a list and weighing my options? There are only two options. I have my baby—or I don't."

I prayed, and after praying, I clearly heard a voice say, "Legally, you have not sinned; but, in the eyes of God—you have. Don't turn away from God because you feel He doesn't love you anymore. God forgave Adam and Eve. He will forgive you too. This baby is a miracle from God, just like your other two children. Trust in God and believe that He will not forsake you."

When I told Nicholas that I was pregnant with his child, he frowned and asked, "Are you sure?"

"Yes, I am sure," I answered.

"May I see the test results?" he asked.

"Of course," I answered as I handed him the test results.

While he read, I said, "I'm not asking you for permission to keep the baby, nor am I asking you for financial help. I'm telling you because I feel you should know."

Nicholas handed me the test results and quietly asked, "When is your next gynecology appointment?"

"In two weeks. Why?" I asked suspiciously.

"Because I intend to be a part of this pregnancy, and my baby's life—if you allow me to," he answered tenderly.

"Ok, now it's time to break the news to my family," I sighed.

Emilia took the news of my pregnancy better than I had expected. She immediately said that she didn't think being pregnant would hurt my divorce because it happened after the divorce was filed and legally separated. She was especially happy that she could be part of this pregnancy.

Rebecca took the news just like any toddler would. All she cared about was that she would have a baby brother or sister to play with.

Alexander was nine years old, and even though kids at that age usually speak their minds, he really didn't show any emotions or said anything. He wasn't upset, so I took that as a sign that he was ok with it.

When Nicholas broke the news to his parents, his mother was not very happy. She was afraid that the baby would ruin her plan of reuniting Nicholas with his ex and his daughters—a plan she had been working on for months.

When Manuel found out about the baby, he immediately accused me of cheating on him. He refused to believe that my relationship with Nicholas began after I filed for divorce and was legally separated. He even went as far as saying that he would tell everyone we knew back in Puerto Rico that I was an adulteress.

Did I defend myself? Why should I? Those that knew me and loved me knew better than to believe his lies. He lied because it was convenient for him to look like the victim instead of admitting that our marriage was over way before we left Puerto Rico.

During the first months of my pregnancy, Nicholas and I took things very slow. He visited us on weekends, or we would go out with all our kids so that they could get to know each other; after all, they were all going to be related to the baby.

In my fifth month of pregnancy, we found out that we were having a boy. Nicholas was in seventh heaven because, like most men, he had always wanted a son. From the moment he heard the news, he began treating me like I was the most important person in the world.

One day, Nicholas called and said, "Things are getting really bad here with my mother—I just can't take it anymore. Make room in your closet for my clothes because I'm moving in. I'll be there in a few hours with my things," he announced and hung up before I could say a word.

"What just happened?" I asked myself while clutching the phone.

Nicholas moving in with us was something that I did not expect—nor want. I felt that the kids and I needed time alone to heal from all that had happened to us in the past years, especially now that the baby was coming. I would have preferred my relationship with Nicholas to continue as it was, with him visiting—not living with us.

I was annoyed because not asking me felt like he was invading my space. He didn't give me a chance to ask my kids how they felt about him moving in or prepare them. I didn't even get a chance to ask God for guidance.

Thank God that the kids did not object when I told them Nicholas was moving in. I really feel that if they would have, I would not have allowed it—or would I?

From the moment Nicholas moved in, I felt like my life was being controlled again. He not only put my clothes in the kid's closet, took over my closet, and moved our furniture to his liking, but our schedules, meals, and even the people we visited were all according to his preference.

Our schedules were so busy that my head was spinning. There was always someplace to go, someone to visit, or something to do. I found it very hard to keep up with Nicholas' busy lifestyle, especially during my last four months of pregnancy. There was no lay-back time in my world anymore—I even lost my private moments with Jesus and my Heavenly Father.

On the other hand, Nicholas was actually very helpful and caring, which I took as a sign that he loved me, even though he never told me. When I asked him why he never told me, he said he didn't have to say it—he had to show it.

Rebecca was late coming into this world, but not this baby. This baby was in a rush and not waiting for its due date, which was a week away.

Contractions began on a cold, snowy Sunday morning. After calling my doctor, we rushed to the hospital, where I was taken to a small examining room.

"It will be a few more hours before you are fully dilated," my doctor said. "I'm going to go downstairs for a cup of coffee. Don't worry; the nurse will page me if anything changes."

The doctor hadn't even been gone a few minutes when the contractions became stronger, and I felt like pushing.

I heard the nurse say, "The baby's head is crowned—we need to deliver this baby now."

Then I heard Nicholas yell, "Get the doctor—quick."

"There's no time. When I paged the doctor, he was in the elevator going down to the cafeteria—this baby is not going to wait for him to come back up—in fact, we don't even have time to get her to the delivery room," she hurriedly said.

There I lay on a short examining table without leg holders, without a monitor, without instruments, and without a doctor.

Thank God that while the nurse was putting clean blankets under my butt and literally tying blankets together to form a safety net for the baby to fall into, my doctor arrived.

My son, Tony, rushed into this world with a big sneeze instead of a cry, January 20th, 1991. The first person to hold him was his overly excited dad. On the other hand, due to tubulation surgery, I could not hold him until a few days later, when the nurse jokingly carried him into my room like a football.

Tony was welcomed with open arms when we brought him home. Rebecca and Alexander loved him. Rebecca thought he was her real-life baby doll.

That same week, I received my official divorce papers, which was a great relief for me.

Nicholas's attitude towards me changed as soon as we brought the baby home. I stopped mattering, and our son became his world. Don't get me wrong. I loved the fact that he loved our son and that his focus was on being the best father and making sure our son had everything he needed—it was just sad to realize that the only reason he had treated me so well was that I was carrying his son. He wanted to make sure that nothing went wrong during the pregnancy.

Once again, I found myself in a relationship with a man that made me feel like I was being used. But even though I was unhappy, I didn't say anything because Nicholas was a good father to our son and treated Rebecca and Alexander as his own.

Our son's christening ceremony was very touching. Afterward, we had a small celebration at the Knights of Columbus across the street from our apartment, where family and close friends enjoyed a night of great food, music, and dancing.

Dancing was both our passions. We were both looking forward to dancing at our son's christening celebration and had promised each other that even if we were busy hosting, we would find time to dance and have fun—something we hadn't done for a long time.

Things didn't go as we planned. Nicholas was distant all night. He stayed close to his family, barely spoke to me, and not once did he ask me to dance.

Towards the end of the evening, our baby's godfather asked me to dance a fast salsa. I didn't think it was wrong. After all, he was Nicholas's best friend since childhood and now my baby's godfather. We were family—so, I danced.

After the party, while we were cleaning up the venue, Nicholas was very cold with me—almost hostile. I couldn't understand why he was so angry. I was sure I hadn't done anything wrong, so I assumed maybe one of his family members had upset him.

When we got home, I was exhausted after a full day of activities, setting up, hosting, cleaning up, taking care of my three kids plus Nicholas' three kids, and barely eating. All I wanted was a warm shower, something to eat, and sleep; instead, the unexpected happened.

After getting the kids settled, as I was about to go into the shower, Nicholas blocked my path and began yelling at the top of his lungs, "You disrespected me in front of my whole family," he snapped. "You behaved like a whore."

I was stunned. At first, I thought maybe he was drunk, but then I remembered that we had not served any alcoholic beverages.

"What are you talking about?" I asked, confused.

"I'm talking about your dancing with Sebastian," he shouted.

"Sebastian is your childhood friend. You said he was like a brother to you. Sebastian is the person you chose to be Tony's godfather. What is so wrong with me dancing with him?" I asked.

Instead of answering my question, he looked at me as if I was his worst enemy and stormed into the kitchen.

I sat on the sofa for hours, confused and baffled, trying to figure out what I had done wrong. It was just a dance—not a slow dance—it was a fast dance where we didn't even touch. I just couldn't understand what had just happened.

From that point on, things between Nicholas and I went from bad to worse. We constantly argued about everything from Tony's health to his mother's behavior towards me.

To the world, we probably seemed happy; however, we weren't. I was unhappy, not just because of my relationship with Nicholas, but because the drama surrounding my relationship with him and his family affected my three children.

I did not want my children to be part of a hostile environment, especially at a time when they were going through so much.

Rebecca and Alexander were finding it difficult to deal with their father moving to Puerto Rico. Tony was hospitalized twice. First, with pneumonia due to the constant exposure to cigarette smoke when he visited his grandparents; the second, when he was operated on due to a urine leakage through his belly button.

Again, my life was a total mess. So, I turned to the only person that never failed me—my Heavenly Father—who I had neglected for a long time.

Shortly after Tony's first birthday, Nicholas came down with what we thought was the flu. He was so sick that when I took him to the emergency room, he was hospitalized immediately. After many tests, we were given a shocking diagnosis.

The infectious disease doctor very sympathetically said, "I'm sorry to inform you that Nicholas has Pneumocystis Pneumonia— a pneumonia that attacks people with HIV. Nicholas has full-blown AIDS with a very low CD4 T-cell count, which puts him at serious risk of dying from almost any type of infection."

The news hit me like if a ton of bricks had fallen on me and crushed me to death. I didn't know much about AIDS, but I did know that people died from it—and—sexual partners caught it.

All that went through my mind was, "He is going to die! I am going to die! Oh my God—is Tony going to die?"

Nicholas took the news very badly. He called the doctor a liar and insisted that the test results were not his. To make matters worse, he had the nerve to say that if he did have AIDS, I had given it to him. He was in complete denial of the fact that he had this virus long before he met me and that he was the carrier.

The doctor turned to me and said, "You need to get tested, and you need to test your baby."

When I got home, I was in a daze, so I did what I always did when I got hit with humongous mountains—I prayed—I vented to my Heavenly Father—I pleaded for Him to spare my son's life. I told Him that I wasn't afraid to die but to please extend my time on earth so that I could raise my children. I prayed harder than I had ever prayed before, and then, I left everything in God's hands.

God answered my prayers with a double miracle. Tony and I tested negative for HIV—something that was considered very rare due to Nicholas, and I's many times, and I had been intimate and the pregnancy, while he had full-blown AIDS.

At the time that Tony and I were tested for HIV, everything was confidential. We didn't even have to give our names to the HIV counselor at the medical center. The counselor and nurses were all very understanding and compassionate, which helped me tremendously.

"You and your baby are very lucky to have tested negative for HIV. Most women in your situation catch the virus from their partners and then pass it on to their unborn child," the HIV counselor said. "However, you are not out of the woods yet. You need to get tested annually, for the next five years, to make sure the virus isn't dormant."

During Nicholas's hospitalization, I had a few conversations with his ex-girlfriend, who shared a few family secrets that Nicholas had kept from me. Nicholas, and his brother, had been drug addicts for many years, and his brother and his wife both died of AIDS—not in a car accident as he had told me.

I also learned that Nicholas and his ex were separated because he almost killed her by bashing her head with a blunt instrument—not because she had cheated on him as he had said.

After Nicholas and his ex-girlfriend split up, he lived the life of a homeless drug addict until eventually he went into rehab, put his life back together, and moved into his parent's house—six months before I met him.

When I discovered all this, I felt betrayed. I asked myself, "Was Nicholas aware that he had AIDS when we were first intimate? After all, he was in a rehab center. They must have tested him. And, if he did know, how could he put my life in danger? Deliberately having sex with someone when you are fully aware of having AIDS is the same thing as committing a deliberate crime. How could I trust a man like this?"

When the time came for Nicholas to be discharged from the hospital, a decision had to be made about where he was going to live and who was going to take care of him. When I asked him what he wanted, he said he wanted to go home—my home. I could have turned my back on him right then and there, and no one would have blamed me. But I didn't because it's not what God, or our son, would have wanted me to do.

Ever since I had met Nicholas, our relationship had taken bittersweet turns, but never in my wildest dreams did I imagine that he would be dying of AIDS or that I would be his caregiver.

Living with AIDS changed our life. I am not going to go into the details of what an AIDS patient or caregiver faces daily. To describe it would be revolting to the person reading and painful for me to tell. What I will say is that watching Nicholas deteriorate was heartbreaking and draining for all of us.

A few weeks after Nicholas had come home from the hospital, he announced that with his disability money, he had rented an apartment one floor below us. He gave me a key and told me that it would be an extension to my apartment and that we could go in and out whenever we wanted. His decision made sense, so I did not argue.

While Nicholas faced the side effects of multiple medications, pain, depression, embarrassment, and whatever demons were in his head; I had to face performing my best at a full-time job, raising three children, running errands, taking Nicholas to doctor and lab appointments, dealing with his mood swings, cleaning up his vomit and soiled clothing, and schlepping him back and forth to his parent's home every day before and after work.

It was hard, but my Heavenly Father did not let me down. He saw how full my plate was and sent me angels to help me. My mother and her husband bought me an old Malibu Classic to help me run all my errands, and they volunteered to care for the youngest children after work hours.

The AIDS counselor referred us to Discipleship Outreach—an organization that helps people living with AIDS and their family, and who helped us in more ways than one. They offered counseling, prayer meetings, education, and support groups for both the AIDS patient and family members. We went to many holiday and family events, activities, shows, weekend trips, and even outings. Their care, understanding, and support helped us get through some very tough times.

At work, my supervisor and my co-workers were very understanding and supportive during this time of my life. They covered for me when I had to run to the hospital or deal with an emergency with the kids, without once complaining.

Without the help and support of all these angels sent from God, my journey as a caregiver would have been much more difficult than it was. I'll always be extremely grateful to them for their help during this hardship.

Yes, I was going through a lot; but Nicholas was going through much worse. There were times when I would be tucking him in before going to my apartment, and he would cling to me as if he were clinging to life itself. He seemed angry, thankful, and scared, so I would stay with him until he fell asleep. When I left him, I felt drained. All I wanted was to be alone and cry, but I couldn't because I didn't want to scare the kids.

Nicholas began drinking heavily. Sometimes he would be so drunk that he wouldn't recognize me. When a neighbor told me that he saw Nicholas crossing the middle of the street, leaving Tony to walk alone behind him, I realized it was not safe to leave Tony with him without supervision. This hurt Nicholas greatly.

Nicholas was hospitalized for the last time in September 1993. After a long conversation with his doctors and hospital social worker, we both felt that he might not be coming home this time.

Every night I traveled from work to the hospital in the city to visit Nicholas and didn't leave him until well past ten at night. By the time I got home, it was midnight. I would take a shower, go to bed, and wake up the next day to go to work and do everything all over again.

Shortly before Thanksgiving, Nicholas's mother passed. The day before his mother's burial, he begged me to take him to the funeral parlor. I spoke to his doctor and was granted a one-day pass.

I arrived at the funeral parlor with Nicholas in a wheelchair.

Everyone was surprised to see him. His father cried and smiled at me and then asked me to sit in the front with the family.

I began to wheel Nicholas to the front of the altar when I stopped. Then, I walked over to his daughters and his ex, who were sitting in the back row, and said wholeheartedly, "It is only right that you and your daughters be the ones to sit in the front with Nicholas's family. It's what his mother would have wanted."

After his mother's death, Nicholas's health worsened. Within two weeks, he stopped walking and barely ate. His weight dropped very fast. He kept asking for Tony.

On Thanksgiving, I went to visit Nicholas with my three kids, my mom, and her husband. With the nurse's help, we wheeled him into the patient's family room, where we took pictures and ate our last family meal together.

I will never forget how he looked. His hair and beard were long. His face was thin and ashen. I don't think he knew that we were there. All he did was twirl his fingers and stare straight in front of him, hardly blinking.

December was extremely exhausting for me. The winter weather made it impossible for me to visit Nicholas regularly, but I tried to go as many times as I could.

December 17, 1993, I received a call from Nicholas's doctor while I was at work. He asked me to come to the hospital as soon as possible because he didn't think Nicholas would make it through the night.

When I arrived, Nicholas' eyes were closed, so I sat by his side and read some passages from the Bible out loud. Occasionally, he would open his eyes and then shut them.

I wasn't feeling well and was having severe cramps, but I didn't go home; instead, I slept on a cot in the hospital family room near his room.

The next morning, I woke up with my period and felt like crap. I felt uncomfortable because I didn't have pads, a change of clothing, or a toothbrush. I washed up with what was available and tried to make the best of it.

When I met with the doctors that morning, they informed me that the only thing keeping Nicholas alive was the feeding and medication tubes. When they asked me for permission to remove the tubes, I declined because that was Nicholas's wish when he gave me power of attorney.

Later that day, while I was sitting by Nicholas' bedside, his father and sisters walked in. I respectfully left the room so that they could visit with him.

I was in the patient family room, resting my eyes, when Nicholas' younger sister, Ursula, stormed in and started yelling at me. She said I had no right to have power of attorney over her brother and demanded that I release all rights over to her father.

"No, I am not giving you power of attorney. Where were you when he was hospitalized, and since? Now, that he's dying—now you want power of attorney?" I yelled back at her.

Ursula was like a madwoman shouting hysterically. She launched at me but was blocked by her nephew.

I turned away from Ursula in disgust and furiously walked to the nurses' station, leaving her cursing at the top of her lungs.

I was shaking and sobbing so badly that the nurses took me to their lounge to wait for the doctor. When I updated the doctor on what had just happened, he said, "You have the power of attorney, which gives you the right to ask that security escort Nicholas' family off the floor."

Out of respect for Nicholas' father, I told the doctor that I would rather go get some air and come back when they were gone.

The doctor said he would have someone escort me downstairs through another exit so that Ursula would not see me.

I thanked him and asked the nurse to please bring my pocketbook and coat from the family room.

Unfortunately, when the nurse tried to get my belongings, Ursula refused to give them to her unless I released power of attorney over to her father.

I couldn't leave without my coat—it was freezing outside, so instead, I collapsed on a chair and cried.

A debate was going on in my head. Part of me wanted to ask security to escort Ursula out, but the other part of me kept thinking about Nicholas' father—a good and kind man who recently lost his wife and would soon be losing his son.

Then, it hit me. He's the one that had the right to power of attorney—not me, but what about my promise to Nicholas?

After what seemed like hours of crying and praying for God's guidance, I was ready to face defeat, for I was too tired to continue fighting a battle that was not even mine to fight.

I entered the family room, sat in front of Nicholas' father, and said, "I'm doing this for you—not for anyone else." I took a napkin and scribbled the release allowing him power of attorney. Then, I snatched my belongings from Ursula's hand, looked into her cold, bitter eyes, and silently said, "God help her."

As I passed the nurse's station, each nurse hugged me. I thanked them for all their help and then slowly walked into Nicholas' room.

I sat by Nicholas' bedside, read a passage from the Bible, and then prayed in a low voice. I took his hand in mine and softly said, "I know I promised that I would honor your request until the end, but I'm tired—I don't have the strength to fight anymore. I'm going home, but I'll be back tonight. I just need to shower and change. Your family is all here. They will stay with you until I return."

Nicholas opened his eyes and looked straight into mine. A tear ran down his ashen cheek.

I smiled, leaned close to his ear, and whispered, "It's ok to go, don't worry about Tony. He is going to be fine."

When I walked out of the hospital, my heart told me that I would never see him again.

When I arrived home, I was so exhausted that I showered and went straight to bed.

Sometime during the night, I was awakened by a bright light shining outside my window. I sat up motionless, watching the bright light grow bigger as it came through the window, glided to my bed, and circled me.

A warm sensation enveloped me as if I had been hugged. I felt sure that it was Nicholas saying goodbye. I closed my eyes and whispered, "Goodbye."

The bright light disappeared just as the phone rang—it was Nicholas.

I can't remember what he said, but I remember telling him that

I would see him later, and then I went back to bed.

The phone rang a second time. This time it was the nurse informing me that Nicholas had passed. When I asked at what time, she said he had passed a little before 4:30 a.m. "It can't be," I thought. "That's the time he called me."

I hung up bewildered as I wondered, "Who was on the phone with me? Who had hugged me? I must have been dreaming!"

After breakfast, I cuddled with the kids and broke the sad news to them.

Alexander said, "Did he die after he spoke to you on the phone this morning?"

"That wasn't Nicholas on the phone; it was the nurse informing me of his death," I explained.

Alexander was very serious when he said, "No, Ma, you were talking to Nicholas because I heard you say his name when you asked him if he was ok. And then, you said you would see him later. A few minutes later, I heard the phone ring again, and I heard you ask someone what time it had happened."

"It wasn't a dream," I whispered. "It was really Nicholas saying goodbye."

I can DO
ALL THINGS *through* CHRIST
who strengthens ME.
PHILIPPIANS 4:13 KJV

CHAPTER SIX
Forbidden Fairy Tale

*"Love is patient and kind; love does not
envy or boast; it is not arrogant or rude.
It does not insist on its own way; it is not
irritable or resentful; it does not rejoice at
wrongdoing but rejoices with the truth."*
(1 Corinthians 13:4-6 KJV)

As the years passed, waiting to die became very monotonous. I worked all day, came home, helped the kids with their homework, cooked, cleaned, went to bed, and started the same boring routine the next morning.

One beautiful spring afternoon, while I was in the ladies' room fixing my makeup before leaving work, my co-worker Valerie who was standing before the vanity mirror next to mine, asked, "How is Rosita?"

"I'm good!" I answered without giving it much thought.

"No, I mean—how are you?" she asked with genuine concern.

I knew Valerie well enough to know that she wasn't prying. She was genuinely concerned and interested in knowing how I was, which is why she deserved more than just a casual response.

"I feel like I've been on an emotional roller coaster ride. I feel numb most of the time. I feel like my body, mind, and spirit are separated from one another. It's like I am observing my body going through motions, but I'm not a part of it. Does that make any sense to you?" I asked.

Valerie put her lipstick down, turned to me, and said, "For the past eight years, I've watched you deal with one mountain after another, and I have been very worried about you.

First, you took care of Nicholas until he died. Then, you lived the next five years fearing that the HIV was dormant and would surface. And, when you were finally told that you didn't have to worry anymore about the virus surfacing—you got hit with the horrible news that you have a lung nodule that could kill you if you don't have it removed. I just can't wrap my head around how you dealt with all that while raising three kids and working a full-time job without having a breakdown."

"I believe in God's Word. He promised that He would give me the strength to deal with everything that came my way, and He did," I said.

"Having faith is great, but do you realize that eight years of non-stop stress in your life can be very dangerous?" Valerie said.

I weakly smiled and said, "Not eight years—it's more like a lifetime of getting hit with one thing after another."

"Built-up stress is like a volcano that's about to erupt. If you don't take time to relax, have a little fun, and take care of your-self—you will explode. Stop and smell the roses. Remember, even God rested on the seventh day," Valerie said.

Just before she was about to walk out the door, she turned to me and said, "Another thing, Nicholas is dead, but you are still alive. You're not getting any younger. Open your heart to love again." Then, she smiled and walked out, leaving me standing before the mirror.

I took a long look at the reflection in the mirror and thought, "What happened to my lovely full long hair, big bright eyes, and luscious lips? All I see is a tired chubby woman with dark circles under her sad eyes."

While I drove home, I thought about the tall, handsome Prince Charming I used to fantasize about when I was young. The romantic prince who treated me like Cinderella and made me feel like the most important woman in his life.

When I arrived in front of my apartment building, as usual, there was no parking. I double-parked, leaned my head back on my seat, and spoke to my Heavenly Father while I waited for a spot.

"Forgive me, Father, for what I'm about to say, and please don't drop a mountain on my head for sounding selfish; but, even though I've asked you to keep men out of my life, would you grant me one more wish before I die. Will you help me find my Prince Charming so that I can live—in real life—the beautiful romantic moments that I lived in my dreams? I know this is a selfish wish, especially because I will be breaking his heart in a few years when I die, but isn't it better to find love than to die without it?"

A few weeks after I had this conversation with my Heavenly Father, two very weird things happened.

I was having lunch with a few of my co-workers when the conversation about online chat came up. I gathered from everyone's input that chatting online with perfect strangers from around the world was the new way of meeting people.

"Everyone I know is chatting. It's so much fun and so interesting, and if you are very careful and don't get hooked into meeting these people in person, it's actually a safe way to socialize," Susan said.

"Sounds interesting, but I do not own a computer," I said.

That night, the most ironic thing happened. I came home from work to find my mother and stepfather bringing boxes into my apartment.

"We have great news," my stepfather said with excitement. "The company that I work for is selling computers for two hundred and fifty dollars each, so I bought one for us—and—one for you."

"Well, say something, Rosita," my mom said. "Aren't you excited?"

"Of course, I'm excited?" I said. "With this computer, I don't have to rush to the library two or three times a week after a long hard day at work for the kids to work on assignments. We can research at home, in our pajamas, at any time. And I can type to my heart's content instead of writing by hand."

While my stepfather installed the computer, my mother, kids, and I gathered around him, talking about all the exciting things we were going to learn with this computer.

Yes, the computer was going to open up a whole new world to my children—but never in my wildest dreams did I imagine how it would change my life.

I had been curious about online chatting since the girls spoke about it at work. It sounded like a fun way of talking to people without going out. Now that I had a computer, I could find out for myself.

It took me a few weeks to familiarize myself with the process of online chatting, which I found very overwhelming at first.

There were hundreds of chat groups to choose from, and each group had chat rooms for every topic or age group imaginable.

Each chat room had thirty or more members continuously typing conversations to each other, and there was an open microphone where members could speak or play music. The members also had the option of typing in a private messenger box, which was called a private room.

After going in and out of dozens of chat rooms, I joined Chat Room 7. I picked this room because they played my favorite music on an open microphone every night and because the members were close to my age.

The first few days, all I did was park my name in the room and sit back and read what everyone else was typing. I had so much fun reading the comical screen names and hilarious things they typed. Many times, I burst into laughter—something I hadn't done in a long time.

It didn't take long for me to realize that being in a chat room was like being part of a soap opera made up of invisible characters, with all types of personalities, conversing with each other just like people do in the real world. There was more drama in these rooms than in my own neighborhood.

In the real world, we have cities, towns, neighborhoods, and homes. In chat, the chat groups are like a city or town—chat rooms are like neighborhoods—and the private messenger boxes are like the privacy of our home.

One night in July of 2001, I gathered enough nerves to type my first sentence in Chat Room 7. My screen name was "Amor Prohibido," which means "Forbidden Love" in Spanish.

To my surprise, my character was received with a typed ovation of warm greetings from each member. The warm welcome from so many strangers made me feel better than I had felt in a long time.

What can I say? From that day on, I was totally hooked.

Chat was a world that I looked forward to entering every night. Why not? It turned my boring life into an incredible adventure, and the best part was meeting people without leaving my home or kids.

One particular Friday night, while Room 7 was in full swing playing my favorites, a mixture of country and oldies, Amor Prohibido was greeted by Walter—her competitive chat room friend.

"Well, Amor Prohibido, I think tonight I will definitely beat you in the Little Black Dating Book contest," Walter laughingly announced on the open mic.

"Oh? Really, Walter? You and who else believes that?" I smirked on the mic. "I bet you one hundred cyber dollars that in less than an hour, my black dating book will be longer than the Verrazano Bridge."

"We'll see Amor Prohibido—we'll see," Walter said before playing his next song.

I envisioned Walter as a short bald chubby man in his late fifties with a penguin walk, whose humor made up for his lack of looks, and who purposely entertained us every night by comically proposing to every woman in our chat room.

Our little black dating book competition started one night when I challenged him by saying that I could get more dates in one night than he could. Chat Room 7 found our competition so entertaining that it became a regular weekend thing to do in the room. It was so much fun that I would end up in tears from laughing so much.

One night, while I sipped my lemonade and sat back to read the conversations on the screen, a character named Francisco caught my eye. I could tell right away that he was very well known in the room by the way the women flirted with him and desperately tried to get his attention.

Francisco had charm, and he knew exactly how to use it. His words made the ugliest woman feel beautiful, as if she were the only woman that existed. His favorite line to the women was, "Only a Goddess could be worthy of a name like yours."

Francisco also had a dark side. He went from being a charmer to being a foul-mouthed, sarcastic, arrogant, and offensive asshole in a split second. I really didn't understand how the women found this side of him attractive.

"I hate women that throw themselves all over men—where is their dignity?" I thought as I finished my lemonade.

My thoughts were interrupted when I heard Walter shout on the mic, "Amor—I have twenty-two names on my list. Do you give up now?"

"Oh, come on, Walter—only twenty-two names? Don't make me laugh. I just added my 30th name," I lied.

Immediately after I said that, the music stopped playing, and a deep sexy voice said on the open mic, "Hello Amor Prohibido, may I join in on the competition?"

Francisco's voice sent shivers from my neck to my very soul. I had to take a deep breath to get control of my unexpected emotions.

"Take control of yourself," I sternly told myself. "Remember, Amor Prohibido is not like those childish, silly women. Amor is different! She is unique!"

"Nope, you cannot join in our competition!" I typed.

"Ok, in that case, will you add my name to your list, young lady?"

"No! I won't!"

"Why not?"

"Because I don't like you!"

"How can you not like me; you don't even know me!"

Instead of answering Francisco's question, I said, "Excuse me. I have a private message to answer."

Francisco was not used to women walking away from him. He wondered why Amor Prohibido affected him the way that she did. Was it her personality? No way! She was nothing but rude to him. "You haven't seen the last of me, Amor Prohibido," he thought.

When I opened the private message that had popped up on my screen, I was surprised to see that it was from one of the serious women in the chat room.

"Amor, be careful with Francisco. He enjoys chatting with women under different character names without telling them who he really is. He has broken almost every woman's heart in Chat Room 7—and has no remorse over it," the woman said.

"Don't worry. I have no intention of falling under his evil spell. He is too obnoxious and definitely not my type," I said.

"Just be careful. Francisco is very mysterious and hurtful. You seem like a nice kid, and I would hate for you to get hurt," she said.

"Thank you. I'll keep it in mind," I said and then clicked the box closed.

Another private message box popped up. This one was from Francisco himself.

"Talk to me!" he typed.

"No, go away!" I answered.

"You know you want to talk to me, so stop acting like you don't," he insisted.

"Oh? So, you are now assuming that I am putting on an act and that I am dying to drool all over you like those silly childish old women? WELL, YOU'RE VERY MISTAKEN!" I typed in bold letters.

"Assume? Assume only means ass-u-me, Amor. I'm not assuming anything. You just don't want to admit that you're dying to know me," Francisco wrote before disappearing.

Strangely enough, after a lot of resistance on my part, and a lot of insistence on Francisco's part, we began chatting and ended up being friends.

Eventually, our friendship turned into a special relationship that felt like the fantasy love I had in my dreams.

I was well aware that Francisco was a playboy and that he and I would never meet; so, to protect my heart, I treated our relationship as a fairy tale, where Amor was Cinderella, and Francisco was Prince Charming.

Francisco and Amor's romance was full of passion, friendship, laughter, and imaginary adventures. Together, they fulfilled their desires in ways that they had only read in fairy tales or seen in passionate movies. They had the perfect fairy tale romance.

Eighteen months after Francisco and Amor had become a couple, they had a very emotional break-up caused by jealousy and lies.

Amor was told that Francisco was cheating on her with other women in chat. Francisco lied and denied it.

Although I had constantly told myself that Francisco and Amor's romance was not real, the break-up and all the drama involved upset me so much that I decided to leave Chat Room 7, change my screen name, and joined another chat room.

A few weeks after the breakup, Francisco came into the chat room I was in, and sent me a private message.

When I didn't answer, he took over the microphone, and after apologizing for interrupting the music, he said, "Amor, I'm sorry for all the hurt that I've caused you. Please answer my private message."

I was about to leave the room when Francisco said, "What I feel for you is not make-believe—it's real. I don't want to lose you. I want our relationship to be real. I want our love to be till death and beyond. I want to marry you."

Then, on the private messenger box, Francisco wrote in huge bold letters, "**Will you marry me?**"

My hands trembled as I typed, "How can I marry you if I don't even know you?"

I had heard Francisco's deep sexy voice a few times, but I had never seen a picture of him. The only thing Francisco had told me about himself was that his real name was Fernando, that he was retired from the army, single, owned a small construction company, and lived in Houston, Texas.

I had very strong feelings for Francisco and loved what we had; but, after a failed marriage and a rocky relationship, I was not about to jump into marriage without having a real face-to-face relationship.

Francisco's next message woke me up from the battle going on in my head. He wrote, "You're right. Before you answer, give me a couple of months to prove to you that I am serious about my feelings towards you and about marrying you. From this moment on, it's not about Francisco and Amor—it's about Fernando and Rosita. Ok?"

"Could this be real?" I asked myself. "Was Fernando the answer to my prayer of finding my Prince Charming before I died, or was he sent by Satan to distract me from my personal relationship with God and His Son? Or was it both?"

During the next months, my relationship with Fernando grew stronger than ever. I was definitely in love.

There was no doubt in my mind that Fernando wanted to meet me in person as much as I wanted to meet him. We both spoke about the need to hold each other and make things real.

Twice, Fernando made plans to come to New York. Unfortunately, both times something got in the way. So, I made plans to go to Houston instead.

Without mentioning it to Fernando first, I requested a long weekend from work and booked the flight and hotel room. I was excited, and I couldn't wait to tell him.

Fernando laughed nervously after I gave him the details of my weekend trip to visit him. I should have taken his nervousness as a red flag, but I was too blind to see it.

The week before my trip, Fernando became distant and seemed to want to avoid any conversation pertaining to my trip.

When I questioned him, Fernando said that he was just nervous to see me because he was self-conscience about his weight.

A few days before my trip, Fernando made a very emotional and intense confession. He spoke for the first time about his family. He said he was a widow with two grown children and three grandchildren. The oldest lived in Mexico with her husband and children, and the youngest was a resident doctor in Houston.

Then, Fernando added, "I don't know how to tell you this, but my son is getting married the same weekend that you are arriving in Houston. Ever since you told me the news of your trip, I have been trying to figure out how to juggle the chaos of the wedding with our first time together, which is why I've been so preoccupied."

"What am I going to do? The tickets and hotel are non-refundable—I can't change the trip," I said.

"No, I'm not asking you to change the trip," Fernando said. "I'm just saying that I'll have very little time to spend with you because of all that's going on with the wedding. The only available time that I will have will be for a few hours on the night you arrive. It's just bad timing, and I hate for you to waste your time and money for nothing."

Anyone who knows me knows that I am very stubborn. While I listened to Fernando, the wheels were turning in my head until I came up with a brilliant solution.

"Coincidently, a few days after I bought my ticket, a friend of mine who lives in Oklahoma City invited me to watch him compete in a motorcycle race. I told him I couldn't because I was going to Houston.

Instead of staying in Houston, I'll change my flight to Oklahoma City, with a stop at Houston. We can have lunch at the airport before I board my next flight. It's not exactly what we had originally planned, but at least we'll get to meet," I said excitedly.

Fernando responded with that same nervous laugh, followed by, "That'll work."

I landed in Houston four hours before catching my flight to Oklahoma City. I was excited and nervous. The plan was for me to meet Fernando near the check-point area where we would have lunch at one of the airport restaurants.

As soon as I entered the main airport lobby, my phone rang. "Mamita (Fernando's nickname for me), I'm caught in terrible traffic, but I should be there soon," Fernando said loudly.

What could I do? I had no choice but to wait—until I couldn't wait any longer because it was time to pass through security and catch my flight to Oklahoma City.

Tears were streaming down my cheeks as I boarded the plane. As soon as I sat, my phone rang.

Fernando's voice sounded just as sad and disappointed as I felt. "Mamita, I just arrived at the airport. Unless your flight was delayed, I believe your boarding—right?" he said.

I could barely answer. We spoke a few words, and then I hung up, promising to call him as soon as I arrived in Oklahoma City.

I felt sad and so disappointed. How could this happen? Probably, because I didn't pray on it and just impulsively did things my way without consulting God.

"Well, if it's meant to be to meet Fernando—it will happen someday. In the meantime, I'll make the best of this trip," I told myself.

Despite everything, I had a great time in Oklahoma City. I stayed at a nice hotel. My friend took me dancing, and we spent a day at the motorcycle race tracks where he took a great picture of me on his bike to show Fernando.

The morning of my return trip, it was raining heavily with chances of a thunderstorm. The weatherman said that heavy thunderstorms and torrential rain were over Houston and heading towards Oklahoma City.

When I called Fernando and asked how the weather was, he said, "The weather is absolutely beautiful here."

When I told him about the weather report I had just heard, he sounded angry when he said, "The weather changes a lot in Houston."

"Odd," I thought.

After I returned home, Fernando and I continued building our relationship and making it stronger. He was so kind, considerate, and loving towards me that I fell in love with him more and more each day.

That summer, he asked me to marry him again. Somehow, not meeting him wasn't that important to me anymore, so I said, "Yes."

We spent the month of June planning every detail of a Hawaiian theme wedding in Montauk. We had so much fun deciding on colors, clothes, decorations, music, and how we would bring all our children and family together for the event.

"Now that we have a vision of what our wedding is going to be like, shouldn't we pick a date? I asked.

"Absolutely, but first we are taking a trip," Fernando announced.

"A trip to where?" I asked.

"I'm coming to New York to meet your children, and then we are all going to Puerto Rico, where I plan to ask for your hand in marriage," Fernando said.

I was ecstatic. "Could this man make me any happier?" I thought.

In July, Fernando's first attempt to come to New York failed because he was bitten by a snake, which I believed after seeing his swollen leg on cam.

His second attempt was planned for August, on the same day that we were all leaving for Puerto Rico. We coordinated his arrival and our departure so that when his plane arrived in New York, he had plenty of time to meet us at the departure gate.

On the day of the trip, everything started off as planned. Before we left for the airport, I checked Fernando's flight, and it was on time. He would arrive about the time we planned to be at the security checkpoint. I was excited, but at the same time, worried that something would go wrong.

My youngest son was vacationing in Puerto Rico, and my oldest son could not take off from work, so only two other people were traveling with us—my daughter and my oldest son's girlfriend.

Waiting at the security check-point line was torture. The closer we got, the more I felt like fainting.

When we finally reached the departure gate, I looked around anxiously for a man that resembled the description Fernando had given me of himself but didn't see anyone. When I checked the flight board, it showed that Fernando's flight had arrived an hour ago.

I called Fernando's cell, but it went straight to voice mail. "Where could he be," I thought.

The closer it got to our boarding time, the sicker I felt.

The four-hour flight to Puerto Rico was in silence. My heart was broken, but I didn't cry.

I was so embarrassed that when we arrived in Puerto Rico, I lied to my daughter and parents and told them that Fernando had an emergency and could not make it.

For days, I checked my phone messages and nothing from Fernando. I was devastated. I didn't know what to think.

"Did Fernando play with me? No, he couldn't have. He sounded so loving and sincere while we planned our wedding. There had to be a good reason," I thought.

There was only one way to find out, so I left him a voice mail message asking him. Two days later he called me.

"Mamita, I just came out of the hospital where I've been since the morning that I was supposed to fly to New York. My son was driving me to the airport when my arm and chest started hurting, so against my will, he drove me to the hospital instead. Apparently, I had a mild stroke. I'm so sorry. You must think that I'm an asshole," he said, sounding very sincere.

In a matter of seconds, the hurt that I had been feeling turned into concern for his health. I felt horrible for doubting him and feeling that he had to apologize for something that was totally out of his control. There was nothing to forgive, and there was no reason to break up.

As soon as I returned to New York, Fernando continued planning our future. He kept telling me that we had hit a few rough patches but that nothing was going to get in the way this time. He was very loving and kept swearing that he would not let me down again.

I wanted to believe Fernando with all my heart, but he had let me down so many times that I just couldn't. So, when he mentioned visiting me before the end of the year, I said, "No, I don't think I can stand being disappointed again. This time—I'm going to visit you."

Fernando's nervous laugh made me shiver. "Mamita, there's no need for you to spend money so close to Christmas. I promise that this time I'll make it," he said.

"I don't think I can take another thing going wrong between us. If you and I do not meet physically before the end of this year—it's over," I said and meant every word of it.

Fernando was quiet for a long period of time, and then he said, "I have something to tell you."

My heart sank to the floor as I braced myself for the worse.

"I don't live in Houston," he began, "I was born in Houston and lived in Houston most of my life, but for the last few years, I have been living in Monterrey, Mexico, with my daughter and her family.

When I first arrived in Monterrey, my passport was stolen. For the last few years, I've been trying to get a new one, but the process is taking a long time because my identification was also stolen.

When we started planning our wedding, I hired a lawyer to speed up the process so that I could go to New York; unfortunately, to this day, I still don't have a passport."

Mexico? I thought, "No wonder when I called him from Oklahoma City, he said the weather was perfect in Houston when the weather report said torrential rain. He was in Mexico."

"Why did you lie to me?" I asked.

"Mamita, I didn't lie. I swear my intentions were to go to New York. I even tried to get false papers to travel but chickened out because I didn't want to get arrested," he said.

"So, where does this leave us?" I asked.

"Nothing has changed, Mamita. We just need to wait until I get my passport," he answered.

Fernando's confession didn't change my feelings towards him, but it did add to the list of disappointments.

"You and I have a lot to talk about, and it's only fair that we do it in person. You may not be able to travel, but I certainly can. I will go to Monterrey in December," I said very seriously.

"Wait. What did you say? You're coming to Monterrey?" he asked in surprise.

"Yes, I'm going to Monterrey. But, let me tell you that if you don't show up at the airport—it's over, mister—for good," I said.

This time there was no nervous laughter when Fernando said, "Mamita, you are an angel sent from heaven. I swear that I will be at the airport."

When I made my decision to go to Mexico, I did not run it by my Heavenly Father. I acted on impulse and planned the trip without His guidance.

I really didn't know if my decision was in God's plan or if Satan was playing with my mind and making me think it was.

I was fully aware of the dangers of going to a strange country to meet someone I had never seen. It was very risky, but I took the chance anyway because I needed to look into Fernando's eyes and hear him out. I needed to leave Monterrey knowing if I was going to marry or break up with Fernando.

During the flight to Houston and then Monterrey, I prayed for God's protection. I prayed that I did not get kidnapped, raped, or killed during this trip and that I returned home safely.

The walk from the runway to baggage claim was nerve-racking. I was so nervous that, while I waited for my bags, I avoided looking at the crowd that stood behind the glass door waiting for passengers.

I acted cool, calm, and collected as I picked up my bags and purposely walked slowly towards the automatic glass doors.

When the doors closed behind me, my heart pounded as I looked at the few people left.

Fernando walked slowly towards me, holding a red rose in his hand.

My heart melted.

When I jumped into his arms, I felt like I had just come home. I don't remember how long we held each other. All I know is that I didn't want him to let me go.

We both spoke at the same time, in between tight hugs and kisses.

The days I spent with Fernando were the most romantic days of my life. He treated me like a princess. He was kind and considerate. He even remembered how I liked my coffee and all the little things that I had shared with him during our online conversations.

Fernando being a widow was one more reason for me to feel that I had found the man of my dreams. He did not belong to anyone else but me. I could be his little girl, his lover, his wife, his everything, without ever worrying about ex-wives like I had with Miguel and Nicholas.

When Fernando spoke of his feelings towards me and our future together, I could see in his eyes that he was honest. I left Monterrey feeling like the luckiest woman in the world and the most loved.

While we waited for Fernando's lawyer to get his official documents, I visited him religiously, once or twice a year. Twice, I brought the kids along.

During every trip, Fernando made me feel like I was the most important person in his life. He took care of me. In fact, every time I arrived in Monterrey, the first thing he did was, take my watch and put it away. When I was with him, I didn't have to plan. I didn't have to rush. And, I didn't have to look at the time.

Three years passed, and Fernando still hadn't received his passport. I was so fed up that all I did was question him. Every time, he avoided the conversation.

Deep down inside, I felt that Fernando was hiding something. So, in the spring of 2006, I went to Monterrey with one purpose in mind—to get answers.

During the cab ride from the airport to the hotel, I was quiet. I dreaded the questions I had to ask because I feared that Fernando's answers would bring our relationship to an end.

That night, I told Fernando how I felt.

"For five years, I have been waiting patiently for you to come home and have believed every excuse you have given me every time you didn't.

It doesn't take this long for you to get your passport, especially when you have a lawyer working on it. I feel deep in my heart that there is another reason. And, if you don't tell me what it is—you will never see me again."

Fernando stood with his back to me, looking out the wall-to-wall window at the busy street seven floors below.

After what seemed like hours, he finally walked slowly towards me and sat down—his face looked as if he had just been told that his best friend had died. My heart sank when I looked into his watery eyes. Then, he hit me with a revelation that crushed my soul.

"Mamita, I swear to you that you are the only woman that I love. However, my ex-wife is not dead as I had told you. She is alive, and I really don't know if I am still married to her or not. I mean—I have been led to believe that I am divorced, but I have not seen the official documents because I moved to Mexico before the divorce was finalized," he said.

I was stunned. I didn't know what to think. I didn't know what to say. I just sat there with tears in my eyes and totally in shock. How could he propose and plan a wedding when he wasn't sure he was legally divorced?

"For the past three years, I've been trying very hard to deal with fixing my legal situation and finding out my divorce status so that we could finally get married. I'm sorry I didn't tell you, but I had no idea it was going to take me this long," he sobbed.

Any other woman would have probably ended the relationship right then and there. I wanted to scream out how I felt, tell him how much he hurt me, even hit him, but instead, I put my arm around him, told him how much I loved him, and held him close while silently feeling totally broken inside.

We both tried to make the best of the rest of the week, but no matter how much we tried, there was a thick black cloud hanging over us.

I spent a few days in bed with horrible stomach cramps, which I'm sure were a result of holding in my anger and tears. Fernando's blood pressure went up the last two days of my trip, which resulted in him being ill and having a fainting spell. We were both a mess.

When we parted at the airport, he swore he would fix things, and we would be married just as planned; and even though I responded with a weak smile—I just didn't believe him.

My return trip included a four-hour stop in Houston, which gave me more than enough time to go over Fernando's confession. I thought back to all the times he had disappointed me, and all the times I believed his excuses. He lied about being single. He lied about where he lived. Was every believable excuse he had given me in the past five years lies too?

It's not fair. In less than a week, I had gone from being engaged to a widowed man who swore I was the only woman in his life to possibly being his mistress—with no rights whatsoever to him or anything that had to do with his life.

Now I understood why, in five years, he never put his family on the phone or took me to meet them when I visited him in Monterrey.

Then it hit me. If Fernando was not legally divorced, that meant that I had broken one of God's commandments. I, who had been so proud of following God's laws—was a sinner.

I don't know what hurt more, Fernando's confession or hurting my Heavenly Father.

"My dear Heavenly Father, I am so confused. I love Fernando, and I don't want to lose him. If there is the slightest chance of us being together, please bring him home," I prayed.

For the next six months, our relationship continued in the same direction, with Fernando promising that he was taking care of his situation so that he could come home and get married.

The roller coaster ride of emotions wore me down. I just couldn't take one more let-down or web of hidden truths. So, I decided to take one last trip to Monterrey, for my birthday, with one purpose in mind—to give him an ultimatum.

Surprisingly, my birthday trip to Monterrey was the best. We both focused on each other and not on asking questions or talking about the past.

Fernando was very loving, warm, and caring. Every moment of our time together was very romantic and passionate.

We went to a museum and walked the romantic streets of Monterrey. We even visited a very old church and exchanged vows of loving each other "till death and beyond."

On my last night, we held hands at the restaurant and gazed into each other's eyes. After dinner, we danced to soft music in our room. We fell asleep in each other's arms as if we were afraid to let go.

In the past, our tearful goodbyes at the airport were routine. Fernando would promise to come home soon, and I would assure him that if he didn't, I would return to Monterrey. This time, all we did was hold each other in silence.

When it was time to part, I held my tears, and with determination, in my voice, I said, "The next time you see me will be when you come home. I will not be returning to Monterrey."

Fernando did not say a word, but I could see the hurt in his eyes.

After passing through the checkpoint, I stepped onto the escalator that went down to the gate area. I turned and smiled as I descended. Fernando smiled back and then looked away as he raised his eyeglasses to wipe the tears.

I wanted so badly to run back to him, but instead, I watched him as if trying to suck him into my very soul and keep him there forever.

In seconds, he was out of my sight—that's when my tears started flowing.

The next nine months were very hard on both of us. I constantly pressured Fernando to come home. Every time, he came up with an excuse, and, every time, I found a reason for it not to be an excuse and pressured him more.

"There are no excuses for you not to come home. I've already told you a million times that you can work on your divorce situation from home," I insisted.

Towards the end of August, I put my foot down and gave him another ultimatum. I told him that if he did not come home before my next birthday—it was over.

I sincerely believed with every fiber of my being that if God wanted Fernando to come home—he would. So, I prayed and then left it in God's hands.

At the end of August, Fernando announced that he finally had a passport and had made plans to come home.

Was I excited? No, not really, because I had heard a similar story for five years.

On September 2nd, my heart sank when Fernando said, "Mamita, I've encountered a little set-back that is forcing me to delay my trip but don't worry—it's just a set-back that can be resolved."

Whether Fernando was telling me the truth or not did not matter. I was sticking to the ultimatum that I had given him. If he doesn't come home by my birthday—it's over.

A few days later, Fernando happily announced that everything was resolved and that he had bought a one-way ticket to New York City.

"Mamita, next month I will finally be home," he said with a chuckle.

Fernando had disappointed me so many times in the past that I just couldn't believe him. All I could do was pray and leave things in God's hands because I believed that if it was in God's plans for Fernando to come home to me, he would.

I also believed that if Fernando didn't come home, it was a sign from God that it was time to let him go. Would Fernando make it home this time, or was I going to be disappointed for the last time? Only God knew.

On the day that Fernando was supposed to arrive, the weather from Monterrey all the way to New York City was very bad. I had received a voice mail message from Fernando very early that morning saying that he was about to board the bus that was taking him from Monterrey to Austin, Texas, where he would be boarding a plane to New York City. He mentioned the weather by saying that he hoped there would be no delays.

The comment about the weather raised a red flag in my already doubting mind. Would the weather be his excuse?

His flight wasn't due to arrive until nine-thirty that evening, so I tried to go about my daily routine until it was time for me to head for the airport. My nerves were a mess. A part of me was excited, and the other was bracing for another disappointment.

When Tony and his friend asked if they could go with me to the airport, I was relieved because I was a little nervous traveling at night by myself, especially with bad weather.

The trip to the airport was long. First, we traveled on the subway, then on the Long Island Railroad, and finally on the airport shuttle. Despite the weather, we made it to the airport an hour before the flight was scheduled to arrive.

The waiting period was torture. Although I laughed at the boy's silly jokes, inside, I felt as if I was going to have an anxiety attack or faint.

The anxiety grew, even more when I looked up at the arrival board and saw that Fernando's flight was delayed two hours.

The next two hours were torture. I kept looking at Fernando's flight on the arrival board until it finally read—arrived.

While Tony and his friend jumped up excitedly, and greeters started getting up from their seats, hurrying to get closer to the arrival doors, I sat frozen.

"Ma, hurry, or we're going to be too far to see Fernando," Tony said excitedly.

I couldn't move. Every part of my body was shaking. "No—you guys go. I'll wait here," I said.

It seemed like hours, but really only minutes, when I spotted

Tony and his friend walking back towards me through the crowd.

And, right behind them, was the most beautiful man I had ever seen—my Prince Charming.

Fernando's arrival made my birthday, Thanksgiving, and Christmas holidays the best I had ever had. He fit in perfectly with our ways. It felt like he had always lived with us. The kids, and their friends, seemed ok with his presence. I was in heaven.

After the holidays, I began noticing that Fernando was quieter than usual. He seemed sad. When I asked him what was wrong, I was surprised by his answer.

"Mamita, I love you and your kids, and I love living with you; but I think I'm going through a culture shock that I can't seem to shake off," he began.

"Everything around here is different from any place I have ever lived. I'm used to greeting and socializing with my neighbors. The other day, I said "good morning" to a few people, and every response was nasty. One person angrily asked, "What's so good about it?"

You live in an Asian neighborhood where most people don't know English. I'm not being racist but living here reminds me of the time I was in combat. Asians were our enemies. Living here is bringing back all the anger I felt back then.

I'm used to living in a spacious house. This apartment is very small and cramped. It makes me feel claustrophobic. We can't even have a family dinner because we don't all fit around your small dinette table.

I'm alone from the time you and the kids leave in the morning to the time I pick you up at work. I'm not used to being alone. I need people to talk to.

I want to take day trips and go out as a family, but between your job and weekend chores, we rarely go out; and the kids are too busy with their friends and social life to hang out with us.

My social security check doesn't go far here. It frustrates me immensely when I cannot contribute to the household expenses. I am used to earning money. In Mexico, it's much easier for me to make money than here. In Mexico, I had a small cybercafé, tutored students in English, fixed computers, and sold software. I need the extra income.

To top things off, the winter weather is killing me. My knees hurt so much that I'm thinking of buying a cane to help me walk."

I listened to Fernando and felt so bad for him. He sounded miserable.

"I understand your frustration. What can I do to make it better?" I asked.

"There's nothing you can do," Fernando said, "I love you, and want more than anything to spend the rest of my life with you — but not here. If I continue living in pain, broke, unhappy, and frustrated, I won't live long enough to make it to Puerto Rico."

We had discussed living in Puerto Rico many times and we were both eagerly waiting for my retirement to fulfill this dream. Unfortunately, my retirement was six years away.

I held my breath waiting for him to say that he was returning to Mexico and that our relationship was over.

"What if I return to Mexico until you retire?" Fernando asked.

I responded with, "I truly understand what you are saying, but if you return to Mexico, I will not be able to visit you because my savings are gone; and, I refuse to be your online fiancé for six more years—I just can't take that type of relationship anymore."

"Listen, I have an idea," Fernando said, "What if I spend winter months in Mexico and return every spring or summer? Can you live with that?"

It wasn't what I wanted, but six months out of the year was better than nothing. After thinking it over for a few minutes, I smiled and said, "Sounds like a plan."

In the middle of January, Fernando returned to Mexico; and I returned to my old life. I missed him terribly, but the months went by so fast that before I knew it—he was back in my arms again.

The first summer that Fernando returned, we took a trip to Disney World for Rebecca's 21st birthday. The kids and I had gone there many times when they were little and loved it. We were all very excited to return, especially to celebrate Rebecca's birthday. I really thought Fernando would love it too, but he didn't.

During the whole trip, he complained about the walking and the heat. He hated everything we did and everywhere we went, except for the steak house. He was an old grouch the whole time. I even overheard him telling his grandchildren, on the phone, that Disney World was the worse place to come to. It hurt me to hear him say that.

When I questioned what was wrong, he simply said that the pain in his leg was killing him, which had to be true, because not only was his knee swollen, but his ankle was swollen and looked bruised.

After the trip, he got grouchier. He would sit in front of the computer all the time and stay on it even after I went to bed. He said he was chatting with his grandchildren and his daughter, but when he constantly shut the computer down when I came near, I started suspecting that he was chatting with another woman.

Fernando constantly complained about not having anything to do in New York and how helpless he felt. He also shared that his daughter was sick, and he worried about her and the children. So, in early November, he returned to Mexico—he didn't even wait for my birthday.

The following spring, Fernando was supposed to come home, but he didn't because his daughter wanted him to build new kitchen cabinets for Mother's Day. Then, when he finished the cabinets, she told him that he had painted them the wrong color; so, he had to re-paint them.

God forgive me but, at that point, I was honestly thinking that Fernando's daughter was not only making up her illness, but she was doing everything in her power to stop him from returning home to me. Well, I wasn't about to let her win; so, I pressured him to return home.

Fernando returned just in time for Tony's high school graduation, which made Tony so happy because he really liked him. I was also happy and excited to have Fernando home, especially because I had a lot planned for us to do together.

After Tony's graduation, Fernando and I decided that it was time to paint the apartment. We had so much fun picking paint colors and working together on redecorating our room. I felt "married," and it was a great feeling. Fernando was happy too because he finally felt useful.

At least once a month, we escaped to Atlantic City, where we would play the slots, go to the buffet, and see some great shows. The times we spent in Atlantic City reminded us of the times we had in Monterrey. The trips became our honeymoon getaway.

In September, we went to New Jersey to attend my oldest son's wedding. It was during that time that I noticed that although Fernando seemed happy, there were moments when I saw a sadness in his eyes.

When I asked Fernando what was wrong, he simply said that his daughter had told him that she was feeling ill again, and his grandchildren kept pleading for him to return.

"You're not supposed to go back to Mexico for another two months. Are you trying to tell me that you're going back sooner?" I asked.

"I thought about it. Melisa is sick, and she can't take care of the kids. She needs my help," he said.

"What about her husband? Why can't he help until you get there?" I asked. "Besides, did you forget our trip to Puerto Rico in November? Your ticket is paid for, and it's not refundable. Can't you return to Mexico when we return from Puerto Rico—as we had planned?"

"Sure. I'll go to Puerto Rico to meet your parents as planned while my daughter lies in a bed sick, and then I'll go on to Mexico," he said sarcastically.

For the life of me, I couldn't understand what was going on in Fernando's head. "Was it really his daughter's illness? I asked myself.

The trip to Puerto Rico did not go as well as I had imagined. My mother obviously did not like Fernando, because she made things very uncomfortable for him. She even went as far as commenting that Mexicans were to blame for crime and drugs in Puerto Rico. I wanted to die when I heard her say that.

Mom did something else that totally upset me. She invited my ex-husband, Manuel, and his wife, to spend time with us—on my birthday. Who does that? It was my birthday. I was with my future husband. The last people we wanted to spend time with were my ex-husband and his wife.

It was very obvious that Mom was out to jeopardize my relationship with Fernando. Surprisingly, while I was upset, Fernando took it like a gentleman, which made me love him more than ever.

We returned to New York a few days before Fernando was to leave for Mexico. We spent the final days in serious conversations about our future.

"Mamita, this trip to Mexico is not only about taking care of Melisa," Fernando began, "I am going back to make sure that the land I inherited from my father is sold. With the money I get from the sale, I will give some to Melisa, and with the rest, we will build our house in Puerto Rico. I will also work on making sure my divorce is final.

I don't know how long all this will take, but I suspect our house will be built way before you plan to retire. Now, my question to you is, are you willing to retire and move to Puerto Rico before your retirement age if the house is built before then?" he asked.

"Are you kidding me? Of course," I answered without a second thought.

When Fernando left for Mexico, although I was sad to see him leave, I was excited and happy because I believed with all my heart that this time he was really going to work on our future.

Finally, the dream of living in our own house in Puerto Rico, where we would spend our days gardening, taking leisure walks, and watching the stars every night, while sitting on the porch on our rocking chairs—was going to come true.

Every conversation that Fernando and I had during his absence reassured me that he was working hard on selling his land and getting his divorce finalized. He didn't avoid the conversation like he used to in the past; instead, he enthusiastically shared every detail of the process. Fernando's enthusiasm was so contagious that I dared to trust him once again.

When May arrived, I began planning Fernando's return. I was so happy with all the progress he had made with the land and the divorce that I wanted our reunion to be private and special; so, I made reservations at our usual hotel in Atlantic City for the weekend of Father's Day.

Early June, Fernando announced that his lawyer had advised him not to leave yet because he had to be in Mexico to sign papers pertaining to the sale of his land.

"I know you are disappointed—so am I, but we're so close to selling this property that I don't want to do anything to delay the process," Fernando said.

"I understand perfectly, Fernando," I said. "Selling the land is what's important right now."

"I'm glad you understand, and I'm really sorry that you have to cancel the Atlantic City trip," Fernando said.

"Oh, I'm not going to cancel it. It's already paid for. Besides, I need to get away and relax from all the craziness that I've had to deal with lately. Who knows, I might even visit the spa on this trip," I said excitedly, "I might even ask the kids if they want to join me."

"Is everything ok at home? Fernando asked.

"Yes, it's just that lately, I've been having a little conflict with Tony. I really don't know what's going on with him, but lately, he's been acting very strange," I said.

"I'll talk to him when I get home. He probably needs a male figure to talk to, and we've always gotten along," Fernando said.

"That would be great, Fernando. Thank you. But, in the meantime, focus on getting the land sold so that you can come home," I said.

Since Fernando had left in 2009, my stress level had reached a boiling point. Between work-related stress, financial difficulties, my relationship with Fernando, and worrying over Tony's change in personality, I desperately needed a couple of days to get away from everything and relax.

Fernando didn't seem too happy about me going to Atlantic City by myself, but I wasn't going to let that stop me from going. This trip was exactly what I needed. Besides, my supervisor had already approved taking Friday and Monday off, and the bus and hotel were paid for. It would be crazy not to go.

When the coach bus heading towards Atlantic City closed its doors, I let out a deep sigh of relief. "Finally, my mini-vacation had begun," I thought as I leaned my head back and closed my eyes.

After checking in to the hotel, I bought coffee and pastries and went up to my room to rest and check my itinerary.

"This weekend is going to be all about relaxing, pampering myself, indulging, planning my retirement, and celebrating," I told myself while sipping coffee comfortably in my room.

"I am going to eat my favorite chocolates and pastries, watch my favorite movies, sleep late, eat all I want at the buffet, sit at the slot machines, have a full spa experience, and not look at the clock until my departing day.

This weekend I was also celebrating. I was celebrating that my three miracles were adults with goals and dreams of their own; and that it was ok to cut the cord and go for my own dreams.

Alexander was married to Victoria, who was a wonderful girl. And, God had given me the gift of witnessing the birth of their beautiful daughter—my first grandchild—Amber.

Rebecca was going out with a very nice young man who seemed to care very much for her. She was working at a pediatric clinic and was planning to attend bartending school so that she could work at a four-star hotel someday.

Tony was a determined young man who set goals and went for them. The past year alone, he had graduated from high school, found a job, bought a car, started a small business selling health products, and was getting ready to start college. Doing all this at the same time had to be stressful and probably the reason for his change in personality.

I was celebrating that my last CAT Scan showed that the mass in my lung was miraculously shrinking, and I didn't need the operation—another miracle from God.

I was celebrating that Fernando's property was finally being sold and that soon we could begin construction on our house in Puerto Rico.

On my bus trip back home, I was all smiles. The weekend had been perfect. I accomplished everything that I had set out to do, including drafting a four-year plan of things I needed to complete before moving to Puerto Rico.

"I'm finally getting off the never-ending roller-coaster ride of unexpected turbulence I have been on for most of my life," I thought. "It's time to take a rest from tribulations, enjoy my family, work on my book, plan a future with Fernando, and begin the journey to my happily ever after."

Suddenly, I heard a voice say, "Not so fast, Rosita, because around the corner lies an unexpected turbulence that is going to knock you off your seat. Buckle up with all your faith because this ride is going to be very rocky—probably the worst you'll ever have."

I can DO
ALL THINGS *through* CHRIST
who strengthens ME.
PHILIPPIANS 4:13 KJV

CHAPTER SEVEN
Possessed By Fear

*"For God hath not given us the spirit of
fear; but of power, and of love, and of a
sound mind."*
(2 Timothy 1:7 KJV)

Never in my wildest dreams did I imagine that just when the future looked so bright, my children and I would be facing a battle so evil that no matter how much faith I had—I was not prepared or strong enough to fight—a long exhausting battle that changed our lives forever.

My youngest son Tony was a normal teenager. He was a loving, kind-hearted young man with a sense of humor and a great personality who loved to play handball, basketball, and baseball.

Tony worked hard to accomplish his goals, even when the odds were against him. At nineteen, he graduated from high school, had a job, started a home business, bought a car, and was planning to start college. He was very persistent and determined to make his dreams come true.

Tony wasn't perfect. He was impatient and a little short-tempered, but not in a rude or disrespectful way. When he showed this side of him, we jokingly said, "It's all about Tony." And we shrugged it off.

After my trip to Atlantic City, Tony's personality and behavior changed drastically. He became someone I did not recognize. He was edgy, spoke fast, and changed topics so rapidly that I couldn't make sense of what he was saying most of the time.

Weekends became a living hell. Every conversation between Tony and I turned into an argument—something that had never happened between us. It got to the point where I looked forward to Mondays, just to get away.

On Friday, July 30th, 2010, voices outside my window woke me up at 5 a.m. I looked out the window and saw Tony talking to one of his friends. I couldn't make out what they were saying.

An hour later, Tony came in. He went to the bathroom and then left. I peeked out the window but didn't see him.

Something wasn't right. "What was he doing outside so early, and where did he go?" I wondered. I was so edgy from worrying that I got dressed and left for work early.

Two blocks from home, I spotted Tony walking across the street, in the opposite direction, as if he were heading home. I called out to him twice, but he kept walking. The third time, he finally stopped.

My heart sank when Tony turned his head and glared at me with eyes full of hatred.

I asked Tony if he was ok. But, instead of answering me, he shrugged and began punching the air with his right hand, body swaying as if getting ready to fight.

I wanted to keep questioning him, but I didn't. Instead, I said, "I'll see you tonight."

His whole body looked tense and angry when he walked away.

I continued my walk to work, confused and worried. By the time I got to work, I was emotionally exhausted. So, instead of going in early, I decided to walk to the church two blocks away and pray.

When I got to the church, I was very disappointed to find that a mass had started—only because I really wanted to be alone with my Heavenly Father.

I sat in the back of the church and silently prayed for my son. When I finished, I leaned back, drained of all energy. I just couldn't get up.

I looked up at the statue of Jesus, at the left side of the altar, where He usually stood smiling with his hands slightly extended. It surprised me that I could see his face so clearly from where I sat.

I searched for comfort in Jesus' face. Instead, I saw something that scared me. Jesus was not smiling. He looked so sad. And His eyes were full of tears.

I blinked a few times thinking it was my imagination, but it wasn't—it was real. Jesus was crying.

My heart sank because at that moment, I felt deep down inside that Jesus was crying for me. It's like He was trying to warn me that something horrible was about to happen and that He had to allow it.

The feeling of doom overpowered me.

After work, instead of going food shopping as I usually did on Fridays, I went straight home. No one was home when I walked into the apartment, which was weird for a Friday night.

I ordered Chinese food, and since I was still alone when it arrived, I decided to eat in my room while I watched TV.

I was about to take the first bite when I heard the front door open, followed by heavy footsteps coming towards my bedroom.

Tony stopped by my bedroom door. He seemed more tense and angry than that morning. He was so angry that he panted and hissed when he hoarsely said, "I don't like you anymore. I can't live here."

Without thinking, I said, "I'm not stopping you from moving out."

"I hate everyone. I'm going to kill myself," Tony shouted. Then, he walked away, mumbling something that I couldn't make out.

"I ordered Chinese food. It's in the kitchen," I called out while trying to get a grip. I know my words sounded stupid after what had just happened, but I just couldn't think of anything else to say.

A few minutes later, I heard the outside door slam close. Seconds later, someone banged really hard on my bedroom window. It had to be Tony.

I sat staring at my untouched dinner. Suddenly, I smelled smoke. At first, I thought someone was smoking outside my window. But my gut feeling was that it was coming from inside our apartment. So, I hurried to check.

The smoke smell was very strong in the kitchen, but there was no visible smoke. I checked the stovetop and outlets—nothing.

I was about to open the oven door when I saw one of my kitchen towels on the floor. I picked the towel up and examined it—part of it was burnt.

"That's why it smelled like smoke. The towel caught fire—but how, when I'm always so careful not to leave it on top of the stove," I wondered.

"If someone hadn't stopped the towel from burning, the fire would have spread to the whole apartment—with me in it," I nervously thought. "Who turned off the fire? It had to be Tony. Who else if no one else was in the apartment but us?"

Suddenly, I started shaking uncontrollably. My body went into high panic mode, and I lost it. I couldn't think. I couldn't pray. I couldn't talk, much less scream. My right arm turned in a weird position as if it were in a sling. Fear overpowered me. I wanted to run, but all I could do was cry.

In desperation, I called my daughter's cell. I tried to explain what had happened, but all I could do was sob. The only thing she understood was, "Help me."

A few minutes after I spoke to my daughter, someone knocked on my door. When I opened it, I was relieved to see that it was my daughter's best friend and her brother, who lived next door.

When they saw the state that I was in, Elaine immediately called my daughter and told her that I needed help.

"Why is Rebecca taking so long?" I asked Elaine.

"She will be here soon; it's just that she and her boyfriend are driving from Jersey," Elaine said.

"Oh my God, I forgot they were going to stay in Jersey this weekend. I just can't think straight," I sobbed.

An hour later, my daughter arrived. I tried to go over what had happened, but I could hardly get through a sentence without crying and shaking.

"Ma, I cannot leave you here in the state that you are in. I'm taking you with us to Jersey so that you can get a good night's sleep. We'll deal with this tomorrow," Rebecca said.

"What about Tony?" I asked. "He wasn't himself. He even said he was going to kill himself."

"The important thing right now is getting you somewhere where you can relax and calm down before you have a stroke. We'll talk about Tony tomorrow morning. I'll call him as soon as we get to the hotel," Rebecca said.

On the drive to New Jersey, my hand stopped shaking, but my mental state got worse. I could not focus. I could not think. I could not do anything. I could hear, but I could not speak. It was like if something had reached into my mind, body, and spirit and ripped out every ounce of strength and faith that I had, replacing it with fear and weakness.

I was possessed by the demon of fear and did not have the strength to cast it out. I couldn't even pray. I was of no use to anyone.

That night, Rebecca, her boyfriend, and Alexander all heard from friends and family describing details of a rampage Tony was on.

A few neighbors texted that Tony was pacing up and down the street talking to himself.

Some friends texted that Tony had been outside their homes threatening them.

Rebecca's co-worker texted that Tony had shown up at her workplace, dressed in a suit, asking for her, and acting incoherently.

When my daughter and son tried to text Tony, he responded with horrible and hateful words. It was obvious that there was something terribly wrong with him.

I received a phone message from my mother saying that Tony had called her, saying that everyone had abandoned him. She said he kept screaming, crying, and talking without making any sense.

This all went on Friday night through Saturday. By Sunday, my daughter told me that Tony seemed calmer on his texts. She said he was behaving more like a frightened child.

When Alexander told me that we were all heading to my apartment to find Tony, I began shaking again. The thought of going back to my apartment filled me with fear.

We arrived in Brooklyn Sunday night. Alexander did not use the apartment keys; instead, he rang the bell.

I stood behind him.

Tony came out of the apartment and opened the building entrance door. He looked horrible. He spoke very fast and was very edgy. He greeted each one with a hug.

When we went into the apartment, I walked straight into my room while everyone else stayed in the kitchen. My room was a mess. It looked like a tornado had hit it.

Apparently, Tony had barricaded himself in my room. There were piles of quilts high on the bed forming a tent, furniture had been moved close to the door, and all the kitchen knives were on the floor.

When I went to the kitchen, Tony was nervously talking to everyone. I hardly understood what he said, except that he was under attack and had to defend himself, which explained the barricade in my room.

I didn't know what was happening to Tony or to me. All I knew was that we were both genuinely terrified of something.

I couldn't watch my son go through such fear, so I went back to my room and sat on my rocking chair until my son and daughter came in.

"Ma, Tony needs help. What do you want us to do?" They asked.

Somehow words came out. "Take him to Maimonides Hospital. Tell them what happened and ask them to evaluate his mental state. I'm afraid that something will make him hurt himself or someone else," I sobbed.

A few hours later, Alexander came home to tell me that Maimonides had referred Tony to Staten Island University Hospital for a psychological evaluation.

"Rebecca and her boyfriend are driving Tony to Staten Island. I cannot go because I need to get my family back to Jersey. Please call me and let me know what happens," Alexander said as he and Victoria prepared to leave.

Somehow, I managed to go to bed until the phone woke me up. Rebecca sobbed, "Ma, the whole process at the hospital took all night. First, they did blood tests, and then Tony was seen by a doctor; and then, by a psychiatrist. I stayed with him throughout the whole process. He seemed so scared—like a little boy. He kept begging me to take him home."

Rebecca could barely talk. I could hear her sobbing. After a minute or so, she continued, "Ma, they hospitalized Tony. He's in the psychiatric ward. It was terrible," she said as she began sobbing again. "He kept begging me not to leave him there, but there was nothing I could do." Then, she broke down and cried.

I felt so helpless with the whole situation. For the first time, I could not help my son with what he was going through. I couldn't even comfort my daughter.

What was wrong with me? I was supposed to deal with the situation—not my daughter. Why couldn't I function? Why couldn't I take charge? This is not me.

Tony was hospitalized for three weeks, and during that time, I went through a roller coaster ride of emotions. The first ten days of his hospitalization, I suffered a breakdown, depression, and severe anxiety, which put me in bed for most of that time. I didn't speak to anyone other than Rebecca, Alexander, and the benefits coordinator at work. I didn't even call the hospital or visit Tony. Rebecca and her boyfriend visited him almost every day, but I just couldn't.

Mid-August, I returned to work and tried to function as best as I could. It was very hard, but my co-workers were so kind that it helped me get through the day.

Every day became a little easier to bear until I visited Tony for the first time.

Visiting a patient at the Staten Island University mental ward was like visiting a prisoner. We were searched and had to leave our personal belongings with the guards.

The visiting room was a small version of an over-crowded school cafeteria with long tables surrounded by chairs placed too close to each other.

When Tony walked in, I hardly recognized him. He was dressed in what looked like pajamas. He had a mustache and beard and looked like he hadn't shaved for a long time. For a split second, he reminded me of how his father looked when he was hospitalized.

Tony was calmer than he had been for a long time. He spoke slowly and took a long time answering our questions. However, his stare and eyes had that same cold, withdrawn, spaced-out look—as if he wasn't really present.

The visit was short—mostly small talk, but it did break the ice and nervousness of seeing each other after that horrible Friday.

After our visit with Tony, we were taken to meet the hospital social worker that had been assigned to him. She introduced herself, exchanged phone numbers, and then told me that she would be calling me the next day to give me more information on Tony.

During the rest of Tony's hospitalization, I only visited him twice because of the distance. Rebecca and her boyfriend visited more frequently. Alexander also went to see him.

A few days before August 19th, I received a call from Tony's social worker asking that I come to the hospital to meet with her and Tony's psychiatrist. She said he would be released soon, and we needed to go over his out-patient treatment plan.

When I heard the words "released soon," panic and anxiety began to kick in. I started sweating, and my stomach was in knots. Three weeks was too soon. I wasn't ready for him to come home—not until I regained my strength.

The meeting with Tony's psychiatrist and social worker was very long and intimidating. The questions seemed endless. Worse, I had to go over every detail of that awful weekend before he was hospitalized. I felt like I was being interrogated by the police for committing a crime. I don't even know if I was making sense because my mind was still in a blur.

It helped that Rebecca and her boyfriend attended the meeting because they could contribute information that I couldn't remember.

After an exhausting two hours, the psychiatrist asked me a mind-blowing question, "Are you willing to accept Tony back home when he is released?"

"Where else is he going to go, if not home?" I asked, not understanding why he had asked the question.

"If you do not want him to return to your home, we will turn him over to the state. The state will send him to live in a psychiatric group home until he can live independently. It's your call," the psychiatrist said.

"Let me get this straight. You are saying that if I don't allow him to come home, he will become part of the system? The courts will decide where he would live and own him?" I asked.

"It's a little more complicated than that and a long process, but basically, it's something like what you are saying," he answered.

"If I decide to bring him home, is there a treatment that will cure him?" I asked.

"Schizoaffective Disorder Bipolar Type is not curable, but it could be managed with medication and treatment. We would transfer Tony to the hospital's mental out-patient treatment program, which has been very effective for our mental patients. The program runs from 9 am to 3 pm, five days a week. It includes individual and group therapy, psychiatric sessions, plus events that will give him a chance to socialize with other patients like him. Breakfast, lunch, snacks, and transportation to and from the home are included. It's a great program, and your insurance covers it. The only requirement is a referral from us and for Tony to take his medications. Call the social worker tomorrow with your decision, and we'll take it from there," the psychiatrist answered and then closed the meeting.

The ride home was quiet, but my thoughts weren't. I had been asked to make a decision—a decision that would not only affect Tony's future but mine and my other children—a decision that I wished I hadn't been asked to make.

As soon as I got home, I called a NAMI (National Association for Mental Illness) counselor that I had been talking to since Tony was hospitalized. Between tears, I told her all about the conversation with the psychiatrist.

"How am I going to care for my son when I don't know the first thing about Schizoaffective Disorder Bipolar Type. I have absolutely no knowledge of mental illness at all," I said.

After a long conversation, she said, "If you're going to be your son's caregiver, it is extremely important that you learn all you can about his disorder and what you need to do to help him through this. I cannot make this decision for you. You are the only one that knows how you feel. What I can say is this, if you do not feel mentally, physically, and spiritually ready to bring your son home—do not bring him home. You don't have to. There are places that will take care of him. And, if you do bring him home, make sure that you follow up with the out-patient plan they give him."

That night, I did what I hadn't done for a long time. I got on my knees and prayed for guidance. Before I fell asleep, an inner voice reminded me that my role on earth was to be my children's mother until they were adults. Although Tony was an adult, at the moment, he was not capable of taking care of himself; therefore, it was my responsibility to do so until he could.

After a long night of praying and soul searching, I knew exactly what I had to do. I was bringing my son home.

On August 19th, Tony was discharged from the hospital.

During the discharge interview, Tony's caseworker gave us pre-scriptions and instructions for the out-patient treatment plan the psychiatrist had told us about during the meeting.

"Thank you for all your help," I said to Tony's caseworker as we stood to leave.

"Tony's condition is not curable, but it is treatable. All he has to do is, take his medication and attend the out-patient program. If he follows this plan, eventually, his condition could be stable enough for him to live a fairly normal life," Tony's caseworker smiled and shook our hands, and she said goodbye.

Tony's first day home went better than I had imagined. He was a little edgy but seemed happy to be home again. When I told him that I had switched rooms with him, he smiled and seemed ex-cited. He spent most of the afternoon and evening rearranging his new room the way he wanted. It almost felt normal, and I was so grateful for it.

The next morning, Tony did a total about-face. He announced that he would go to the treatment program but that he would not take his medication. He said the medication made him feel like he was going to faint, and he didn't need it.

As soon as Tony said this, fear overpowered me, my stomach started to tremble, and my heart sank to the floor because I knew that without the medication, he was not eligible for the program.

The first thing I did was call Tony's social worker, who con-firmed my fears. She said the only thing left to do was for me to take him to a local psychiatrist as soon as possible so that they could help him understand the importance of taking his medicat-ion.

Luckily, the psychiatrist we were referred to had an office at our neighborhood hospital. When I called for an appointment, I was happy to hear that he was part of a team that was working with a new psychiatric pilot program that treated Tony's disorder.

All the positive energy God had given me the night before Tony was discharged—was slowly disappearing. I was a mess again. I was so full of fear that I jumped every time Tony made a loud noise. And I was worried about leaving Tony alone all day while I worked, especially now that he refused medication. The moments talking to my Heavenly Father were the only moments where I felt peace.

A few hours after I had spoken to Tony, his mood totally changed from anger to excitement.

"Ma, there's an Audio Technician school in Manhattan that I want to go to," Tony said excitedly as he showed me the school website on his computer. "What do I have to do to enroll?"

After reading the information on the school website, part of me thought that getting a certificate in Audio Technology was not a wise decision. However, the desperate part of me thought that it was perfect. Not only would Tony be doing something he liked, but he would have a place to be while I was working. What harm could it do?

"Ok, I'll call the school and set up an appointment," I said while trying to sound very positive and excited for him.

When I went to bed that night, my mind replayed all the ups and downs of the day. I couldn't wrap my brain around the changes in Tony's mood from one moment to another. And how his mood swings affected me.

Without medication, Tony was acting similar to the way he acted weeks before he was hospitalized—mood swings, edgy, talking fast and sometimes not making much sense, and very impatient. Thank God the psychiatric appointment was in two days.

The day before the psychiatric appointment, I came home to find Tony had dismantled the lock on our entrance door. All the pieces were on the kitchen table. After a long hard day at work, it was the last thing I needed.

When I asked him why, he said, "Someone tried to break in. They want to hurt me. We have to change the lock."

He was so upset and frightened that I played along and took him to the hardware store to buy a new lock. But, when we tried to install it—it didn't work, because when he took the old lock out, he damaged the door.

We couldn't sleep with the door open, so I called a locksmith who installed a heavy-duty safety lock that cost me over $300. Thank God for credit cards.

The morning of Tony's appointment with the psychiatrist, he was quiet and seemed upset. The hospital was close, so we walked. When we were halfway there, Tony's whole-body language changed. He started walking as if he were going to fight someone, and then he started yelling at me, saying I was forcing him to do things he didn't want to do. People were looking at us. I was embarrassed and very fearful of what he would do next.

When we arrived at the doctor's office, Tony became quiet again and stayed that way all through the intake process and the long hour in the waiting room.

After the two-hour psychiatric session, Tony returned to the waiting room a totally different person. He hugged me and then told me that the doctor wanted to see me.

The psychiatrist began by explaining Tony's disorder in detail. Then, he informed me that because Tony was an adult, doctor/patient confidentiality prohibited him from sharing information with anyone without Tony's consent, not even with me.

This psychiatrist seemed very caring and interested in how Tony felt and what he thought. He showed genuine concern when he said, "I cannot give you the details of what Tony has shared with me, except to say that he has been through a horribly traumatic experience.

As his caregiver, it is important that you learn about his condition in order to help and support him during trying times. It's important that you encourage him to follow his treatment and supervise to make sure he is following it.

It's also very important that you both be very patient during the treatment process because it will not show progress overnight. We will begin Tony's medication treatment with a low dose and slowly raise it until we get to the dose that works. He will also be attending weekly therapy sessions and monthly psychiatric sessions. And you will be attending family support sessions that will help you—help him. If Tony complies with all the steps required for his treatment, I am confident that he will eventually live a fairly normal life—even with his condition."

On the walk home, I really felt positive about the treatment plan the doctor had for Tony. I could actually see the light shining at the end of our dark tunnel. But, when I mentioned how I felt to Tony, he said, "I don't want to take medication, and I don't want to go back to this doctor."

Once again, my heart sank, and the tiny bit of hope and joy I felt was taken over by doom, anxiety, and fear.

Tony had to take his medication twice a day. It was easy to supervise his morning dose because he was so sleepy that he would take it and go back to sleep until almost noon. While he slept, my anxiety and stress level was lower, which helped me think, plan, and educate myself on Tony's condition. The evening dose was another story.

In the evening, Tony was at his worse. He was sarcastic, angry, and edgy. He blasted his music and sang along in anger. I feared the neighbors would complain or call 911. When I asked him to lower the music, he would answer in a sarcastic manner.

None of us could sleep because Tony kept pacing from his room to the kitchen or would go in and out of the apartment until way after midnight.

Sleep was so important for us. Rebecca and I had to get to work, and her boyfriend had started a new job. We all needed to perform our best at work, and without sleep—it was extremely hard to do so.

One time, when Tony was still outside at two in the morning, Rebecca tried to convince him to come inside and came back in tears, saying, "I can't do this anymore, Mom, I just can't."

If it weren't for Rebecca's boyfriend, Tony would have stayed in front of the building all night. He was the only person who could calm him down and talk him into going to bed. Not that he went to sleep, but at least he went to his room.

At work, I was under a lot of pressure because I was only working half a day and had to complete a whole day's work in four hours. My supervisor had shared with me that they were getting complaints about my work not being done on time. Thank God that many co-workers supported me and covered me when they were able to.

I really didn't know how long I would be able to live this way. My nerves were shot because I always feared the worst.

All I could do was pray, which is what I did the day before Tony and I were going to the audio school orientation. I worked until lunchtime, and then I visited the church next to my job, where I prayed and cried for my son, my family, our situation, and for me. I asked God, in the name of Jesus, for strength to deal with our situation and for peace and harmony at home. I asked God to hug Tony and give him peace and to take away his anger and fear. I prayed that he be accepted to the school he wanted to go to and that I could afford it. I left everything in God's hands, for I knew that only He could work miracles.

Miraculously, that night was the first night that we all got a full night's sleep. It was the first time, in a long time, that Tony seemed more relaxed and actually went to bed early.

The next day, I got home from work around 1 pm. All seemed to be running smoothly until around two when Tony started blasting his music and singing in a loud, angry tone.

My heart ached as I listened to his words. "My mom has to work…I'm home alone…nobody to hug me," he sang angrily.

I hated when Tony got like this because I feared what would happen next. My nerves were a mess because it was the first time since he got ill that we were taking public transportation, and I was very concerned about being in public with him in this state. What if someone looked at him the wrong way? What if he lost it and I wasn't able to control the situation?

My anxiety grew as we walked to the train station. Tony was silent, but the muscles on his face were tight, his eyes looked angry, and his whole body was tense as if he were getting ready to fight.

As soon as we walked into the audio school, Tony's mood completely changed. He seemed more relaxed. As we waited to be called, he seemed excited and happy while he glanced through the magazines and looked at the posters on the wall.

My heart sank when the school administrator informed us that the total cost for the Audio Technician course was $16,900, and financial aid was only going to cover $2,880. However, God worked a miracle because even though I had a bankruptcy, the school was willing to lend me close to $5,500 to be paid back in monthly payments over two years. And Tony was able to get two student loans that covered the remaining $8,000. All I had to lay out was $450 for registration, books, and equipment.

Praise to God! Tony was admitted and was starting the following Monday, August 30th.

When we left the school, Tony was so happy. And so was I because this school was going to keep him busy from midday to seven in the evening, which is something that he needed badly — to keep busy.

We celebrated by eating at a Mexican restaurant near the school. All through the meal, Tony talked about how happy he was to have been admitted. He also spoke of getting a job because he felt bad that we were paying all this money.

When I told him that God had worked a miracle and that I loved him and all I wanted was for him to do something that he really wanted so that he could achieve his goals in the music world, he nodded sadly.

As we left the restaurant, Tony did something that he hadn't done in a long time. He put his arm around me and kept it there until we reached the train station. I felt so happy that I almost cried. He almost seemed like his old self.

As soon as we arrived at our neighborhood, he changed again. His walk tense, angry stare, and tight fists. He even said something to a man that he said looked at me in a strange way.

"Forget everyone and everything. Concentrate on your future," I said. That seemed to calm him.

Tony was so happy that I was afraid to remind him of the court date that he had the Friday before he was to start school. When I mentioned it, he became very depressed.

"What if I go to jail and can't start school, Ma?" Tony asked in tears.

"I don't think they are going to put you in jail for jumping the turnstile in the train station. They'll probably just make you pay a summons. The only way that you would go to jail is if you don't show up in court. We'll pray and leave things in God's hands," I answered calmly.

That Friday, we were both worried and edgy. I felt confident that he would not be put in jail but was afraid that he would be given community service and wouldn't be able to start school on Monday. I didn't share my worry with him; instead, I prayed.

While we waited in the long line outside the courthouse, we didn't speak. When we entered the courthouse, we were directed to a desk to sign in before going through the metal detectors. The police officer told us that Tony's name did not appear on the list of court cases that were going to be heard. He said, "The District Attorney is not ready for your case. If you don't hear from us in ninety days, call this number to see if the case has been suspended or for instructions."

Neither one of us questioned or said a word. We both walked out of the courthouse in shock. Once outside, I turned to Tony and said, "God works in mysterious ways."

Tony made the sign of the cross and said, "Moments like this we don't question, we just walk out."

There was no doubt in my mind that God had worked this miracle. And I really think that Tony felt the same way. Well, I hoped he did.

That same Friday, Tony had a psychiatric appointment. When we arrived home from the courthouse, he was so tired that he slept for a few hours.

As we walked to the doctor's office, Tony complained that the sun was bothering his eyes and kept insisting that it was because of the medication.

After Tony's session with the psychiatrist, I was once again asked to join them.

"Tony keeps insisting that he has to start working," the doctor began, "I reminded him that he was just recently discharged from the hospital and has started medication that still needs to be adjusted. I'm glad that he is happy about starting school, but right now, he needs to take things one step at a time. He should focus on this treatment first, then school, and later on a job. If he takes on too much at once, especially at the early stages of treatment, he will be overwhelmed and stressed."

"Ok, I won't go to work, but I am going to school," Tony told the doctor in an angry tone.

Most of the way home, we walked in silence. At one point, Tony said, "You just wished me out of your life forever."

"I would never wish you out of my life. I love you," I answered, confused.

"We just passed a light post, and instead of you walking past the post on the side I walked on, you walked on the other side. In other words, the light post was between us," Tony said and continued to explain, "I learned in school that electrical posts carry energy and if two people that love each other walk on opposite sides of the post, it means one of them is wishing the other out of their life."

Quickly, I tried to think of something to say that wouldn't upset him.

"I didn't know that. I'll try to remember next time," I said calmly while thinking, "How am I going to remember all the things that upset him?"

"Well, since you didn't know it, I guess it doesn't count," Tony said.

Saturday morning, Tony slept late, which gave me a chance to drink coffee in peace and then start my weekend cleaning.

While I did the laundry and cleaned, I worried about the unknown for the day. "God, please let there be harmony and peace at home," I silently prayed.

Around noon Tony came into the kitchen. He turned the stove on, full flame, to grill a bagel. Before he got ill, he was always careful with the stove. I felt nervous. I didn't know if I should lower it myself or ask him to do it. I didn't want to say anything that would trigger something.

"What if he's alone and forgets to turn the stove off?" I thought as I glanced to make sure he turned it off.

Tony stayed in his room most of the afternoon, listening to music and watching TV.

"I need to run to the store; do you need anything?" I asked.

He didn't answer, so I walked over to his bed and kissed his forehead.

"Are you ok?" I asked.

"I'm OK," he answered in a loud, angry tone.

The nerves in my stomach turned as I walked out of the room.

Once outside, I took a deep breath and then began walking slowly to the grocery store. I had walked just a few steps when I realized that I had not combed my hair or put on makeup. In fact, I had not even looked at myself in the mirror before leaving the apartment.

"What have I become?" I silently vented to my Heavenly Father. "I never go outdoors without combing my hair and putting on makeup. I hate this new life that I have entered—a life I never asked for nor dreamed would happen to us. Tony's condition is devastating for him. He is suffering most of all. However, so is everyone else. Everything is changed. His condition has changed him, us, and life as we lived it. I can't even sit with my daughter and talk like before because, in Tony's mind, he believes we are plotting against him. I miss visiting my son, daughter-in-law, and granddaughter, but I can't because I don't want to leave Tony alone. And they cannot visit us until he is stable enough to be around a lot of people. My parents are suffering because they live far away and are too old to travel. They are confused and concerned about the whole situation. Thank God they don't know all the details. Even my daughter's boyfriend is suffering because he is in the middle of a situation that is not his responsibility, but he can't escape it because he knows he is the only one we have that we can count on right now. This will sound selfish, but what about me? My whole world has been turned upside down, just when I had begun planning my retirement and my future with Fernando. I gave up my room. My things are all over the apartment. I have no privacy. I feel displaced."

Guilt swept through me for thinking so selfishly. "I am Tony's mother, and I chose not to run away from this situation. I will care for Tony for as long as my health allows. I will do everything I can to help him stick to his treatment so that someday he can be stable enough to live on his own," I silently scolded myself.

I had just finished dinner when Tony walked into the kitchen freshly showered, smelling of aftershave, and dressed very nicely.

"Wow, you smell good," I said.

Tony smiled as he walked to the stove. He served himself, ate, and then told me the food was delicious. A few minutes later, he said he was going for a walk and would be around.

As soon as he left, I smelled something weird. Just as I had feared, Tony had forgotten to turn the iron off. Thank God I caught it in time before it burned right through the bedspread.

I worry that he doesn't take his medication. I worry that he will have a relapse. I worry that he may harm himself or someone else. I worry that he leaves the stove or iron on. I worry every second of the day.

Tony wasn't in a very good mood when he returned from his walk. He was getting upset over everything. First, he got upset when his sister and boyfriend were too tired to pay attention to him. I don't blame them for resting. I'm sure the situation was taking a toll on them too. Then, he got upset because there was nobody outside to hang out with.

Even though I didn't feel up to it, I asked him if he wanted to watch a movie with me in his room, which he agreed to.

Before I started the movie, Tony said he was going to take his pills. As he walked to the kitchen, I heard him mumble something about not needing to take medication anymore. It's like he was talking to someone.

All through the movie, he complained of a bad headache. So, I gave him two Tylenol. After the movie, he went outside twice. He didn't return to his room until 1:30 am.

Sleeping in Tony's old room made me realize how much noise he was subjected to—so different from my old bedroom, which I considered a quiet haven where I could tune out the world and sleep peacefully.

The new sleeping area was making me jumpy, nervous, and edgy. The bed was so close to the entrance door that I could hear people trafficking in and out of the building, running up and down the stairs, and talking loudly all through the night. At one point, I actually heard someone trying to put a key in our lock. I felt like I was sleeping outside, instead of in the safety of my home—I barely slept.

With Tony's disorder, noises like these could easily make him think that someone was breaking in or that he was in danger. No wonder he constantly patrolled the front of the building as if guarding it against intruders and insisted on changing the lock.

"It's time to leave this place. I don't feel safe here anymore," I told myself.

On Sunday, August 29th, the day before Tony was to start school, I surprisingly woke up late, and so did everyone else.

After drinking coffee, I watched one of my favorite Sunday morning Christian programs. The theme was "fear" and how we should not allow it to take over our lives because it gave Satan power. And how important it was to have faith and trust in God, no matter what the situation. I hung on to every word that was said as if they were speaking directly to me.

Hard to believe that until a month ago, I thought I was fearless. The only time that I felt fear was when I was on a plane or car. But that was because I had a phobia of flying and driving.

Now, I was possessed by the demon of fear. And no matter how much I prayed for God to destroy it—it was still inside me. More than ever, I had to be strong and continue having faith that God would eventually destroy this fear.

Tony got up around noon. He was quieter than usual but seemed ok. Mid-afternoon, he came to the kitchen dressed in shorts and a t-shirt.

"I'm going to go with some friends to shop for t-shirts for school. I'll be back before dark," Tony said.

"Don't stay out too late. Remember, you start school tomorrow," I said, trying not to sound worried.

"I have to get back early because I have to shave, trim my hair, and get my clothes ready for tomorrow," Tony said.

When Tony left, I prayed, "Oh God, please don't let anything happen to stop him from starting school tomorrow. I know I'm being paranoid, but can you blame me?"

The extra sleep and Tony being in good spirits made me feel like my old self again. So, while Tony was out shopping, I got busy preparing a delicious Sunday meal, hoping that we could all dine together—something we hadn't done for a long time.

Dinner was ready. It was getting dark outside, and Tony was not back. Worry took over.

Hours later, I was a basket case. My instincts told me that something was terribly wrong. I could feel it.

At nine-thirty, the phone rang. "God, please let it be Tony," I prayed.

It wasn't Tony. It was a police officer from the Coney Island precinct.

"Earlier this afternoon, violence broke out between a few gang members at the beach area in Coney Island, and there were multiple stabbings. Your son was identified as one of the stabbers and has been arrested," the police officer said.

I was numb. I couldn't think. All I could say was, "My son is on medication. He also needs his asthma pump," I babbled without making much sense.

"I'm sorry. We cannot allow him to have any medication. Everything was taken from him when he was arrested. He will be arraigned tonight at the downtown Brooklyn Criminal Court. You can speak to the assigned legal aid lawyer then," the police officer said.

I did not make it to Tony's arraignment on time. Bail was posted at ten thousand dollars, and because he did not have the money, he was sent directly to Riker's Island Prison.

I was devastated and worried about Tony's mental state. The only information that the clerk at the courthouse gave me was the name of the legal aid lawyer that was assigned to him.

Tony's lawyer called me very early the next morning. After speaking to him, I knew in my heart that he was an angel sent to us by God to help us during this horrible time.

I explained to Tony's lawyer that Riker's Island was hours from where we lived, and, although I wanted desperately to visit Tony, I just couldn't take any more time off from work to travel that far. He assured me that he would try to visit or speak to him to let him know and that he would keep me updated.

Monday night, Tony's lawyer called again.

"I'm so worried about Tony being without his medication. There's no telling how he will act without it," I cried.

"I called the prison psychiatrist this morning to request that he contact Tony's psychiatrist. He assured me that he would do everything possible to evaluate him and get him back on his medication," the lawyer said.

"Thank you so much. You have no idea how much I appreciate your help," I said.

I spent the rest of the week trying to get a loan to post bail but couldn't because of my bankruptcy. The morning that I was going to request a loan from a bail bond place, my mother called saying that they were able to get a loan and would be sending the bail money by Western Union.

How could I not believe that when everything seems impossible, God works miracles?

Right away, I called Tony's lawyer, who suggested that I wait until the day after Labor Day, Tuesday, September 7th, to post bail.

"The faster I post bail, the faster Tony will come home. Why wait?" I asked, confused.

"I understand where you are coming from, but trust me on this. Even if you post bail Friday, Tony will not be released until after

Labor Day," Tony's lawyer said, trying to convince me.

"Ok, it makes sense," I said.

Friday morning, I had the money in my hands. I was so tempted to run and post bail right away, but a little voice kept telling me to follow the lawyer's advice. And so, I did.

Saturday morning, I was very restless, so when Rebecca and her boyfriend invited me to go to New Jersey to visit my oldest son and family—I agreed.

Alexander and Victoria had a lot of Saturday errands to run, so we all tagged along. When we were coming out of Walmart, my cell phone rang.

"Ma, it's me, Tony. I'm home," Tony said, sounding very tired.

"Oh my God, you're home?" I said excitedly.

"Yeah, but there's nobody here," Tony said.

"Ok, listen. We're in New Jersey but stay there. We will all be there later this afternoon," I said.

Then, Rebecca's boyfriend interrupted me saying, "Tell him to stay there. You stay here, and Rebecca and I will go pick him up right now."

When I told Tony, he sounded relieved.

Later that afternoon, we all ate together—for the first time in a long time.

My son had been set free, with a court date and no bail. Once again, God worked a miracle and made the impossible come true.

The whole ordeal of being in prison and not being able to start school affected Tony greatly. He didn't even talk about the arrest until a few days after he was released when he told me all about it.

Tony began by saying, "Ma, I didn't stab anyone. My friends and I were hanging out by the beach, and a fight broke out. It was crazy. Someone hit me, and I hit him back. The next thing I knew, I was in handcuffs and dragged to jail.

I was so scared that I wet my pants. I kept asking them to call you so that you could bring me a change of clothing, but they didn't listen to me.

I fell asleep and woke up in another prison. They told me I was in court waiting to be arraigned. I stunk. I wanted to go home and take a bath.

A lawyer spoke to me. He was very nice. Then, we went before the judge, who said I had to pay a lot of money for bail. I didn't have money, so they sent me to Riker's Island.

My lawyer told me not to worry. He said he was going to call you," Tony said.

"I was frantic," I said, "I couldn't get answers from anyone. When I got to court, you had already been transferred to Riker's."

"People in my cell kept beating each other up, but I think because I smelled so bad, they left me alone. I slept most of the time," Tony continued.

They didn't give me a change of clothing until after I saw a psychiatrist who gave me the same medication I was taking. Then, I was moved to a cell with less people.

Saturday morning, they gave me my smelly clothes back and told me to get dressed cause I was going home. Before I left, they gave me a court date, prescription, and a metro card.

People on the train kept talking about me cause of the way I smelled. It was embarrassing," Tony said with tears in his eyes.

"Tony, you've been through too much in such a short time. Since you won't be starting at the audio school until October 10th, how do you feel about staying with your grandparents until then?" I asked, hoping he would agree.

"Yeah, that would be nice," Tony said without even thinking about it.

"Ok, I'll call your lawyer, and if he says it's ok for you to travel, you can go," I said.

On September 10th, Tony traveled to Puerto Rico.

While Tony was safely in Puerto Rico, I was able to rest, re-energize, and think of ways to deal with making life less stressful during this trying time.

Our apartment, where my children grew up and where we shared so many fond memories, did not feel safe anymore. In fact, it no longer felt like home. We needed to find a new place to live.

Trying to juggle my work responsibilities while taking care of Tony's caregiving needs took a toll on my job performance and my health. I had to find a way to care for Tony and keep my job at the same time.

I felt in my heart that Tony had not committed the crimes he was being charged with, but there was nothing I could do to help him—only God could. I kept praying for a miracle.

Through all this, my health had deteriorated. I had suffered episodes of anxiety, panic, depression, and a nervous breakdown. I needed to be strong, get a grip, and take control before I totally lost it.

I prayed day and night for a solution to our problems because I knew deep down in my heart that although we were facing some really hard times, God had not forgotten us. I believed and had faith that He would show me the way.

After days of praying, ideas started popping in my head even while I slept. Some of the ideas seemed almost impossible, but I looked into them anyway because I felt that's what God wanted me to do.

Within the next three weeks, doors started opening, and miracles started happening.

Of all the apartment complexes I had applied to, the only one that accepted our application was a few blocks from where my oldest son lived. It was less rent, in a quieter and better neighborhood, and was in better condition than the one we were currently living in.

The apartment was perfect, except for one thing—it was in Somerville, New Jersey. The commuting time for me and Rebecca to get to work on the express bus would be almost two hours each way. For Tony to get to school, the local bus would take about three hours each way. This time frame did not include the train we all needed to take after arriving at the Port Authority in Manhattan.

At work, I put my pride aside and shared my dilemma with the benefits coordinator, who helped me apply for a partial leave of absence from work, which allowed me to take hours or days off, to take care of everything related to Tony's condition. I would be earning less money, but the stress of being fired would be eliminated. It was exactly what I needed.

Tony's lawyer, and his assistant, continually kept in touch with me. They both seemed very caring and interested in helping Tony with his case. I shared with them all that had happened to Tony in the past year, his goals and dreams, how he used to be, and who he had become because of his condition. I had no doubt God had sent these two angels to help Tony.

It was amazing how much had been accomplished in such a short time. By the middle of October, we had signed the apartment lease, my partial leave of absence had been approved, Tony had returned from Puerto Rico and had started classes at the audio school. Tony's lawyer had shared that things were looking favorable in Tony's case. How can I not believe in God's miracles?

The last night in our old apartment, I thought back to the words I had heard in my head when I was returning from my mini-vacation in Atlantic City, "Around the corner lies an unexpected turbulence that is going to knock you off your seat. Buckle up with all your faith because this ride is going to be very rocky — probably the worst you've had."

With tears in my eyes, I spoke to my Heavenly Father, "You were warning me. Weren't you?

You were trying to prepare me for an evil attack and a long exhausting battle. If I had been stronger in my faith, I would have understood. I would have known to turn to my Bible and read Ephesians 6:10-20, where you clearly tell us how to prepare for Satan's attacks.

I would have been a strong warrior instead of allowing myself to be possessed by fear and become so weak that Satan's army almost devoured me.

I learned my lesson. From now on, when you warn me — I will listen. I will follow your instructions. I will put on the Armor of God and become the Princess Warrior you always tell me that I am.

Thank you for not giving up on me. Thank you for grabbing my hand and pulling me up before I drowned. Thank you for lifting me up when I fell. Thank you for giving me strength when I had no energy left.

This journey has just begun. It will be very unpredictable and very challenging. I'm not going to lie. I'm scared. But, with you by my side, I believe I can survive anything. You have shown me time and time again that no matter how dark it gets, no matter how scary the attack is, and no matter how impossible it seems—you will not forsake me."

I can DO
ALL THINGS *through* CHRIST
who strengthens ME.
PHILIPPIANS 4:13 KJV

CHAPTER EIGHT
Jesus Help Me—I'm Sinking!

"Do not fear, for I am with you; do not be dismayed, for I am your God. I will strengthen you and help you; I will uphold you with my righteous hand."
(Isaiah 41:10 KJV)

Schizoaffective Bipolar Type Disorder, a combination of Schizophrenia and Bipolar symptoms, is a mental hurricane that invades a person's mind, destroying everything in its path. There is no peace for those who live with this condition because the mind is congested with voices and conversations all talking at the same time that never shut up—not even during sleep. Life as the person knew it—stops existing. The goals and dreams—disappear. Love, emotions, thoughts, and dreams—fade away.

This illness not only crushed my son's world but it also crushed everyone around him. I can only describe it as an evil entity with one purpose—to make life so unbearable that we lose our faith, give up, and allow it to devour us. It's never-ending torture that we could only endure by holding on to our Heavenly Father and His Son, Jesus Christ.

The move to the small quaint town of Somerville, New Jersey, had many perks that we would have noticed if we weren't still numb from all we had gone through since last summer. It also had a lot of challenges that we weren't sure we could handle.

Commuting was a huge challenge for all of us. Rebecca and I took the first express bus to Manhattan and then a train to Brooklyn. Commuting time was close to three hours, making us late to work every morning. Rebecca couldn't deal with the commute, so she quit her job. Thank God she found a new one within walking distance from home.

Tony's commute was worse because he left for school in the afternoon when the local buses ran, making his commute close to four hours. After school, he had to rush to the bus terminal before the last bus to Somerville left, bringing him home after midnight.

Aside from the commuting, I was facing financial difficulties. My paycheck had shrunk in half since I had started temporary family leave, making it almost impossible for me to afford Tony's expenses. Thankfully, my Beloved Jesus and His Father did not forsake us.

On January 18th, two days before Tony's birthday, we received a very uplifting email from Tony's lawyer, "I am very pleased to hear that you and Tony are doing well and have settled in. He deserves a good situation that will allow him to proceed with his life and to thrive. As for the case, our sense of the situation is that there is good reason to remain optimistic about the case resolving well. While there is never a guarantee in these cases, until they are over, I feel comfortable saying that you and Tony should continue to make your life plans—to laugh, to love, and to work—and not allow the case to occupy too much of your energies or worries." This e-mail lifted our spirits. We knew things could still go wrong, but it gave us hope.

Experience had taught me that buses from New Jersey to New York were hardly on schedule, which was a concern because I did not want Tony to be late to his court appearance on February 25th. So, even though I could not afford it, I booked a room at a hotel near the courthouse to avoid traveling from Somerville.

On February 24th, I went straight to the hotel after work. Tony had class until ten, which gave me five hours of alone time to unwind, pray, and prepare emotionally for the next day.

When Tony arrived, he seemed in good spirits. We ordered room service, watched TV, and prayed before going to bed.

I couldn't sleep. I kept glancing across the room at Tony while he slept. How I wish I could protect him like I did when he was a little boy. But I couldn't. Only my Heavenly Father could keep Tony out of jail, so I desperately prayed for a miracle.

In the morning, we walked to the courthouse in silence. During the long wait to enter, I kept praying silently. Posted on the door outside the courtroom was a long list of all the cases that were going to be heard. We searched the list but did not find Tony's name. When we asked the person at the information desk, he confirmed that Tony's case would not be heard and suggested we call Tony's lawyer.

Tony and I nervously walked down the long hallway past the crowded courtroom entrance, seeking a quiet place to make the call. After a few tries, Tony's lawyer finally answered.

"I left you a message late last night, which I'm assuming from your phone call you didn't receive," he said after I anxiously asked him what was going on. "Rosita, I am very happy to inform you that all the charges against Tony have been dropped, and the case has been dismissed."

When I heard his words, my knees weakened, and I felt faint. After thanking the lawyer and telling Tony the news, all I could say was, "Thank you, my Heavenly Father," —over and over again.

It was a miracle, and Tony and I were very aware of this.

That night, I thanked my Heavenly Father and His Son, Jesus Christ, for saving my son from going to jail. I asked that every time I had doubts, they remind me of all the times they had saved us and all the miracles they had given us. I felt a warm hug—then I drifted to sleep believing I was in my Heavenly Father's arms.

When we turn a situation over to our Heavenly Father and His Son, Jesus Christ, they want us to let go of it and leave it in their hands. If we continue worrying about the situation and try to solve it our way, God probably sits back and says, "Fine; you think you could do this better. Go right ahead. Let's see what happens when you do things your way."

In other words, God and Jesus are the drivers—we are the passengers. We are not supposed to touch the wheel while they are driving because if we do, we can cause a detour, an accident, or worse, death. I learned this the hard way.

Shortly after receiving the miracle of Tony's freedom, Tony's Social Security Disability was approved, and the roller coaster ride we had been on slowed down enough for me to breathe.

During the calm, I had this crazy idea that I shouldn't sit and wait for God to do everything. It just seemed wrong, like I was taking him for granted. So, I decided to give God a break and drive the car, without asking Him if that was what He wanted me to do; and without paying attention to the warning signs along the way.

One day, Tony approached me with a dilemma. He said the medication made him dizzy, and he was afraid of fainting on the train. He sounded very serious when he announced that he was not taking his medication anymore. I could tell he was determined to get off the medication, whether I agreed to it or not. So, I prayed. But, instead of waiting for God's guidance, I did things my way.

After researching, I learned that because Tony's dose was very low, there were cases where patients could be taken off the medication and do very well.

In between doctor's appointments, I weaned Tony off of the medication slowly while watching out for any symptoms of a relapse. I didn't see any, but then again, I wasn't with him all day.

Shortly after Tony was completely off the medication, I began noticing him very edgy. I blamed it on school stress.

Then, I began noticing other signs. When he got home from school at midnight, he would play music very loud for hours. He stuttered a lot and started a sentence without finishing it. His personality changed within minutes. He kept going in and out of the apartment, late at night, like he used to do in Brooklyn.

One day, when he looked at me with that horrible look that he used to give me before he was hospitalized, I knew he was relapsing. So, I took him to the psychiatrist and confessed what I had done. Immediately, Tony was put back on medication.

Tony's relapse was my fault for taking matters into my own hands without waiting for God's guidance and without consulting the psychiatrist. Never again will I wean Tony out of his medication unless his psychiatrist instructs me to. Thank God nothing horrible happened.

When Tony received his social security retro money, he bought a car. He wasn't driving to school yet, but he drove to Brooklyn on weekends to visit his old friends.

One stormy night, returning home from Brooklyn, Tony lost control of the car and hit a side rail on the highway. Miraculously he was okay, but the right front and side of the car were wrecked. I really don't know how he managed to drive the car home.

After this incident, Tony changed again. Gradually all the symptoms of a relapse returned. At night, when he should have been sleeping, he blasted his music. I couldn't sleep. I'm sure the neighbors couldn't either. I feared that he wasn't taking his morning medication, although he swore that he was.

Worry, fear, and sleepless nights caused my anxiety to get worse.

"My Heavenly Father, why is this nightmare repeating itself exactly one year after Tony's hospitalization?" I prayed. "Last year, it almost killed me. Help me because I don't think I can survive it this time."

I don't remember the dream I had that night, but I remember hearing a voice telling me to beware of Satan's attack. When I woke up, I was full of fear.

Unlike last year, I listened to God's warning. I prayed for strength. I prayed for protection. And I prayed to be dressed with the Armor of God and for all His soldiers to help me fight whatever evil was lurking.

A few nights later, during a sleepless night, Tony sat near my bed, and with a smirk, asked, "Am I adopted?"

"Of course not, sweetie," I answered. "Why are you asking me that?"

"I don't know," he said.

"I gave birth to you Tony, you are not adopted," I said.

"Can I have a hug?" Tony asked.

I was exhausted. All I wanted was to sleep. I put my arms around him and gave him a tight hug.

Tony returned my hug with a cold, stiff one. Then, he let go and went into his room, slamming the door behind him. He spent the next hour going back and forth from his room to the kitchen. I wondered what he was doing, but I was too tired to get up to find out.

I couldn't sleep, so I read an inspirational booklet one of my co-workers had given me while I prayed for God's guidance.

It didn't take long for God's words to start jumping out of the pages, one after the other.

"The burdens will not stay; just trust My Word and keep the faith—I will lead the way."

"Don't worry or anxious be. Put your faith and trust in Him, and all your fears will flee."

"When storms begin violently raging with lapping waves tossed to and from, lean on Jesus and press forward – by all means, with bold courage onward row. O'er restless sea we'll sail in life for some days are bleak and drear; yet with Jesus standing by our side, release those dark and gloomy fears. Relax, oh weary sailor, though faced with rushing, billowy tides. Steer towards the nearest lighthouse where our Lord humbly abides. Peek out in faith; link your hand in His and believe He'll lead the way; His beam – the Holy Spirit, His voice – the Holy Word each day. As we persistently paddle onward, someday with the assurance, we'll reach the golden shore, Hallelujah! With love, Jesus will happily greet us, welcoming us home forevermore."

I hung on to every word I read because I felt my sanity depended on them. I was still reading when my alarm clock rang. I was too exhausted to go to work but had no choice.

Hours later, when I arrived at work, I received a phone call from Rebecca.

"Ma, there are two cops here, and they want to speak to you," Rebecca said.

I sat expecting the worse.

"Madam, your son stopped us earlier and asked where he could get a gun permit. When we questioned him, he laughed and said he was kidding. He didn't seem to be acting normal, so we took down his address and came to check on him," the officer said.

I told the officer how Tony acted since the car accident and asked that they please look for him before something happened.

After hanging up the phone, I cried.

I was a mess. Thank God that when my co-workers heard me crying, they all came to hug and support me.

I didn't know if I should commute home or wait for the police to call me. I wasn't in any condition to travel, so I decided to wait.

The next phone call was from the car dealer where Tony had bought his car.

"Your son brought his car in wrecked. He demanded that we exchange it for another car. He was acting very strange, so we had no choice but to call the police. I called your house, and your daughter gave me your number. I'm really sorry, but we had no choice," the dealer said.

The third phone call was from the police.

"Madam, your son was picked up for disturbance at a local dealer. He is not in his right mind. He told us that you had committed suicide. We took him to the hospital for a psychiatric evaluation," the officer informed me.

I thanked the officer and thanked God that Tony had been sent to a hospital instead of being arrested. These officers actually sounded like they cared. Nothing like the ones I had spoken to in Brooklyn when he was arrested the last time.

Before I left work, I called the hospital to get an update on Tony. All I was told was that he had been transferred to a clinic.

On my commute home, I kept asking myself why Tony had told the officers that I had committed suicide.

Rebecca called while I was on the bus heading home.

"Ma, are you ok?" Rebecca asked.

"I don't know. I just can't understand why we're going through this nightmare again," I cried.

During the rest of the bus ride, I wondered why Tony wanted a gun and why he said I committed suicide.

I became paranoid and thought, "What if Tony discharges himself and comes home? I didn't fear him—I feared what was going on in his head and how to handle it if he did appear."

I feared going into the apartment by myself, so when the bus entered Somerville, I called Alexander and asked him to meet me at the bus stop.

At the apartment, Alexander asked me to stay outside while he searched the apartment. When he came back, he said, "Ma, it's empty, but his room is a mess. There's broken furniture—including his television," Alexander said. "I think it's best if you stay with us tonight."

At Alexander's, I tried to call the hospital and get more information but didn't get any.

"Ma, it's Friday night. You may not get any information until Monday," Alexander said. "You haven't slept well in days. Get some sleep."

The only information I got on Saturday was that Tony had been transferred to a Mental Clinic, forty-five minutes from Somerville. They said that unless Tony asked someone to contact me, they could not give me any more information.

That afternoon I went back to my apartment. While I was home, I received a collect call from Tony. He sounded anxious, edgy, and made no sense. He told me to pick him up. When I asked him where he was, he insisted that he was at the Somerville Medical Center. I tried to explain to him that I had been told that he was at a clinic forty-five minutes away from Somerville, but he didn't believe me. He insisted that he was discharged and was waiting for me to pick him up.

It was obvious, by the way Tony was talking, that he was not on medication. I wondered why but couldn't do anything but call the clinic. When I did, they again told me that they could not give me any information.

Tony kept calling me, but because there was nothing I could say to calm him, I decided to let his calls go into voice mail while I cleaned the mess in his room.

In every message, Tony sounded hoarse and desperate. It broke my heart to hear the anguish in his voice. I felt helpless. There was nothing I could do but to leave Tony in God's hands and pray that someone at the clinic could help him.

After praying, I heard a voice I felt was from my Heavenly

Father, saying, "Common sense would tell you that hospitals are never fully staffed on weekends. They probably have Tony under observation until a psychiatrist sees him on Monday. Have patience."

"Oh my God, I'm so sorry. Once again, I laid my troubles at Your feet, and instead of trusting that You had things under control, I'm worrying," I prayed. "Please forgive me; I'm only human. Please teach me to relax while You lead."

Monday, I received a call from a social worker at the clinic who informed me that Tony had given permission for them to speak to me. She asked me the usual questions, and I gave her as much information as I could—including the names of all the psychiatrists and therapists he had seen and the hospital in Staten Island.

When I told the social worker that Tony had called asking that I pick him up, she said, "Tony will not be discharged yet. We began treatment and medication this morning. He will probably be too tired to speak to you for a couple of days, but I'm sure once he feels better, he will call you. If you research the clinic, you will find that it is one of the best psychiatric clinics in New Jersey. I assure you he's in good hands."

While Tony was in the hospital, I was able to rest, re-energize, and think straight. I took time to do some more research on Tony's condition and read many stories told by people caring for others with the same symptoms.

I learned that Schizoaffective Bipolar Type Disorder was not curable, but it could be managed with medication and treatment. It took time, but with commitment, support, and patience, many were able to work and even get married and have children.

I also learned that some people with Schizoaffective Bipolar

Type Disorder could still have setbacks or relapses, even when taking medication. There are many causes for relapsing, but most are due to consistent stress caused by constantly hearing voices and seeing things that aren't there.

One particular story helped me realize just how stressful life was for someone with Tony's condition. It spoke of a young man who went from being active and sociable to staying in his room and not wanting to interact with anyone—not even his family. One day, this young man saw a zebra on television and began screaming. After an evaluation, his psychiatrist determined that to the young man, the zebra was a giant monster that was trying to eat him. In his state of hallucination, he saw the zebra jumping out of the television and launching at him.

Tony's whole life had changed. Not only was he dealing with the horrible symptoms of his disorder, but he was also dealing with taking medication, psychiatrists, therapists, and hospitals—all of which he hated. Despite it all, he tried very hard to continue reaching his goals and to hold on to his life. Unfortunately, because of his condition, simple things like school responsibilities, commuting, being around a lot of people, being in unfamiliar surroundings, being given too much to do at once, or being spoken to very fast, were huge challenges that caused him a lot of stress and anxiety.

More than anything, I wanted Tony to be stable enough to live as normal a life as he could—despite his disorder. But, if he didn't take his medication, he would probably continue relapsing.

Tony's relapse proved that he wasn't ready to manage his treatment on his own. He needed supervision with his medication, not just in the night like I had been doing, but in the morning too.

In order for me to supervise Tony's medication, treatment, doctor's appointments, and be close enough to get to him in case of an emergency, I couldn't work forty-two miles away. I had to find work close to home.

The thought of leaving the job I had worked in for over twenty-two years, and planned to retire from in five years, brought tears to my eyes because I would be giving up a perfectly good and secure job with a pretty good salary, plus all the benefits that went with it—including health insurance. Who in their right mind does that?

Then, I would have to start job hunting in a small town that didn't have many job openings. At my age, who was going to hire me?

The thought of resigning and job hunting frightened me. However, the fear of Tony relapsing was stronger.

I didn't know what to do, so I prayed and asked for a sign that would reassure me that I was making the right decision. A few days later, not one but several signs appeared.

The first sign came when I received a letter from the benefits department informing me that the partial leave of absence I was on would end September 30th. Effective October 1st, I was expected to return to my full-time hours, which would be impossible for me to do with the commuting, and days off I needed to care for Tony's medical appointments.

The second sign came when my orthopedic doctor gave me the bad news that the extreme pain I was suffering from on my left foot was due to a condition called Morton's Neuroma. The treatment required that my foot be wrapped, wear a special boot, and use crutches for at least six months while I healed. How was I going to maneuver myself up and down the stairs during my daily commute and at work?

The third sign came during an extensive meeting with Tony's social worker and psychiatrist, where they informed me that Tony would be discharged on August 23rd and that he would be attending an out-patient program every day from nine to three. As his caregiver, it was my responsibility to make sure that he attended. How was I going to do this if I was away from home from six in the morning to nine at night?

I had no doubt that these signs were my Heavenly Father's way of telling me that resigning from my job, and looking for work in Somerville, was the right decision. The next day, I submitted my resignation letter, effective September 30th, 2011.

When I told Rebecca and Alexander about my decision, they were surprised but supportive. They were also concerned about my financial situation after leaving my job.

"I won't lie. It's going to be very difficult financially. But, if I find a job really quick, it won't be so bad," I said, trying to reassure them.

"Ma, you might not find a job in the same field you are in now. And, if you do find a job, you probably won't be earning nearly as much as you do now," Alexander said.

"Yes, I'm aware of that. I'm also aware that, at my age, I might not find a job that easily," I said, "I was actually thinking of applying for an office job at a school. They don't pay much, but the hours are exactly what I need."

"What about unemployment benefits?" Alexander asked.

"I won't be eligible for unemployment benefits if I resign unless the hardship of commuting counts," I said. "It's going to be ok. If things get really bad, I'll withdraw money from my annuity account."

"Isn't that your retirement money, Ma?" Rebecca said.

"Yes," I answered.

Tony came home on August 23rd, in very bad shape. He vomited constantly and seemed totally spaced out. When I called the hospital, I was told that Tony's body was reacting to a significant increase to his regular antipsychotic medication, plus 1500 mg of a mood stabilizer added to his medication treatment. They assured me that he would be better in a few days.

In Tony's condition, he could not be left alone. Once again, I had to take time off from work. Thank God I was still on a partial leave of absence.

By the end of August, Tony was feeling much better and able to start attending the six-week out-patient program at the psychiatric center close to home.

The program offered therapeutic one-on-one and group sessions, psychiatric sessions, social gatherings, lunch and snacks, and round-trip transportation to and from home. To me, it sounded great, but Tony hated it.

September 30th, after an emotional farewell get-together with old friends and co-workers, I left the comfort and security of the place that had been a second home to me.

On my way home, I silently said goodbye to places I felt I would never see again. I thought of all the reasons that had brought me to this day, and I realized what this day meant. I was embarking on an unfamiliar and unpredictable journey, not knowing the challenges I would face or where the road would lead. The only thing I was sure of was that my Heavenly Father, and His Son, Jesus Christ, would be there every step of the way.

October was very challenging. It began with a call from the outpatient clinic informing me that because my health insurance had expired at the end of September, and Medicaid would not cover the full cost of the program, I had to pay the balance for Tony to continue in the program. I had no choice but to take him out of the program, which made him very happy—but gave me anxiety.

I knew I wasn't eligible for unemployment benefits, but I applied anyway, hoping for a miracle. When I received the rejection letter, although I felt the decision was correct, something pushed me to request a determination hearing. To the request, I attached a letter stating all the reasons why I had resigned from my job and included a copy of a letter my employer had given me stating that they would not contest unemployment benefits.

On October 13th, I received a letter from the Administrative Judge Division stating that the original determination had been withdrawn, pending further fact-finding. I had no idea what this meant and left it in God's hands.

In the meantime, our financial situation grew worse. The money I had withdrawn from my annuity account was disappearing very fast. If I didn't find a job by November, the only money I would have would be Tony's social security money and what Rebecca gave me—which would cover the rent but not pay the rest of the bills, food, and expenses.

To top things off, I hadn't heard back from any of the jobs I had applied for. It felt like everything was at a standstill.

I'm human—and it's natural for humans to worry and get nervous when they don't see a way out of a situation. I was sure

God would not punish me for feeling this way, especially when he knew I loved Him and His Son, Jesus Christ. I trusted and believed with all my heart that they would not forsake us.

I knew God would not forsake us, but as the days passed without a solution, my anxiety and stress level grew. I didn't know what God wanted me to do. Was I supposed to wait and see if my claim for unemployment benefits was approved, or was I supposed to do something to trigger the solution?

I was trying very hard not to show my impatience and worry, but no matter how much I tried, I was getting very edgy—and it was showing. Not a good sign because I didn't want my kids to think I had lost my faith.

While I was going through all this anxiety, Tony announced that he wanted to return to the audio school in Manhattan. My main concern about his decision was whether or not he would be able to deal with the same challenges he had faced before so soon after being discharged and with a higher dose of medication. I secretly prayed that Tony would change his mind and then left the decision in God's hands.

By the first week of November, I began losing my patience. I tried calling the unemployment office many times but could not get through. I finally found an email address, took a chance, and send them an email.

The next day, I received a response to my email that read, "Due to the complexity of your issue, your email has been directed to the Adjudication Division." The response confused me even more.

God speaks to me in mysterious ways. He answers my questions through the Bible, a book, a person, a situation, a dream, or even a daydream.

That night, while watching my favorite Christian program, I felt God speak to me.

"Sometimes, we take God for granted," the reverend said. "We become so comfortable with receiving miracles that we lose the true meaning of the experience. We don't feel the emotions we used to feel when we were desperately asking for the miracle. We expect the miracle, and when it comes, the gratification is not as strong as it once was.

God doesn't want us to become platonic in our faith. He wants our faith to grow and get stronger, but it's not going to happen if we lose the essence of the whole experience of miracles.

When this happens, God might make us wait longer for the miracle to arrive so that during the waiting period, our feelings will awaken. We will seek God's comfort. We will seek God's arms. We will cling to Him just like a child clings to his parents when hungry and waiting to be fed. The longer it takes, the harder we will pray. The more we pray, the stronger our faith becomes.

We need to feel the edginess and emotions we felt when we were a novice in faith so that we are totally aware that God is working on something impossible to anyone else but him—a miracle."

God was telling me to believe, trust, and have more faith than I ever had—and to be patient and wait. So, that night, I prayed harder than ever.

I asked for patience because I was afraid my patience would wear out, and I would lose it despite my faith. I asked God to strengthen my faith so that I could show my children that even though we were going through a storm, I believed God would help us.

The next morning, I had the weirdest dream. Someone handed me a note that read, "I have waved the curse. You must...," and then I woke up.

In my dream, there were words after "you must," but no matter how hard I tried, I couldn't remember them.

The words were puzzling. "What did they mean?" I thought. "If the note referred to a real curse, wouldn't it say, "I have lifted the curse? Besides, do curses even exist?"

Then I heard a voice say, "It took a lot of God's soldiers to crush the curse, but it's done."

Suddenly, I felt that everything was going to be ok. The long wait had to happen so that I could become stronger in my faith and recognize that God was working on a huge miracle.

The miracle arrived on November 9th, when I discovered that six weeks of retro unemployment benefits had been direct deposited in my bank account. A few days later, I received the official acceptance letter without any explanation as to why my claim had been accepted after it was denied.

This is what a miracle is all about. When an entity that has the power to approve or disapprove something denies you, and then without an explanation or reason, it's approved—it is a miracle; and, the reason why it's a miracle is because it wasn't the human entity that made the approval possible—it was God.

Shortly after, Tony received approval from his school to return to classes beginning in January. But, instead of being excited with the news, he seemed edgy and stressed.

"Ma, I don't want to return to the audio school. I feel that pursuing an audio engineering career is not going to help me get a job," Tony began.

I was surprised but listened.

"I feel that commuting to New York might be a problem again. It's going to be hard for me to face the same type of individuals. I feel that I should get out of New York altogether," Tony continued, "What I want to do is attend college near here."

What can I say? I had left my concern about Tony returning to school in God's hands. This was the answer to my prayers. Not only did Tony not want to commute to New York, but he wanted to go to college.

"What should I do, Ma?" Tony asked, confused.

"I think you should pray and sleep on it. If you wake up in the morning feeling good about your decision, then it's the right choice. Leave everything in God's hands," I said, hoping that he would.

The next morning, he seemed much calmer; however, he became a little stressed by the end of the day because when we searched for colleges, he realized the process would be a long one.

While researching, I found a college nearby that had a program for the disabled. I emailed the Coordinator of Disability Services, asking for an appointment for Tony to meet with her.

I let Tony meet with the coordinator, knowing full well that college was a long shot for many reasons. Would he be able to take fewer classes and still be covered by financial aid? Would he be able to deal with the stress of college, stamina, bullying, and campus life?

How I wish I could keep my son in a bubble protected from the bad guys. But I couldn't because that would enable him. He needed to feel useful. He needed to live as normal a life as possible within his condition. And, I had to let him try while standing by him, supporting him, and being there for him, every step of the way, for as long as he allowed me to.

Tony came home full of information and excited to enroll in college. However, before making a final decision, we encountered a dilemma. How was he going to get to school? We had three options, public transportation, a cab, or Tony's car.

The most logical solution would be Tony's car. However, due to our financial situation, we had not been able to repair it since the accident. The estimate for fixing it was over a thousand dollars. That option was not going to work for us at the moment.

The college was just a town away but tricky to get to by public transportation. It would take Tony almost an hour to get to the nearest train stop, and then he would have to walk a long distance from the train station to the school. We tried to avoid this option.

When I called the cab company, they gave me a quote of seventeen dollars round trip daily. The cost would be six hundred eight dollars monthly, double the cost he paid when he commuted to New York. Although the best option, we just couldn't afford it.

After crunching numbers to find a way to pay for the cab and not coming up with a solution, I became so frustrated and stressed that my anxiety level skyrocketed.

When God wants a miracle to happen in our life, He will move mountains. He will even change laws and policies that no person on earth has the power to do. All we need to do is pray, trust in God, and let Him do the driving. It's so easy, but yet so hard for me to do sometimes.

While I struggled with my stress, I heard a voice say, "Why are you stressing out? You put Tony's college situation in my hands, and now you want to take it back and do it your way? Do you think you can find a better solution than I can? If you can, I'll let you drive."

"No, I'm sorry, my Heavenly Father. I am not taking a chance on messing up again. Tony's college situation is in your hands. All I ask is that if you want me to get involved, please let me know, and please let me know what you want me to do," I prayed.

A few days later, Tony announced excitedly, "Ma, I found an accredited college that offers online courses. I've enrolled and will begin classes in the middle of January."

I sat in awe. College and transportation situation resolved—just like that. Thank you, Jesus!

"What happened to Fernando?" you might ask. Well, during those horrible last months in Brooklyn, Fernando and I did not communicate much. The few conversations we had were quick because I was always involved with work or something related to Tony's condition. It seemed like our relationship was at a standstill.

It's weird, but I never insisted that he return or even prayed about it. I assumed that he understood what I was going through and was giving me space to handle things, waiting for things to calm down so that we could pick up where we left off.

When I moved to Somerville, Fernando tried many times to get romantic on the phone, but when he did, I changed the subject because, honestly, my emotions were numb. In fact, I actually thought it was inconsiderate of him to expect me to be lovable when I was going through so much and more inconsiderate when he cut me off when I tried to vent.

Around the time that I left my job, I did not hear from

Fernando for over a month—something that had never happened. I worried that he was sick. So, when I didn't hear from him on my birthday, I sent him a short email asking if he was ok.

Fernando's response hit me like a ton of bricks. He didn't mention my birthday or the photos I had attached. All he wrote was that he had been so busy that he had lost track of time. He did say he loved and missed us. But that was it.

Instead of leaving well enough alone, I went into his Facebook page, searching for something that would explain things. Well, they say, "Search, and you will find." And that's exactly what happened. Somehow, I found his ex-wife's page, and the last post on her page was from Fernando, where he wrote her a story about old people dying together and never-ending love.

"Why did Fernando send his ex-wife this story?" I wondered. So, I asked him in an email.

His response was, "I give up. I don't want to continue this way. Good luck."

Fernando's words were cold and direct, with absolutely no compassion.

"This is it. It's over, and without an explanation," I whispered to myself. "What a Christmas present."

Fernando breaking up with me in such a cold way brought back the same symptoms I felt when I had the nervous breakdown.

I spent a lot of time talking out loud to my Heavenly Father, "I hate Fernando. I've never hated anyone in my life, not even my father, but I hate Fernando. If hate is a sin, Fernando has caused me to sin—and that makes me even angrier. You say to forgive those that hurt us. He hurt me. He lied to me. He used me. He played with me—not only me but my kids too. How can I forgive him? I don't want to remember Fernando anymore. I don't want to remember his face, voice, singing, smile, or idiotic ways he used to make me laugh. I want to erase his memory forever as if he never existed in my life. Maybe it's in your plan for Fernando to be in my life, but right now, I don't see it happening. In fact, I certainly won't be praying for it to happen. It hurts too much. What I do pray for is that you help me let go and move on."

I really wanted to call Fernando, curse him out, and tell him what a coward and asshole he was. I wanted to hibernate under my covers and not wake up for days. I wanted to cry until I had no more tears. Instead, I prayed for the courage to hide my feelings so that I didn't spoil the holiday season for everyone around me.

To make matters worse, the upstairs tenants, who were normally quiet during the week, were babysitting a couple of toddlers that ran, stomped, jumped, and played ball from seven in the morning till the late hours of the night—every day, including weekends—which was shooting my anxiety and stress level to its highest peak.

As if it weren't enough, shortly before Christmas, I received a letter from the Medicaid office stating that Tony was no longer eligible for Medicaid, effective December 31st.

The news was too much to handle. I felt like I was losing control—as if I was disappearing and some stranger was taking over my body and mind.

I wanted to get under the covers and never get up. But I didn't because the holidays were upon us, and hibernating was not on my to-do list. Instead, I put all my "end of the year" hardships on hold, put on a happy face, and focused on holiday decorating, gifts, cooking, and family time—leaving everything in God's hands, praying that everything be resolved the following year.

The year 2012 began with the issue of Tony's Medicaid, which had to be resolved before his next prescription refill. After many phone calls and much research by a very nice representative that took her time to figure out the problem. She said the termination was a mistake due to an error in the system. And, though not our fault, Tony had to re-apply for Medicaid.

On the day of the Medicaid appointment, it was breezy, cold, and snowing. The interviewer was a very warm lady, who I felt from the start had been sent by my Heavenly Father because of the way she continually spoke of Jesus and her faith during the whole interview.

After the interviewer reviewed Tony's application and documents, she gave us the wonderful news that he had been re-approved. Tony and I left the Medicaid office in awe. Neither one of us doubted that we had just received the first miracle of 2012.

Tony's decision to get an associate degree online was definitely a blessing because it kept him busy. Plus, it made him feel like he still had some control over his life. Although there were days when the medication made him tired, and he couldn't focus on his schoolwork, which frustrated him, he was very committed and tried his very best to keep up with his schoolwork.

The school policy for disabled students was very helpful. It allowed Tony to request extra time to submit assignments or complete tests. It also allowed me to act as his tutor, which he didn't mind.

Tutoring was hard for me at first because I had to read all the lessons, go over his homework, and help him study for tests. All this took a lot of time, but eventually, I got a grip on it.

Once Tony adjusted to his online classes, I felt it was time to make a decision on the car which had been sitting in the parking lot for seven months.

"We have two options. We can repair it, or we can sell it. What do you want to do?" I asked Tony.

"If the car can be repaired, and we can afford it, I would like to keep it," Tony answered.

"Yeah, I would like you to keep it too. Having a car is not a luxury—it's really a necessity. It will come in handy for running errands, doctor's appointments, and emergencies," I said. "Who knows, maybe I can overcome my phobia of being in a car, if you help me get back to driving."

"I still have the money I saved up for prescriptions, school, and commuting," Tony said.

"Hopefully, it doesn't cost too much to repair," I said. "We'll know once we get an estimate."

We got three car estimates, and all three were much more money than Tony had.

"My Heavenly Father, I don't know if praying for a way to get money to repair Tony's car is important to you or not, but if it is, could you please help us find the money to fix it," I prayed, and then left the situation in God's hands.

Not long after my prayer, I received my tax refund. And even though I had planned to save the money for emergencies, I decided to help Tony with the car repairs.

Tony was happy when the car was running again. At first, he was a little nervous about getting back behind the wheel, but he felt confident again after a few tries.

I, on the other hand, became extremely anxious every time he went for a drive. I kept thinking something was going to happen, to the point that if I heard sirens, I immediately thought Tony had gotten into an accident. My anxiety grew, even more when he drove me to places.

One morning, when Tony was going to drive me to a job interview, the thought of him driving on the highway brought on a panic attack that was so bad that I couldn't leave the house. That's when I knew my car phobia was much more serious than I had thought it was.

"My Heavenly Father, I don't understand why, if I trust and have faith in you, I still suffer anxiety and phobias when I'm in a car. Without a car, I can't go job hunting or drive to work when I get a job. Please help me get rid of this phobia," I prayed.

The next morning, I found a website that helped people with phobias. It said to start from scratch and take baby steps.

"Tony, I need your help to beat this car phobia," I said. "First, I'm going to sit in the driver's seat for a few minutes every day until I feel comfortable enough to start the car. Once I can do that, I need you to teach me to drive again."

"Sure, Ma," Tony said, confused.

Tony was a great teacher. It's amazing how, despite his disorder, he was able to focus on his schoolwork and teach me to drive. Without my Heavenly Father and Tony's help, I would never have gotten the nerve to try to beat my phobia of driving.

The first couple of months of the year, I was so busy tutoring, and taking care of the car situation, that I did not have the time or energy to think about the break-up with Fernando. But, when things calmed down, the question of why he had broken up with me haunted me night and day.

Fernando had been my best friend, my confidant, my shoulder to cry on, my love, my future, and my Prince Charming. Sure, our relationship had conflicts just like any relationship, but there was no doubt in my mind that he loved me and really wanted to spend the rest of his life with me—so, why breakup without a reason? I deserved an explanation.

While I tried to figure out what went wrong, my inner voice said, "You know perfectly well that you have fallen for every single lie Fernando told you since you met him. If he does give you an explanation, what guarantee do you have that it's true? God puts people in your life for a reason, and if someone walks away, it's usually because whatever purpose God had for that person to be in your life has been fulfilled, and the person is no longer needed in your life. Fernando became a mountain, and God moved it, so why do you want to bring the mountain back? Bringing him back, even for an explanation, is like playing with fire. And there's a possibility that God will let you get burn. Don't you see that?"

"Yes, I do see it," I answered.

With all that I was going through, I could not afford to waste what little energy I had waiting for Fernando to give me an explanation for our break-up. It was time for me to close this chapter of my life, so I answered his break-up email, thinking that I would find closure by doing so.

I wrote, "The emotional turmoil caused by the "cold turkey" way you walked away, at a time when you knew I was going through hardship, did not allow me to respond to your email when I first read it. You didn't ask for a response; however, I feel a response is needed, not for your sake, but for mine. Thank you for being part of our life, whether it was for a reason, a season, or to build beautiful memories that I will keep close to my heart for a lifetime. May you find the peace, joy, and happiness you are searching for, as you continue your journey. Who knows, maybe our paths will cross again someday. If not, just know that you will always be in my heart."

The letter was short and sweet, and the weird thing is that I meant every word of it. I sent it right away before I changed my mind.

A few days later, I opened a confusing email from Fernando that said, "From the looks of things, this is not going anywhere."

I guess I must like being hurt because instead of leaving well enough alone and praying on it, I answered by saying that he had broken up with me and that he had taken whatever little bit of sanity I had left with the break-up. I ended with, "I'm tired."

Well, the Pandora's Box was open. Fernando answered by saying that he accepted any guilt and asked to speak to me over the phone instead of by email. I agreed and set up a call for the following night.

The night before the call, I couldn't sleep. My inner voice said, "Why did you answer Fernando's email? Open your eyes and see that Fernando wants nothing to do with your family, you, your feelings, your situation, or the hardships you are facing. He does not care! How many times do you have to be hit upside the head, or how many times does he have to break your heart for you to face the truth? It doesn't take a rocket scientist to read between the lines."

"Look at you," the voice continued, "Just one e-mail, and you're back to crying, feeling down, hurt, and sick to your stomach. He isn't doing this to you—you are. You have a disabled son to care for. You have no health insurance, which means you cannot afford to get sick, and certainly, you cannot afford to end up in the hospital. For your family's sake and yours, you need to come to your senses."

Everything my inner voice told me made sense. But did I listen? No, instead, I spoke to Fernando the following night.

"I don't consider you my husband or fiancé," I began, "You weren't there for me when I needed you the most. You allowed two and a half years to pass by without coming to see us and hardly communicated. Your actions prove that I am not as important to you as you led me to believe."

"Rosita, I love you. And I want to spend the rest of my life with you," Fernando began. "I know things have been crazy between us. But the only reason I haven't come home is that I need to be here to sell this land. If I don't sell it, I can't build our house."

Hearing Fernando's words only confused me more. If he loved me, why did he break up with me?

"I sort of understand where you are coming from, but I don't see how you coming home for a few months like you used to is going to jeopardize selling the land. If your lawyer needs you, all you have to do is fly back," I said.

Fernando agreed, but vaguely. And then, in a matter of seconds, his personality changed from loving to obnoxious. He even insulted Jesus, which he knew would hurt me. When we finished our conversation, I really didn't know where we stood. All I knew was that I had opened up a door that should have stayed closed. Now, I had to suffer the consequences.

Although I truly felt that Fernando and I loved each other, living apart for so long had weakened the support system that kept us strong as a couple. The fireworks that existed for so many years had turned into a dim and disappearing candlelight.

Aside from our relationship going sour, many factors were probably keeping Fernando away. He was over sixty-six years old, and his health was not good. Why would he leave his home and family to build a house and live on a strange island with strange customs at this point in his life? Would I? No!

Then, there were the factors on my end. What if Fernando did move to Puerto Rico with us and then got sick. Would I be able to handle caring for him while caring for Tony? No!

When I thought of these factors, it didn't make me feel better. But it did help me understand the many reasons that kept Fernando and me apart. It also prepared me for the possibility that he and I might never live our "happily ever after."

Sadly, my suspicion was confirmed a few days later when Fernando and I had a conversation that I felt was the most honest one we had in a long time.

"Living in Mexico is very dangerous. They're killing people every day, for no reason," Fernando began, "I was hoping to use the money from the sale of the land to help my daughter move to Texas with her family and to build our house in Puerto Rico. Unfortunately, the land is not selling. Rosita, I love you. And I really want to spend the rest of my life with you. But, if in the process of going towards my happiness, something bad happens to my grandchildren because I wasn't here to protect them, I would never forgive myself."

"It's very honorable of you to put your family over your happiness. In a way, I don't blame you. I just wish you would have been honest with me instead of blindsiding me," I said.

Fernando had finally shed some light on something realistic instead of one of his fantasies. His honesty was what I needed to open my eyes finally and realize that I was heading to Puerto Rico without the man who had promised to love me till death and beyond.

"My Heavenly Father, please give me the strength to accept this reality. Please open the necessary doors so that I can move to Puerto Rico without Fernando's help," I prayed.

I had lost my faith in Fernando, but I had not lost my faith in my Heavenly Father and my Beloved Jesus. I believed with all my heart that if it was in God's plans for us to have a house, he would open the doors, no matter how impossible it seemed.

With this belief in my heart, I withdrew what was left in my annuity account and headed with Tony on a mini-vacation to Puerto Rico to begin the process of building our future house. Once again, I was a passenger on a journey that God was driving me to. I was excited and anxious to know how this trip would end.

My goal on this trip was to hire someone to build the foundation of the house. Later on, I hoped to get a loan to build a small wooden house on the foundation.

When I told my mom my plans, she wasn't very happy. She said bugs were attracted to wood, and a hurricane would destroy it. She was right, but a small wood house was all I could afford; therefore, I was sticking with my decision.

Before I left Puerto Rico, I opened up a savings account where I deposited the money I had left from my annuity account, authorizing my stepfather to withdraw money to buy material for the foundation and pay the person building it.

Even though the construction of our house could take years, I left Puerto Rico with a strong feeling that no matter how long it took, we were actually going to have a house someday, with God's help, instead of waiting and depending on Fernando's promises.

A few weeks after returning from our trip, I was blessed with a memorable family outing to Wild West City in New Jersey with all my children, my granddaughter, and my daughter-in-law — something that we hadn't done in years and that I will never forget.

During this outing, I was grateful for so much. I was grateful for Tony's effort to come with us, which I know was very hard for him to do with his condition. I was grateful for the many funny faces my granddaughter made when she heard the sound of cowboys shooting their guns and for the way she danced on her chair during the lunch show at the saloon. I was grateful for the great cowboy hat my daughter bought me. I was grateful for being with my family and for not getting car phobia during the long ride to and from. Thank you, my Beloved Jesus, for a blessed day!

Challenges began surfacing once again shortly after our family outing. Alexander lost his job, and he and Victoria were having a real hard time living on one salary. Their economic situation was so bad that if he didn't find a job by the end of September, they would have no choice but to move in with us or someone else.

Rebecca, who had suffered back pain for many years, shared that the pain was so bad that she could hardly breathe or walk. After many tests, the doctors found that her left lung was full of fluid. Tony and I prayed with her. After praying, I reminded her that God worked miracles, and the same way He worked miracles with me—He would work miracles with her.

After everyone was asleep, I prayed again, "Dear Jesus, I know you have a reason for this, but Rebecca's too young to be suffering this way. Please look into her heart and remember all she did for me when I lost my strength. You used my daughter to get me through the worse moments of my life. Please give Rebecca the strength that she needs to deal with this situation with her lungs. Please heal her—please."

I also prayed for all the challenges we were facing, "Soon, my unemployment benefits will end, and I too will be in the same situation Alexander and Victoria are in if I don't find a job. I leave our situations in your hands, my Heavenly Father. I have faith that the necessary doors will open to resolve things. Please guide us to those doors. And please give us the wisdom to recognize them and faith to go through them."

All doors led to Alexander and his family moving in with us. And, although it was very hard for all of us to give up our private spaces, as a family, we were willing to make sacrifices to keep a roof over our heads.

Shortly before the move, Tony asked me to go to church with him. I can't remember why I didn't go, but I wish I had because he came home late. When I asked him where he was, he said he had gone shopping for t-shirts—which was true because he showed them to me.

Monday morning, Tony seemed quiet. A few times, I heard him talking to himself in the kitchen.

Tuesday, instead of watching TV in his room, he came to watch TV with me but kept his eyes closed. That's when I felt something was very wrong.

Wednesday, without me asking, Tony shared that he was hearing voices again and that they were telling him to do things he didn't want to do. He seemed very scared. He didn't even want to go into his room. I immediately called his doctor and made an appointment for the following day.

Thursday, Tony's psychiatrist raised the dose on his antipsychotic medication from 2 to 5 mgs. He also prescribed an anti-anxiety medication.

Tony was back to square one. He was terrified of his room. Even on a higher dose of medication, he was still having bad thoughts that were so terrifying to him that he cried or moaned out loud as if he were being tortured. He was suspicious of everything and everyone. He was so scared of being alone that he moved to the living room with me until he felt safe enough to return to his room.

When I updated Tony's doctor on all he was going through, he said it would take time for his body to adjust to the new dose. He also said that if he didn't adjust within a few weeks, he might have to be hospitalized.

"Dear Lord, I don't know why this is happening again, but I beg you—heal Tony! Please don't let him be hospitalized again. Please protect us all, and please do not allow something horrible to happen," I prayed.

When I told Alexander about Tony's relapse, I'm sure he and his wife had concerns about moving in—I know I did, but it was too late for them to change their plans.

If it weren't for Tony's relapse, I would have been thrilled to have my whole family under the same roof again—especially my beautiful granddaughter, who brightened up my day with her hugs and smiles. Instead, I was so worried about how Tony would react that my anxiety level shot up.

Could you imagine how we all felt? Alexander, and his wife, had given up the comfort of their home to move in with us. My granddaughter no longer had her beautiful room full of toys to play in all day. Rebecca gave up the privacy of her room and was being schlepped from her room to the living room, to Tony's room. Tony was in a state of fear. And I was trying to deal with Tony's relapse, all the changes, and my ridiculous anxiety attacks. We were all stressed, even Alexander's dog. It was a hard time for all of us, but I had faith that soon we would adjust.

It broke my heart for all of us to be in this situation. However, I thanked my Heavenly Father for having a roof over our heads, for being together, and for building memories with my grand-daughter, who made me forget all we were going through every time she fell asleep in my arms.

Tony's psychiatrist had once told me that, even on medication, Tony could still have relapses. This relapse was more intense than the last one, and it lasted longer.

Aside from hearing voices, I could tell by the fear in his eyes that he was terrified of something or someone—invisible to my eyes. He was so scared that he didn't want to be alone. This worried me a lot because it seemed to go further than just hearing voices.

I once read that it was common for someone with Schizoaffective Bipolar symptoms to hear diabolic voices and images. My question is—is what they hear or see part of their mental disorder—or is it real?

I believe that just like my Heavenly Father, His Son, Jesus

Christ, the Holy Spirt, Mary Mother of Jesus, their saints, and all their guardian angels exist—so does Satan and all his demons. The Bible mentions it clearly, and I have had enough personal experiences to know this for a fact.

Was Tony really suffering from a mental disorder, or was he possessed by something evil? I did not believe that he was possessed because I didn't feel anything evil around us. However, looking back to the last two years, some unexplainable things had happened that supported this theory.

When Tony was hospitalized the first time, just like now, he insisted that he heard diabolic voices that were going to get him. Both times, he was terrified of staying in his room. During each episode, he destroyed or got rid of something that he thought was evil.

During each relapse, we all had the sense that some negative energy was around us. And we were all going through some abnormal challenges in our lives.

Even my mother called to tell me that strange things were happening on her end. She said something kept getting in the way of everything they were trying to do. She even said that her husband had mysteriously hurt his back while helping with the foundation of my house.

Was this all coincidence? Was this all a normal part of Tony's disorder, or was he being stalked by something evil? Many would say there was a logical explanation, but I couldn't help but think that evil played a part.

Whether it's normal or evil, Tony was not strong enough to fight it—but I could. And the only way I could was to turn it over to my Heavenly Father because I trusted that He, His Son, Jesus

Christ, and all His soldiers, would cast all evil out and protect us.

If it was evil, and it didn't go away no matter how much we prayed—then, it was because God was allowing it for reasons that I probably would never know.

One day I had a brilliant idea, which I'm sure my Heavenly Father, put in my head. I ordered a cot and moved temporarily into Tony's room, hoping that if I shared the room with him, he would not feel scared. Rebecca returned to the living room, which was not the ideal place for her because she was in the middle of human and dog traffic, but it was the only choice under the circumstances.

As soon as I moved into Tony's room, he calmed down a little. He slept longer, was not eating much, and hardly came out of his room—but at least he wasn't yelling out or moaning like before.

Tony shared with me that he was still having bad thoughts. He also said that he had them all along, even when he felt better.

"Did I tell you I'm sorry for all that went down in Brooklyn?" Tony asked one day when he was opening up.

"There's nothing to forgive," I said. "Hold on to your faith, and don't let go of it, no matter what the voices tell you. You're not alone in this. We love you, and we're here for you always. And I will always pray for you."

Tony hugged me tightly. "Please, dear Jesus, heal my son," I silently prayed.

Hurricane Sandy hit New Jersey. The storm caused devastation throughout the East Coast. Many areas were underwater and without power. Banks, supermarkets, and even gas stations were closed.

The storm did not hit us as badly as it did in other areas where flooding forced people to go to shelters, Thank God; however, for us personally, it was devastating.

For three days, we did not have internet, cable, or phone service. We barely had contact with the outside world, and we couldn't find a store open to purchase the necessities we were running out of. Emotionally, things were awry. We were all edgy.

Through it all, I prayed and tried to bring comfort to everyone—especially Tony. I continually reminded him that we had been lucky, as others had it worse. We were lucky, but with all we had been going through, how much more could we all take without breaking down?

Storms do pass, and within a week, everything at home and around us returned to normal—except for my health. On top of an increase in my anxiety and panic attacks, I had crying spells for no reason, fast heart palpitations, and I jumped every time someone spoke loudly, or I heard a noise. I'm sure my behavior was adding more stress to our situation, but no matter how much I tried or prayed, I couldn't control myself.

On my sixtieth birthday, I thought about how different my life was from what I had envisioned it would be when I reached this age. I was supposed to still be working at my old job. My children were supposed to be on their own, living their own life. Fernando was supposed to have started construction on our house, and we were supposed to have been planning our future together.

Instead, I was unemployed, without a penny to my name, living off my kids, taking care of my disabled son, sleeping on a cot in my son's room, suffering from panic and anxiety attacks, and without the man that had promised to take care of me for the rest of my life.

To top things off, Fernando was playing with my emotions again. I spoke to him a few times after my trip to Puerto Rico, and every conversation was confusing. In a few conversations, he said he was going to finish the house as soon as the foundation was complete; in others, he said he loved me but couldn't leave his daughter and grandchildren in Mexico to pursue his happiness. Then suddenly, he stopped calling and writing and disappeared without an explanation. My emotions kept bouncing from being happy to being disappointed.

My mental health was going downhill very fast. I became depressed. Aside from cooking, running some errands, and watching TV in the living room when Rebecca was working, I spent a lot of time with Tony, in his room, with the door closed—hardly speaking to the rest of the family.

"This sucks. I don't want to live this way," I vented to my Heavenly Father. "I have reached rock bottom. I need to find a part-time job so that I can cover my part of the household expenses, plus my personal expenses, without leaving Tony alone for a whole day. But I can't find a job if every time I get into a car, I get an anxiety and panic attack. What do I do? Please help me."

Christmas was quiet and peaceful—Thank God. But, when I returned from New Year's Eve food shopping, something unexpected happened that freaked me out.

While taking groceries out of the bags, I saw a wall of dark swirls in front of my eyes. At first, I thought the swirls were on the kitchen wall. But they weren't. It was my vision.

My first thought was that I was having an eye stroke, so I searched the internet for answers. I was relieved when I read that what I had experienced could be from a torn retina, which is still serious but not as serious as an eye stroke.

I didn't want to spoil the rest of what was left of the holidays, so when my kids asked why I kept putting wet towels over my eye, I told everyone that I had allergies.

On New Year's Eve, before the stroke of midnight, I prayed, "Thank you, my Heavenly Father, and my Beloved Jesus, for all the blessings you gave us during the year.

I'm thankful because even though it's been very stressful for all my children and me to be living together—we are not homeless.

I'm thankful because you're using my parents to supervise the construction of the foundation of our house. I believe with all my heart that you will provide a way for us to finish the house.

Thank you for giving me the gift of spending time with my beautiful granddaughter, whose innocence you have used to teach me a lesson. She has adjusted well in our current situation, going with the flow while learning to talk, and play. I truly believe that it's because she is sure that, no matter what, her parents will protect and take care of her.

Thank you for always protecting us and keeping us safe from harm and evil. Please strengthen our faith so that we can accept and deal with whatever comes our way—while trusting that you have control over each situation.

Please fill our home with faith, love, hope, health, and harmony—and help me find the energy and time to take care of my health and financial situation, no matter what challenges I face.

I have no clue what 2013 will bring our way, but one thing I know for sure is that you will be walking by our side every step of the way. Without a doubt—I am sure that you will always protect us—and will never forsake us—Amen."

I can DO
ALL THINGS *through* CHRIST
who strengthens ME.
PHILIPPIANS 4:13 KJV

CHAPTER NINE
Be Still And Let God!

*"They that wait upon the Lord shall
renew their strength; they shall mount
up with wings as eagles; they shall run,
and not be weary; and they shall walk,
and not faint."*
(Isaiah 40:31 KJV)

Do you know the feeling of making a New Year's resolution and starting the year determined to stick to it? Well, that's exactly how I felt the first week of 2013. I was determined that no matter what challenges came my way, with God's help, I was going to find a solution to my financial crisis, have my eyes checked, and get treated for the anxiety, phobias, and panic attacks that were preventing me from being the warrior that I used to be.

In January, I called Mental Services and was very lucky to get an appointment right away for a psychological evaluation. I sat with the evaluator for an hour, tearfully pouring my heart out to her. She listened and wrote on her pad. When she finally spoke, she said she was referring me to a therapist and a psychiatrist for possible medication therapy.

After meeting with the therapist and psychiatrist, I was diagnosed with depression and chronic anxiety caused by the traumas I had experienced, not only in 2010 but since I was a little girl. The psychiatrist felt that, with management therapy and medication, eventually I could start feeling my old self again.

I don't know if it was the crying, venting, or the help that I was finally going to get; all I know is that when I left the clinic, I felt better than I had in a long time.

The pain on my wrist was so bad that I could barely open a jar. When I went to the arthritis specialist, he informed me that my wrist was not curable at my age. All he could do was prescribe a shot of cortisone to lessen the pain. In addition to Osteoarthritis on my right knee and Morton's Neuroma on my left foot (both very painful and causing me to limp), Carpal Tunnel on both of my wrists, and heel spurs on both my feet—I had Progressive Tendinitis on my right wrist.

The visit to the ophthalmologist was disturbing. He informed me that I had a tear in my retina, which required immediate laser surgery. He said the surgery was very expensive, but if I didn't have it done soon, it could lead to a detachment, which would cost three or four times more to treat. The doctor said I had two options. He could refer me to a private clinic close to home or to a hospital in Newark that took charity cases.

The whole weekend I researched, prayed, and debated on what to do. Every time I thought about surgery—I had an uneasy feeling, so I decided to put it on hold until I felt good about it.

It's weird but, even though I was deteriorating physically and mentally, my faith was stronger than ever. I was confident that my Heavenly Father was not going to abandon me.

Towards the end of January, an unexpected miracle occurred. The disability lawyer, who had rejected my case months before due to lack of recent medical history on all my conditions, called asking to go over my medical history.

Once again, I went over all my conditions and the reasons that forced me to resign from my job. I explained that I could not continue any of my treatments after leaving my job because I had lost my medical insurance and could not afford to pay for doctors and medication. I also mentioned my recent visit to the therapist, psychiatrist, arthritis specialist, and ophthalmologist.

I was stunned when he told me that he was accepting my case. I didn't question why he changed his mind because deep in my heart, I knew God was working on another miracle.

Applying for disability meant that I could not work while waiting for the claim to be approved, which could take up to a year. "How are we going to survive financially until then?" I asked my Heavenly Father. I began getting answers to my question sooner than I had expected.

A bill passed extending unemployment benefits, which allowed me to continue receiving unemployment benefits until the end of February, around the time that I usually received my tax refund.

When I finished working on my tax returns, I was disappointed to find that my refund would be less than I was hoping for, which worried me.

That night, God spoke to me in a dream. He pointed out that I had made a mistake with some entries on my tax form, and he told me what the amounts should be.

The next morning, I researched my entries on the IRS website and found that I was entitled to certain tax credits I had not entered. After making the corrections, it turned out that my refund would be more than I had expected. Glory to God!

It's mind-blowing how Jesus and His Father work. My tax refund arrived the same week my unemployment benefits ended.

Two months into the year and things were actually falling into place, except for my mental health, which seemed to be deteriorating more each day.

One beautiful spring morning, I woke up feeling like crap. I had an upset stomach. I felt lightheaded, drained of all energy, disoriented, and my head felt like it was about to explode. I also felt panic and anxiety symptoms creeping up for no reason. It was like I was walking around in circles, trying to find my way out of a complicated maze that was closing in on me while the exit was shrinking and disappearing.

"What's happening to me?" I asked my Heavenly Father. "Is it depression? Is it a different type of panic attack?"

"Please, Jesus, help me," I continued. "Take away the fear. Take away the worries. Hold me! Keep me safe! Help me breathe! Don't let me go. Take this panic attack from me! Make it go away!"

"How I wish I had my own room where I could close the door, crawl back into bed, and be alone. Will I ever have days like that again?" I asked myself.

The weird feeling lasted for days. I didn't want to face or talk to anyone. When I passed Alexander in the kitchen, nothing came out of my mouth—not even hello. When Tony got edgy, I panicked. When I spoke to my mom, I felt like she was trying to control my life and everything I did.

"Is it possible that my symptoms are coming from worrying over the disability claim, therapy, the kids, the house, and my financial situation?" I asked myself, "Because every time I think about these things, my anxiety and stress level go up to the point where I can't breathe, my insides tremble, I feel scared, my legs get weak, my stomach is in knots, and I can't focus—all symptoms of a panic attack."

When I told my therapist how I was feeling, she said, "Your anxiety is getting worse because you are worrying over things that might never happen. The extent of your worrying is not only bad for your health, but it's creating a negative environment for those around you.

Let me give you an example of what I mean. You worry when Tony goes out alone because you fear he might be bullied by gangs, and if a fight breaks out, he will be blamed because he is the one with the mental illness. You worry that if he is driving, he might get into an accident—get hurt or hurt someone else. You worry that he might leave the iron or stove on. So, what do you do? You do everything for him and keep him safe in his room instead of teaching him to be as independent as he can be within his condition. What you are doing is enabling and crippling him—instead of helping him."

"That's ridiculous," I interrupted, annoyed. "Tony is my son. Of course, I worry about him and my other children. There is nothing wrong with that. I care about them. It's natural to worry about them."

"Caring usually produces positive results," my therapist continued. "On the other hand, worrying about what you think will happen in the future, which most of the time will never happen, is a waste of time. It's also a waste of time and energy for you to worry about things that are out of your control—like the decision on your disability claim."

"So true," I thought while my therapist wrote on her pad. "Also true is the fact that I put situations in God's hands, and then I waste my time worrying, instead of trusting and believing that God has the situation under control, and it will be resolved in His time—not mine."

"I'm a mess. When will I learn to sit back and let you drive without worrying?" I silently asked my Heavenly Father.

"How's your son doing?" the therapist asked.

"He sleeps a lot, barely comes out of his room, only goes out when he has an appointment or to the movies. His driving skills are slower. Sometimes he doesn't put his signal light on until he is almost at an intersection. He is slow to react, which worries me when he is driving. He still doesn't feel safe enough to be alone, so I'm still sleeping on a cot in his room," I answered.

"And your other kids?" she asked.

"I haven't been spending quality time with my children or my granddaughter. I hardly speak to them. I know my actions are hurting them, but I can't help myself. I miss hanging out with my granddaughter. They keep her from me because of the way I've been acting. They don't even let her say goodnight like before. I was invited to my granddaughter's birthday party, but I didn't go because I didn't want to be around so many people. Instead, I bought her cupcakes from the supermarket as a "before birthday party" cake, which I don't think her parents were very happy about."

"How do you feel about Fernando's disappearance?" my therapist asked, waiting patiently for me to answer.

"The way he disappeared without an explanation or reason is torturing me," I answered, clearing my throat as I tried to hold back the tears. "I mean, things had been rocky between us for the past few years due to my situation and his, but no matter how bad things got, we always communicated. I'm angry at him, but deep down inside, I know that as long as I am caring for Tony, I can't give Fernando the attention he needs, which is one of the reasons why our relationship turned cold and distant since 2010."

"If you had one question to ask Fernando, what would it be?" Therapist continued.

"I would ask him—why?" I answered.

"What do you need to help you ease the pain?" she asked.

"Closure," I answered, without thinking it twice.

"One way of getting closure is to write Fernando a letter telling him how you feel."

"I wrote him a letter last year when I thought he had broken up with me, and all I did was open up a Pandora's Box of pain. I don't want to do that anymore," I said.

"Yes, but you haven't told him how you really feel about his disappearance. Writing your feelings will help you. It's up to you if you mail it or not. But, if you do mail it, you have to be prepared to handle his response. If you don't mail it, you could rip it up and use this step as a "closure" so that you can move on," the therapist suggested.

It took me a couple of weeks to get enough nerve to write Fernando an email telling him how I really felt.

"You swore you loved me and we'd be together "till death and beyond," and then you took me on an emotional roller coaster ride, led me on, and then disappeared without an explanation. You took the cowardly way out—just like my father did," I began. "I'm angry! I'm hurt! I want you to hurt as much or more than you hurt me. I don't wish you luck! I don't wish you happiness! I don't wish you peace! I pray that what you did to me haunts you in your sleep and during every waking moment of the rest of your life. I pray that every time you kiss a woman, you see my face and the tears you caused me. I pray that every time you sing a song, you will remember the hurt you caused me and will hurt just as much. I pray that telling you how I feel will give me the closure that I need so that I can move on with my life. God forgive you because I can't," I ended and clicked send.

The next day, I took a very necessary step. I sold the ring that represented the promise Fernando and I had made to each other ten years ago when we visited the little antique church in Monterrey, where we vowed to love each other till death and beyond. Now, it didn't represent anything. It was time to let it go.

It's so hard to fight off the symptoms of anxiety when I feel pressured, which is what my parents do without realizing it. Ever since my trip to Puerto Rico, every time my mother calls, she asks when I will start building the house. I avoided the conversation, mostly because I wanted to wait for the outcome of the disability case before going further. Unfortunately, one day I wasn't able to evade the subject.

"Building a cement house is about as expensive as building a wood house," Mom began.

"I don't have money to start the construction of the house yet," I said. "I used my tax refund on therapy, doctors, medication, and household expenses. Until my disability is approved, and I start receiving benefits and hopefully retro money, I cannot start the house."

"We know; that's why we took out two loans today and told the builder to begin construction on the house as soon as he finishes the foundation," Mom said. And then, she went on and on about the floor plan and how the house was going to be built—while I sat there, not knowing what hit me.

I tried to argue with her and remind her of my original plans and financial difficulties, but it was like talking to the wall. She did not want to hear it. So, I agreed—with the condition that I pay them back as soon as I had a set income—no matter how long it took.

"My Heavenly Father, what just happened?" I prayed. "All I want is a small country wood house to live the rest of my days in peace. The way Mom describes the house is out of my price range. This scares me. Mostly because Mom has very expensive taste, and when she shops, she always goes overboard. This house is going to end up costing me a fortune."

"Stop complaining. Be grateful and appreciative," my inner voice said. "Obviously, God is using your parents to help build the house that you have been praying for. If it would have been God in that telephone conversation, instead of your mother, would you have argued with Him? No, you wouldn't. So, accept what God is giving you, and stop complaining."

The following morning God spoke to me through a daily devotional I read. He said, "Do not be afraid. Do not worry because I am in control. Have patience!"

One day, Alexander and I had the opportunity to have a conversation. After telling me about all the hardships he and his wife were facing, I told him that we were a family and that we would find a solution together. He said he didn't want to accept anything from anyone because that would be the easy way out. He sounded just like me.

"Ok," I said, "but just know that whatever we can do to help, we'll try to do."

Later that evening, Alexander came to the kitchen, touched my arm, and said, "Don't worry. I'm looking for a solution."

The touch on my arm meant so much to me. It felt like a hug. I wanted to hold him like when he was a little boy; instead, I just stood there and smiled.

Mother's Day was nice. Alexander and Victoria brought food from a smokehouse place in North Jersey. I called Tony to come to the kitchen, and we all hung out there for a while. All of us eating together was the best Mother's Day gift.

During the month of May, I thought about the mental block I was having when it came to writing my story. So, I prayed on it.

I received an answer to my prayer at the end of Mathew 23:23-24 that said something like this, "You're trying to write a life story that is wrong from start to finish because you are focusing on colons and semicolons."

"What does this message mean?" I asked my Beloved Jesus.

"Are you trying to tell me that the reason why I'm stuck is because I'm adding too many small details that have nothing to do with my faith, miracles, and my relationship with you and our Heavenly Father? Or are you reminding me of the purpose of our book—to give testimony—which I find so hard because a testimony is supposed to empower and help those who read it. It's supposed to show others that my faith is so strong that even in the middle of extreme adversity, I hold on to it with dear life. How can I do that if I fall apart at the first sign of a hardship?" I vented frustrated because I did not know what the message meant.

During a gospel concert, Rebecca prayed for a way to help us during our financial situation. After the concert, she received a text from a job application source, and when she returned the call, she was told that she was hired.

"God always finds a way," she said. "It's a miracle."

"Yes, it is a miracle, and don't forget it," I responded.

I received a letter from the social security office informing me that before they could make a determination on my claim, I had to undergo a mental and physical evaluation with their psychiatrist and doctor.

When I researched these evaluations, I read an article that said most people failed because the doctors who worked for the social security administration made the tests really hard. It even mentioned that most of these doctors were very rude throughout the test. After reading the article, I felt like I would be on trial with a judge and jury.

"I'm definitely not going to lie or try to exaggerate my condition. My emotional state is unbalanced. My anxiety, phobia, fears, not wanting to go out and do things, the slurred speech, bad memory, eye, and arthritic conditions are all real," I said to myself. "So, why worry?"

A few nights before the mental evaluation, I dreamt that I was battling two demons. Just when I thought I was going to be defeated, I heard the words, "Fear is a choice" (the exact words I had heard in a movie a few months before). In the dream, after I heard these words, I became strong and killed the demons.

The day before the mental evaluation, I read about unconditional trust, belief, and faith. It reminded me that no matter how impossible a situation seems, if we believe without a doubt, and without fear, God could work a miracle—if he doesn't, it's because the road you were following was not the right one.

The mental evaluation was humiliating. The psychiatrist conducting the evaluation was cold. She asked me questions but wouldn't let me finish responding when she went on to the next question. She didn't even cover the most important symptoms of my anxiety and phobia attacks.

One weird thing did happen during the mental evaluation. I spoke in a slow, loud voice instead of my normal voice. I heard myself and just knew it wasn't me. I didn't feel like I was possessed by an evil entity, but it did feel like a takeover of some kind. My gut feeling was that God had sent an angel to speak for me during the interview. It was all so weird.

The physical evaluation turned out to be a totally different experience from the mental evaluation. The doctor was very compassionate, very thorough, asked questions about my disability, and listened carefully to all my responses. He even showed concern over my blood pressure being extremely high and suggested that I get treatment as soon as possible.

A few days after the physical evaluation, I had a dream about the story I had been trying to write for years. In the dream, I saw a bouquet of roses. The thorns represented the hardships that I had faced during my life. The roses represented the miracles that had been born out of the hardships.

I played with titles that matched my dream, *"Thorns and Roses—Hardships and Miracles"*—neither seemed right.

When I wrote *"Bouquet of Miracles,"* it felt so right that I prayed and asked God if it was the title that He wanted me to use for my story.

The next morning God sent me a sign. I found a bouquet of roses on the kitchen table, with a note, "To Mommy, just for being you. I love you. Rebecca."

"These are the best gifts—the unexpected ones," I said to myself, smiling. Then it hit me. The bouquet of roses that Rebecca left me was God's way of telling me that the title of my story should be *"Bouquet of Miracles."* I felt good chills.

When I shared my dream with Rebecca, she said she had this strong feeling that she should get me the flowers but didn't know why. The feeling was so strong that she had to buy them.

God works in mysterious ways. He used a dream, and my daughter, to help me choose the title of my story and testimony. "Thank you, Jesus," I said softly.

During a conversation with my disability lawyer, I was very surprised by how negative he sounded about my claim. He kept telling me that even if I passed the two evaluation exams, my case could still be denied.

Well, I didn't care what he said. In my heart, I felt that it would be approved. The lawyer was not making the decision on my claim; not even the social security adjudicator was making the decision on my claim—God was making the decision on my claim.

In August, I received a letter from the disability office stating that I had met the medical requirements for disability (thank you, Jesus), but before they could make a final decision, they needed to investigate if I met the non-medical requirements, which were work history, age, etc.—all of which I was sure I met. The bad news was that because I did not have medical records going back to when I lost my health insurance, they used the date I started mental therapy as my disability date—which meant I was not eligible for retro money going back to 2011.

I was disappointed because I counted on the retro money to finish the house but accepted the decision with gratitude because I felt it was God's will.

Alexander and his wife, who had desperately been searching for work, were offered good job opportunities in Tennessee, a home, and daycare for my granddaughter—opportunities they couldn't refuse. They were moving the first week of September. I supported them wholeheartedly, although it saddened me to know that my little princess would be so far away.

I silently thanked God for all the news I had received—both good and bad. I prayed that my disability would be officially approved and I would be receiving benefit checks before my son moved in September so that I could have money to pay my bills.

Great News! The official award letter from the disability office stating that my first benefit check would be deposited into my bank account the second week of September arrived sooner than I expected. I knew deep in my heart that my Heavenly Father worked this miracle. His hand was in it every step of the way.

A few days later, I received a benefits letter from the disability office telling me how much I would be getting in benefits. It was less than I had expected, which meant that I had to do some serious budgeting before signing the lease renewal on our apartment.

In the middle of all that was going on, Tony began experiencing symptoms of a possible relapse, and it might have been my fault for being so preoccupied that I mistakenly gave him his night dose in the morning. A few days later, he began hearing voices again, said the television characters were talking to him, made weird noises with his mouth, held his head constantly, and gave that eerie cold stare.

When Tony and I told his psychiatrist that the symptoms had returned, he said Tony could have episodes even though he was taking his medication. He recommended that I give him the anxiety medication when he was having an episode.

After we left the psychiatrist's office, we went to one of our favorite restaurants, where we bumped into Victoria, Amber, and Rebecca, who were about to leave. My granddaughter decided that she wasn't leaving with her mommy and auntie; instead, she wanted to stay with her grandma and uncle. So cute!

Well, for someone who had just eaten, she ate two big chicken fingers and fries. Then, as we were leaving, she said, "Grandma, let's get a Reese's cake." Of course, we bought it.

Towards the end of August, I discovered something that did not make me very happy. There was mold all over Tony's room, the big closet in the dining room, and the bottom shelf of a unit next to my dining table. By the end of the week, mold was creeping up everywhere, including Alexander's closet.

The cleaning process was huge and required lots of bleach, which concerned me, but I had no choice but to start on it first thing the next morning. I prayed God protected us from getting sick.

The closer it got to Alexander's moving day, the more emotional I became about not seeing my granddaughter. So, we planned an "Amber Day" to spend time with her and spoil her before they moved.

On Amber Day, Tony, Amber, and I walked to the mall, where we met up with Rebecca. We all had lunch, and then we took

Amber to Macy's, where we bought her some cute outfits and a sweat jacket, which she loved. We had a wonderful time laughing at her cute silliness. It was her special day and the last one I would be spending with her. It was a very emotional day for us, but I held my tears so that I didn't spoil the day.

On the morning that Alexander and his family were moving to Tennessee, we all got up at four-thirty in the morning to say good-bye. Amber was half asleep when I hugged her. When I hugged Victoria and Alexander, I was too emotional to say anything, but when I watched them walk towards their car from my kitchen window, that's when the tears began.

As I watched Alexander get into the moving van he had rented, I went down memory lane to when he was a baby. Alexander was tough and resilient since the day he was born. He beat the odds many times. Now, there he went with a family of his own. I had no doubt in my mind that he would always protect and care for his family. He was tough but with a heart of gold.

"Will I see them again, or was this our final goodbye?" I asked myself in silence. "I'll write them an email expressing how sad I felt when they left so that they don't interpret my silence as not caring."

The next morning when I opened the refrigerator and saw Amber's left-over chicken nuggets and fries, my eyes filled with tears. I was going to miss them all terribly, but mostly I was going to miss the one person that brought a smile to my face every day in the midst of my sorrow — my beautiful granddaughter.

By the middle of September, we were all fighting a very bad cold that was getting worse as the days passed. Tony felt better within days, but I got worse. My chest was hurting so bad that I had to go to the doctor, who put me on bed rest due to a bad case of bronchitis, probably from the mold clean-up.

While I was sick in bed, the mold in the apartment continued to spread, forcing me to realize that our living environment was unhealthy and that it was time to move. The problem was—I had no money. So, I prayed and left it in God and Jesus' hands.

A few weeks later, I received three preapproved visa card offers. I was approved despite my bankruptcy record. This was definitely an answer to my prayers.

I was so excited that I began searching for an apartment. Unfortunately, every apartment was more expensive than the one we had.

After re-budgeting, I realized that the credit cards would help with the moving expenses, but they would not help pay rent and monthly bills. I had to face reality. I could not afford an apartment in New Jersey—not on my disability check, which wasn't even enough to pay rent.

There was only one place we could afford to move to—Puerto Rico—even if we had to live with my mother until the house was finished.

I dreaded telling Rebecca what I had decided; however, even though I wouldn't be moving for another year, it was only fair to let her know my decision so that she had plenty of time to weigh her options.

When I spoke to Rebecca, I could tell she was taken back by the news of my moving to Puerto Rico sooner than I had planned. Rebecca doesn't like to show her feelings, so when she didn't say much, I knew she was holding in her emotions.

My heart ached for Rebecca. She had gone through so much since the summer of 2010. She gave up a lot to move to New Jersey with us. And now, all her family was moving far away and leaving her alone when her health was deteriorating. I had no doubt that she felt like her whole world was crashing down on her.

It killed me to do this to my daughter, but I had no other choice. Hopefully, she'll move to Puerto Rico with us—maybe.

My 61st birthday was blessed. I spent the day with Tony and Rebecca, who gave me flowers, packages of my favorite coffee, balloons, and good wishes. We ate pizza and a cherry cheesecake. I also spoke to my mother, Alexander, Victoria, and my princess granddaughter Amber. My aunt also emailed me birthday wishes. All in all, it was great.

Shortly after my birthday, I made a really huge mistake. I wrote Fernando an email asking how he was. His response was a simple "ok."

"That's it?" I thought angrily. "After almost a year and a half of not communicating, he answers my email with one word?"

"What did you expect?" my inner voice said. "The man does not care! Stop humiliating yourself. He doesn't deserve you. You need to move on, focus on your journey, and not let anything or anyone detour you. When are you going to learn?"

I had opened Pandora's Box again, but thankfully this time, it wasn't for long. Fernando and I emailed each other a few times, and then he disappeared again. I learned from his emails that he was still living his days acting like everyone else on this planet did him wrong and that everything that happened to him was someone else's fault. In some emails, he spoke as if I had disappeared instead of him. As usual, he played the victim.

One December morning, I was blessed with breath-taking scenery outside my kitchen window. The back lawn and parking lot were covered with a blanket of untouched snow. It was so beautiful that I drank my coffee standing by the window.

When I finished my coffee, I moved to the living room window, where I stood mesmerized. The front lawn was even more beautiful than the back. Every tree, bush, and path was covered with glistening virgin snow. To witness this miraculous wonder the last winter I was spending in the states was a gift. Thank you, Jesus!

Tony and I wanted to enjoy our last winter holiday, so one day, we took a long stroll to town. It was freezing, but we didn't care. We took pictures and silently enjoyed the winter wonderland around us.

Christmas came and went too fast, and New Year's Eve 2013, our last in New Jersey with my daughter Rebecca, was upon us. I baked lasagna, garlic bread, and Tony baked cookies. It snowed on and off all day.

We tried to enjoy every moment as best as we could while holding in our emotions, especially Rebecca, who was staying behind. The past few months had been very hard on her. Not only did she go through the emotions of saying goodbye to her brother, sister-in-law, and niece, but, in ten months, she would be saying goodbye to us too.

"Is it going to be easier in Puerto Rico?" I asked myself silently. "I don't know because the journey is full of uncertainties. All I know is that we are not going alone. God is going with us!"

Before I went to bed, I prayed, "My Heavenly Father, I feel positive about my decision to move to Puerto Rico but scared at the same time. Please help me complete all the steps needed to embark on our journey to Puerto Rico, and please help us find a way to finish the construction of our house so that we don't have to live with my parents very long. I pray for mental and physical health and happiness for my children, granddaughter, myself, and my parents. I pray that you take away all my fears, anxieties, and phobias, especially the fear of driving, and make me resilient and courageous. Amen."

The New Year began with a snowstorm, followed by a blizzard towards the end of January. Temperatures plunged to a wind chill of -12 degrees. It was so cold that Tony and I decided to hibernate until the weather got warmer—the perfect time to work on my story.

While I hibernated from the cold and worked on my story, I thought about my decision to move to Puerto Rico. I really didn't want to move, but there were too many reasons why I had to.

Stress, whether good or bad, can trigger any illness to get worse. Tony was very excited about the move, but the stress involved with the move took a toll on all of us. I was not surprised when he began to show signs of a slight relapse.

One night he yelled so loud that I got a panic attack. He confessed that the symptoms had started months before but was scared to tell me because he didn't want to go to the hospital. On the next visit to the psychiatrist, the dose on one of his medications was raised again, plus he was prescribed extra anxiety pills to take during the day.

I felt so bad for him. Since his first hospitalization, we really hadn't fallen into a routine because of so many changes. All I could do was reassure him that everything was going to be ok and that I loved him.

Rebecca was not well either. She was in so much pain that her job forced her to go on temporary medical leave. I prayed that she would be healed and could return to work before we moved. She's a workaholic; maybe it was God's way of forcing her to rest.

By April, things began looking brighter. Tony was doing better. He had a few stressful classes but seemed to be dealing with them well. I was making some progress with my driving. I actually drove to my therapy appointments, the mall, and on the highway. I was a little nervous, but no phobias, shaking, nor crying spells. Thank you, Jesus!

Rebecca gave me some good news. She was going to Puerto Rico with us for a few days. I was so happy because it meant more time to spend with her. She also announced that she was moving in with her boyfriend, who lived with his mother until they found an apartment. Her boyfriend, Simon, cared a lot for her. He was there for her during her medical tests when I couldn't be. I was very happy to hear this news because I was very worried about where she would live and her being alone.

Spring to summer, I was extremely busy changing health care services, psychiatrists, doctors, arranging for the car to be transported, hiring a moving company, and packing.

In September, I purchased our airline tickets, scheduled the pickup dates for the car and moving company, reserved a hotel room to stay from October 31st to November 7th, and reserved transportation to take us to the airport.

When October arrived, I began to panic and have doubts. I felt emotional about leaving Rebecca, especially with her health problems. Thank God I had already said goodbye to Alexander, Victoria, and Amber because I wouldn't have survived saying goodbye to everyone at once.

My Heavenly Father sent me a message. He said evil was lurking and to be on the look-out. He also warned me about war and bad times. He kept telling me to use my weapons of prayer and faith. I had no idea what the warnings were about; nonetheless, I recited my protection prayer.

By mid-October, I began feeling ill. The cleaning, organizing, and packing, were getting to me. I felt very tired, and my back was hurting a lot. I prayed and tried very hard not to think of the pain.

One morning while watching a Christian program, I felt Jesus was speaking to me when they spoke about not being offended by what others say about you and how it was best to walk away. I wondered if Jesus was trying to tell me not to let anything my mom says offend me.

I received an unexpected call from Fernando. He sounded surprised to hear that I was moving to Puerto Rico. He choked up when he said he loved me. He said going to Puerto Rico was his dream, but unfortunately, due to his health problems, he didn't want to burden me. What he said was clear, and I'm grateful he was being honest about not going to Puerto Rico. I took it fine— mostly because I had stopped counting on him long ago.

I hated that I wouldn't be spending Thanksgiving with Rebecca. So, I cooked a huge Thanksgiving meal in October and invited Rebecca's boyfriend. A few days after, I received pictures of my sweet Amber. It made me so happy. Thank you, Heavenly Father, for those precious memories.

The last week in our apartment, I was very busy dealing with the movers, Salvation Army, and the cable company. I didn't get emotional until Rebecca started moving her things to her boyfriend's apartment.

On the evening of October 31st (Halloween), Tony and I said goodbye to our apartment. I don't know how Tony felt, but for me, the Somerville apartment had been a temporary refuge very badly needed after that horrible summer in 2010. It served its purpose, and now it was time to leave.

Rebecca still had some items in the apartment, so she stayed behind, waiting for her boyfriend to pick her up. I really believe she wanted time alone in the apartment to say goodbye and probably cry—something I did not have the privacy to do.

The hotel was very close to places I needed to get to and the psychiatrist's office. Our room was very nice with a small kitchenette, microwave, and coffee maker. Comfortable enough for us to rest and re-energize before completing the last steps that had to get done before leaving for Puerto Rico the following Thursday.

Monday, we took the car to be washed and detailed. Tuesday, we said goodbye to Tony's psychiatrist and receptionist. It was sad. We really liked them, and Tony got along with them.

I had a weird, good, and bad driving experience. The "good" part was that God filled me with the warrior spirit that I needed to drive the car and merge three times on the highway without any fear whatsoever. The "bad" part was that I got an unexpected panic attack when Tony drove on Highway 22 back to the hotel. I really don't understand what happened. I felt confident when I drove but then panicked when someone else was driving. So weird.

Thursday arrived too fast. It was time to leave the country I considered home and embark on our journey to Puerto Rico.

The trip to the airport was emotional. When the driver exited New Jersey, I said goodbye to the town I had called home for the past four years and where my daughter would continue living without us. The ride continued to Staten Island, where I said goodbye to my favorite places. When the driver reached Brooklyn, that's when my eyes filled with tears. I said goodbye to the borough I had grown up in most of my life and to the areas we had lived. I said goodbye to the place I had worked in for almost twenty-five years.

The plane ride began smoothly, until twenty minutes after lift-off when rough turbulence caused the plane to literally shake and go up and down, non-stop, until we arrived. Honestly, in all my years of flying, it was the most frightening plane ride I had ever experienced.

"What a way to start our new life—with turbulence. Could this be a warning of what our life is going to be like?" I silently asked myself when we landed.

The hustle and bustle of picking up baggage, waiting for my parents to arrive at the airport, and then going to eat breakfast kept us busy for the first few hours after landing.

We stopped by my parent's house, where we would be living until the basic necessities were installed in our house. Then, we went next door to see our house for the first time.

Opening the door to our house was emotional to everyone else but me. I had dreamed and prayed for this moment for decades, yet for reasons I could not explain, I wasn't as happy as I thought I'd be.

The house was bigger than I imagined. It had a long narrow front porch connected on the left to a large open carport that led to a back-laundry area. If I had been consulted, the carport would not be next to the kitchen door where gas fumes enter the house—

it would have been separate from the house, and a terrace would be here instead.

The house had three bedrooms, two bathrooms, and a small kitchen connecting to the living room. The living room door opened to the front porch, and the kitchen door opened to the car-port.

My bedroom was bigger than any bedroom I'd ever had, with a connecting bathroom and a huge closet with sliding mirrored doors. Tony's bedroom was bigger than the one he had. The small-est room was perfect for an office where I could write to my heart's content.

When my stepfather said, "We made the house the way we wished we had made ours." —that's when I realized why I wasn't feeling as happy as they were. This house was built the way they wanted it, not the way I wanted. No wonder I didn't feel like it was mine.

"Am I a terrible person for feeling this way?" I silently asked my Heavenly Father.

The five days that Rebecca stayed with us were memorable for me. The three of us scrubbed, hosed, and cleaned the house from top to bottom. I watched Rebecca and Tony washing the window screens and smiled.

I wished that Rebecca was staying but understood why she wasn't. It would be very hard for her to find work in this town. She wasn't going to leave her boyfriend behind. Plus, she is very frightened of island creatures.

The day we went shopping for appliances turned out to be a nightmare. Right in the middle of the appliance store, Mom and I had our first disagreement over the refrigerator I picked—

a refrigerator that I was paying for—so, shouldn't I buy the one I liked?

Rebecca went on my side, saying, "Mom, you buy what you like. It's your money."

Tony went on my mother's side because he didn't understand why I was arguing with my mom. All he knew was that my mother was upset, and he couldn't bear to see her upset.

As always, when my mother is upset, it's always my fault. I'm the bad one.

Five days passed too fast. Before I knew it, it was time to take Rebecca to the airport, where we would be saying our final good-byes.

I held my tears until they announced that her flight was about to board. I hugged her tightly. Neither of us said a word.

I watched my daughter as she moved up the line to the check-point area and then onward to the line at the gate. For a few moments, I didn't see a young woman; instead, I saw my little princess playing with her dolls and fighting with her brothers. I saw her on her first day of pre-kindergarten when she ran after me crying because she didn't understand why I was leaving her with strangers. I saw her struggle as she grew up. I saw how resilient, strong, and courageous she was throughout the hardships we all went through when Tony became ill. I saw how she took charge when I was weak.

"My Heavenly Father, please protect my daughter Rebecca, and always keep her safe," I silently prayed as I watched her dis-appear among the passengers that were moving up to board the plane.

"God bless you, my sweet princess," I sobbed as I buried my face on Tony's chest and cried.

When we were sure that Rebecca's plane had taken off safely, we left the airport.

My parents and Tony conversed during our drive home while I sat in the back seat, looking out the window deep in thought.

"This is it," I thought. "We're not here on vacation. This is where Tony and I will be living from now on. I won't have Rebecca or Alexander to run to if we need help like we did back in Brooklyn and New Jersey. Tony and I just have each other."

I was having trouble breathing as my thoughts rambled on, "This new journey is full of too many unknowns. We don't know if the mental health system has all the advantages that we had in Jersey. I'm concerned about how isolated our house is. What if I need crisis intervention for Tony? Who do I call?"

I began feeling caged in as I continued silently talking to myself, "My worse fear is to end up dominated and controlled by my mother, trapped with no way out. If that happens, my anxiety, depression, and phobias will increase to the point where I could lose my mind."

Fear, anxiety, and panic were taking over. I began the breathing technique my therapist had taught me while I prayed silently, "Please help me keep strong, my Heavenly Father. Please help me hold on to my faith. Please take away my fears.

Please don't let my mother's personality and hurtful words kill the self-esteem that I have fought so hard to build.

Please keep Rebecca, Alexander, Victoria, Amber, and Simon, all safe and protected always.

Please send all our guardian angels to protect us and keep us safe, and please be by our side every step of the way during this new journey."

"Get a grip," I silently said to myself. "Remember, we are not alone. God, Jesus, the Holy Spirit, and all their saints and guardian angels are with us. They will protect us. They will keep us safe. They will give us the energy and courage to face whatever challenges appear on this journey."

Slowly, my breathing returned to normal. I stopped sweating, and my palpitations slowed down. By the time we arrived at my mom's house, I felt calmer.

I can DO
ALL THINGS *through* CHRIST
who strengthens ME.
PHILIPPIANS 4:13 KJV

CHAPTER TEN
In God's Time—Not Mine!

*"All things work together for good to
those who love God, who have been called
to his purpose."*
(Romans 8:28 KJV)

Life in Puerto Rico turned out to be very different from what I had expected. The transition was overwhelming, full of stress, uncertainties, disappointments, and unexpected challenges that we're still facing after living here for almost three years. If it weren't because I really believed that God brought us to Puerto Rico for a reason, I would have returned to the states months after arriving.

My first disappointment was to realize that the area of Puerto Rico I moved to was nothing like the Puerto Rico I had lived in years before. It's a different culture full of unfriendly strangers that speak a Spanish dialect that I am not used to. And neighbors louder than the ones I had in New Jersey who play loud music constantly—so loud that my heart pounds with each beat of the base.

My property is situated between mountains. Aside from a few houses, we are mostly surrounded by abandoned plots full of tall trees covered with ivy that attract all kinds of bugs and dangerous insects. It's like living in the middle of a forest.

I can't even enjoy a morning cup of coffee on the porch without mosquitoes, humongous spiders, which I call "mother spiders," centipedes, iguanas, lizards, salamanders, snakes, and all kinds of bugs showing up without being invited.

I had a nerve-racking experience with a spider one beautiful sunny day when we were about to wash the car. I grabbed a rag that I intended to use to soap up the car, walked around with it for a few minutes, and when I wet it, a spider the size of my hand came out of the rag, jumped on my hand, on to the sink, and out the laundry area. I can still feel its heavy crawly feet on my skin. Yes, heavy!

One day I sprayed half a bottle of bug killer on a tarantula that was on the path that leads to the porch. As I sprayed, the tarantula moved towards me. I remembered what a store owner told me, "If a spider runs from you, it's harmless, but if it goes towards you — run!" So, I kept spraying while backing up, and then I ran. When I checked a few hours later, the tarantula had died. Thank God!

A few months after we moved in, a salamander appeared inside the house. Tony and I freaked out. We couldn't catch it, so for months, I slept with the light on, afraid that it would be in my bed at night. This salamander must have been pregnant because a few months later, we began to see baby salamanders. By the time the salamander family had grown to six, we had already gotten used to them. Now, we only have two. On the rare occasions that we see them, they run and hide. The good thing about these creatures is that they eat bugs — especially spiders — which I am very grateful to them for eating. The bad thing is that they poop all over, and I must clean it.

I've seen three snakes around the trees and grass. The other day I saw a baby snake on top of the washing machine — too close for comfort because where there are babies—the mother is not far.

The first couple of years, we hardly saw centipedes, and if we did, they were tiny. Lately, I kill two or three a day around the terrace—some have made their way into the house. I just pray they never stay and grow inside because they are poisonous and very dangerous.

There is one insect that is really driving my anxiety level sky high, termites. When we first moved in, I noticed piles of what looked like sawdust on the floor in my bedroom closet. I thought it was leftover shaved wood the builders forgot to pick up when they built the shelves. I vacuumed, but weeks later, the sawdust re-appeared.

Last spring, right after the first big rainstorm, my bedroom was invaded by a swarm of flying termites that were coming out of my closet. The swarming happened three or four times a week from late March to early August.

I researched and found out that I had a very bad termite infestation that would cost thousands of dollars to get rid of. So, since I didn't have the money to eliminate the termites, I had no choice but to put up a mosquito net on my bed and spend hours a week sweeping or vacuuming hundreds of termite wings and squiggly-looking wormy termites.

On top of the termite infestation, would you believe the house has mold? I'm beginning to think it followed me from our old apartment. I have to constantly wash the clothes in the closet, even if I haven't worn them. There's mold on the roof, ceilings, walls, walkways, and driveway. It's horrible.

The health care system in Puerto Rico sucks. Hospitals and doctor's offices are so far away that an appointment takes all day.

Every patient is given the same time for their appointments, so even though they say, "by appointment only," you still have to arrive early enough to put your name on a "first come-first served" list. If you don't get on this list before 8 am, chances are you will not be seen until late at night. This is the same system they had back in the seventies, and I don't see it changing because it doesn't seem to bother anyone. For them, it's a time to socialize—for us, it's stressful, uncomfortable, draining, and ridiculous.

Living in Puerto Rico with a mental illness, especially Schizophrenia Affective Bipolar, is very challenging. Sometimes I wonder if I made the right choice in bringing Tony to Puerto Rico, where mental health services are so unreliable.

Back in New Jersey, we were surrounded by professionals I could turn to if Tony had a bad relapse and needed crisis intervention. I was able to reach his psychiatrist on an emergency line at any time of the day or night. If Tony went out alone and a disturbance occurred, the police were trained to treat mental health patients with human dignity and compassion. They would take him to a mental clinic for a psychiatric evaluation instead of jail like they did when we lived in New York.

In Puerto Rico, the closest psychiatrist is very far away and can only be reached during office hours—if they answer the phone. Support groups and crisis intervention are only available in the psychiatric hospital in San Juan—too far for us to go. If a disturbance occurs, police who are not trained to deal with the mentally ill will simply arrest them and put them in jail, where they will be treated as criminals.

Don't get me wrong, the move to Puerto Rico has helped Tony in some ways. He sleeps in his own room alone and spends time in the living room, porch, and yard; instead of staying all day in his room like he used to in New Jersey. He even helps with chores around the house and outdoors.

Unfortunately, no matter how many times they raise the dose on Tony's medication, the voices and conversations he hears in his head and around him have not disappeared. In fact, they have gotten worse. He hears people talking inside the house when it's just him and me. He hears all the neighbors talking about him. He even hears people talking about him in my parent's house when no one is there. Sometimes, he says the dogs in the neighborhood are talking about him. And many times, he says he has heard me say things that I haven't said. I've heard him arguing with these voices and telling them to leave him alone.

One day, I was curious to know if the voices might be dangerous, so I asked, "What if the voices told you to hurt me, yourself, or your grandparents. Would you do it?"

Right away, Tony said, "No, I would never do that!"

"I'm not a psychiatrist, but I do know that the voices cannot hurt you. They can torment you, but they cannot physically hurt you," I said.

"Are you sure?" he asked.

"Yes, I am sure," I said.

Thank God Tony trusts me enough to share how he feels and what he is going through most of the time. I imagine the voices in his head are all over the place, scaring and confusing him. It's heartbreaking.

My mental disorder of chronic anxiety, phobias, and panic attacks cannot compare to the torture my son goes through with his mental illness; however, the combination of dealing with all the challenges we faced in the first few years of living in Puerto Rico, dealing with Tony's symptoms and my symptoms, plus dealing with my mother, affected me greatly.

My condition is manageable if I recognize what triggers my anxiety and panic attacks so that I can avoid or handle an episode before it escalates to a dangerous point. Sounds easy, but it's not because some triggers I cannot avoid.

When Tony has a set-back and gives me that blank stare and cold, stiff hug—I feel fear brewing inside me. When my mom says or does something that crushes my self-esteem and makes me feel worthless—I fear I go back to being that scared, abused child that longed to escape her awful and painful childhood. When an unexpected challenge or change takes place that makes me feel disorganized—I fear I might lose total control of myself.

Every time I face one of these triggers, I'm possessed by fear, and anxiety kicks in. For reasons that I cannot explain, I feel like I'm fighting an evil battle that can only be won with God's soldiers, His shield, and all His weapons. So, I pray because if I don't, fear, anxiety, and panic will consume me. I pray, and then I breathe. I pray, and then I sit still. I pray and slowly organize my thoughts until God gives me the strength and courage to get a grip on the situation.

Back in New Jersey, when I told my therapist that I would live next door to my mother, she was very concerned because she knew my history with my mom. Believe me, I was concerned too.

Don't get me wrong. I love my mother, but I can't stand her controlling ways. She dictates and expects everyone to do things her way because she believes that her way is always the right way, and if someone disagrees with her, she'll make their life miserable.

Her husband goes along with her because if he doesn't, she will give him hell. Aside from controlling, she has constant personality changes and outbursts. She offends people one moment and then is nice the next.

Mom and her husband have a great heart and will go out of their way to help those in need. But, every time they help me, what they expect in return is for me to give them total control over my life—something that I will not do. I've come too far and been through too much to let that happen.

Sad to say, but my mother terrifies me. Her ways are escalating my anxiety, and it's making Tony's stress worse because when I'm upset—he gets upset. Every time she yells or comes over to complain about something in that weird way of hers—I literally tremble. When she calls me, without even knowing why she is calling, I get a knot in my stomach and feel like throwing up. She makes me feel exactly like I did when I was a little girl—all my childhood fears surface.

I pray every day that I can deal with living next door to mom and her husband because they have done so much for us—and, because I do love them—I just don't like their meddling and controlling ways.

I have a house, which is something I have prayed to have for decades, but because my parents come to my property and do whatever they want without consulting me, I feel more like a tenant than the owner.

I have no privacy. I feel like I'm living under a microscope. I'm not kidding when I say that my mother and her husband spy on us. One day I caught my stepfather peeking into my kitchen when he thought I wasn't home. They also lurk outside our windows to listen to our conversations. Don't you think that is an invasion of privacy?

I probably sound very bitchy and ungrateful, but it doesn't end with their spying—their meddling is worse. Let me just give you a few examples of how their meddling caused chaos.

When we moved in, my parents told me that because the power and water go out constantly where we live, I had to purchase a water tank and a generator. I only had enough money on my credit card to buy one of these items. Since to me, water is more important than electricity, I decided to buy the water tank and wait to buy the generator the following year.

My parents did not agree with my decision. They insisted that the generator was more important and even went as far as saying that they knew everything about having a house and land in Puerto Rico—and I knew nothing. Arguing with them was making me sick to my stomach—so, I gave in.

Keep in mind, I knew nothing about generators, but since my parents had a generator, I trusted that they were guiding me in the right direction with this purchase. And I believed them when they said that it wouldn't cost more than five hundred dollars.

I was wrong!

Everything related to purchasing the generator turned out to be a total disaster. First, I had to pay for a cement generator house to be built and a cement path leading from the driveway to the generator house. Then, I had to pay a licensed electrician to install all the parts needed to connect the generator. By the time I purchased the generator, I had maxed out my credit card and had no choice but to use the emergency credit card I was going to use to buy a washing machine and some furniture.

Wait! This was not the end of the generator fiasco—now comes the juicy part. From the get-go, I wanted to purchase the generator before building the path and generator house. However, my stepfather insisted that I wait. Bad idea! You see, when the generator he chose was delivered, he realized that the exhaust port of the generator was on the opposite side of the exhaust window built in the generator house for fumes to escape. So, to fix the problem, another exhaust window had to be added.

By the time all this work was completed, months had passed before we were able to test the generator. It took a few tries before the generator turned on. This should have brought up a red flag, but my stepfather didn't seem to think it was strange, so we stored it until we needed it.

A year later, the power went out. When we turned the generator on, it didn't work.

"Did you turn it on a couple of times during the year and change the oil and gas," my stepfather asked.

"No, you didn't tell me I had to do that," I answered, confused.

"That's why it doesn't turn on, because it sat for a whole year without maintenance," my stepfather answered, looking at me like I was dumb.

The warranty had expired, and the only place that could fix the generator was hours away. We didn't have a big car to take the generator to the facility, and they didn't make house calls. So, the generator was stored again, hoping that when it was needed—it would work.

A few days later, my parents began insisting that I buy a water tank and heater. Hello? That's what I wanted to do in the first place, but now I had no money.

I was not going to allow another purchase chaos to happen — not after the generator fiasco. This time, I was going to pray on it and then research instead of relying on my parents. I had to put my foot down because I wasn't rich. I needed to spend my money carefully. So, when they insisted on taking me to the company they had bought their water tank from, I stalled by telling them that I wasn't ready to buy one yet.

I knew my parents would keep pressuring me to get the water tank, and I really didn't want to tell them I was broke. So, I prayed, asking my Heavenly Father for guidance, and then I did some research.

Miraculously, I found a credible company that not only sold and installed water tanks and solar heaters but they also financed them — despite my bankruptcy. I was so happy and proud of my accomplishment and thankful to my Heavenly Father for guiding me in the right direction.

When I told my parents the day the equipment would be installed, they hit me with some unexpected bad news. Our roof had not been treated against leaks nor painted — something that had to be done before the installation.

"How much is this going to cost?" I asked my stepfather.

"Not much," my stepfather said.

Wrong again!

It cost over five hundred dollars, which I had to borrow from Tony, in order to get the roof completed before the water tank and heater were installed.

In less than two months, I was already knee-deep in financial debt and had no money left to invest in the house — something my parents did not understand. Thank God I was able to finance the washing machine and some furniture, and Tony had enough saved to buy the air conditioner for his room.

In the middle of all this chaos, I was informed that the psychiatrist Tony was supposed to start seeing had taken ill and closed his office. Thank God that through the Medicare Helpline, we were able to find another one. His office was far, but the closest we could find—and he did not speak English—or so he said.

The whole ordeal of finding a psychiatrist before Tony's medication ran out and all the chaos with my parents caused me so much stress that I was constantly getting anxiety and panic attack symptoms. All I wanted was a chance to relax, without drama, and without any more complications.

No such luck! You see, my parents were already working on their next meddling scheme.

When we moved in, my parents mentioned that for security reasons, we should get a dog. I clearly told them we planned to do so, but not until we were settled in.

The dog conversation did not come up again until December when Tony told me my parents had mentioned that a neighbor's dog had given birth.

"Why would my parents mention this to Tony when I had told them we weren't going to get a dog until we were settled," I suspiciously wondered.

Caring for a pet is therapeutic for people with disabilities, which is why we had decided that because of Tony's condition and mine, it would be best to adopt a service dog that was trained, neutered, and had all its shots, not a neighbor's dog. It was extremely important for Tony to choose his dog and be involved in every step of the adoption process, plus be trained to interact and care for his dog.

A few days later, my parents announced that they had picked a puppy for us. And that we could pick up the puppy when it was six weeks old.

I was furious. I could not believe that they had taken it upon themselves to not only commit to taking this puppy but to choose it—when I had told them we were not ready to get a dog yet.

Taking in a six-week-old puppy from a neighbor that we didn't even know—was not what we had planned.

Bringing a dog home when we were all under so much stress was a bad idea. Too much was going on—the responsible thing to do was to wait until we were settled and things were calmer so that the dog could come home to a quiet environment. We didn't even have the necessary supplies, toys, and food a dog needed.

So, why didn't I say no to my parents?

When I told my parents how I felt, they were offended and hurt. And then, although I was right in bringing the matter to their attention, somehow, they made me feel guilty for hurting them—so, I ended up giving in, even though it was eating me inside.

Tony had been so excited about going through the process of picking his first dog. It was so important to him and to me that he goes through the process. Unfortunately, my parents ruined the experience we had been planning and looking forward to for so long.

A couple of days before the puppy turned six weeks old, Tony and I visited the neighbor and asked to see the puppy. The puppy was a mixed black male Shih Tzu. He was in a box with the rest of the litter, which also needed homes.

Without thinking, praying, or even researching, and probably out of anger towards my parents, I asked Tony how he felt about taking home two puppies so that he could still have the experience of choosing one.

Tony was excited. We were taking home the black male that looked like a Shih Tzu and his brother, a blonde male that looked like an English terrier—nothing at all like his brother. We named the black dog Bambi, and his brother, Fluffy.

It didn't take long for me to realize the huge mistake I had made in bringing home two puppies. If I had to do it over again, I wouldn't. At my age, and especially when we were still in the middle of settling in, it was a huge and stressful challenge. It felt like I had brought home twins that grew into toddlers in a few weeks and were into everything.

My alone time and writing time went right out the window from the moment the puppies came home. I couldn't enjoy sitting and resting for more than two minutes before I had to get up to break up a fight. They literally brought out the worst in me. At my age, the last thing I wanted was to be yelling or disciplining—I thought these actions were way past me when my kids grew up.

I was so stressed that I researched websites looking for suggestions on how to deal with the siblings. Every single professional dog trainer website warned against taking home siblings. I even wrote to two dog owners who had experience with having multiple dogs in their homes, asking for suggestions. One of them said that because of my age, and health problems, their only suggestion was to give one away. She said if I thought they were a handful now, it was nothing compared to when they got older—especially if they turned aggressive, which could be a danger to us.

All the information and suggestions I received really scared me. My anxiety shot sky-high, thinking that these sweet little puppies could actually turn against us someday due to aggressive behavior.

A few months before they turned one year old, Bambi began showing signs of dangerous aggression. One time, after feeding him, he guarded his bowl and would not let me near it. He continued doing that until one day, he literally launched at me, barking aggressively. He made it a habit to do this every day during his morning feeding. My anxiety was so bad that I would cry.

One day, the groomer mentioned that Bambi had become very aggressive but that she handled him. This worried me, so I spoke to their veterinarian, who suggested neutering them. After the surgery, Bambi's aggression disappeared for a while.

When they were old enough to be fed once a day, Tony took charge of feeding them. I was so afraid of leaving Tony alone with them during feeding time that I stayed in the kitchen washing dishes just in case Bambi got aggressive.

One day, Bambi guarded his bowl after Tony fed him. Tony and I decided not to pick up Bambi's bowl and wait to see what he would do. I kept washing dishes, and Tony stayed in the spot where he usually stood when he fed them.

For no apparent reason, Bambi started barking and launching aggressively at me, just like he used to do when I fed him. If Tony had not gotten in front of me, Bambi would have bitten me.

I began shaking and crying. I told Tony I could not have Bambi in the house anymore. Tony sadly agreed.

We tried to find him another home, but because I was honest about his aggression—no one wanted Bambi. We had two choices—put him to sleep—or keep him. We kept him.

When I began caring for Tony after his first hospitalization, the mental health counselor warned me about the ups and downs of being the caregiver to a person with Tony's diagnosis. She said it was a 24/7 job that could easily take a toll on my health if I didn't take care of myself and find time to enjoy life. She warned me that my life would change, but what I didn't know was that in the process, I was going to end up giving up all the things that I love to do, which are a big part of who I am—not to mention the goals and dreams I had for my retirement years.

Being a caregiver while having mental issues of my own was hard before I moved to Puerto Rico. Going through the challenges of the first years in Puerto Rico, Tony's symptoms, and dealing with my parents made it even harder.

Even though my faith was strong, deep down inside, I felt it was unfair how life had changed for us since I returned from my trip to Atlantic City. Deep down inside, I missed the person that I was, my job, my freedom, and my privacy.

I missed taking time to myself to go to a mall, the spa, or just getting my hair done. Things I didn't do anymore because I was afraid to leave Tony alone for long periods of time, especially when it was time for his medication. I needed to see for myself that he took his medication, or else my anxiety would build up and fear of him relapsing would take over—something that I struggled with and prayed someday I could overcome.

I missed listening to my favorite oldies and singing and dancing to my favorite songs while doing my chores. I missed alone time to read, write, or cry over a good drama movie. I missed being able to close my door for a few hours to write without interruptions. These things may not be important to some, but doing these things made me happy. I felt alive.

I felt robbed of the joy of being a grandmother, being close to my two oldest children, and all the wonderful things that I should have been living and experiencing at my age. I felt trapped. I felt like I was living under a microscope, constantly being watched. I felt like I was living in "home confinement," where I had to do and say only what those around me wanted me to do and say in order to keep harmony.

I felt overwhelmed because, on top of being a caregiver, I had a house and land to maintain and clean and two dogs to help take care of. I had so many chores to do and errands to run that I didn't have enough hours in the day to complete everything. I was always backed up, and catching up drained the little energy that I had.

Not only was my energy low, but my health was deteriorating. I suffered from the symptoms and pain of osteoarthritis in both knees, carpal tunnel in both wrists, tendinitis in my right hand and wrist that shot pain to my arm and shoulder, high-risk blood pressure, and high cholesterol. My vision had also deteriorated. I saw more swirls, dots, and funny-looking shapes out of my right eye than ever before. I worried that these conditions would worsen, but specialists were too far, and besides, I couldn't leave Tony alone to go to an all-day appointment. All I could do to survive each day with all my ailments was to pray and use home remedies when I needed to.

During our first years in Puerto Rico, I had a very hard time adjusting and calling this place home. I lost my passion and joy and turned into a bitter, indifferent, distant, cold, and robotic woman who made everyone around me feel as miserable as I felt. Instead of being happy for being in the place my Heavenly Father

and Jesus brought me to, I vented and constantly complained—
not to those around me, but to my Heavenly Father and Jesus.
With all that I was going through, can you blame me?

One day I was so tired of the person I had become that I prayed,
asking my Heavenly Father to fill me with good emotions and feelings and take away the bad ones. After praying, I held on to the
words in the Bible that say, "I can do all things through Jesus
Christ who strengthens me." I also held on to one of my favorite
quotes, "Everything happens for a reason."

The verses from the Bible, my favorite quote, and the belief that
sometimes God allowed turbulence in my life because He planned
to turn it into "good" motivated me to look for the good in every
negative situation. I realized that not all the challenges that I faced
remained negative—some, my Heavenly Father had turned into
positive results and even into miracles.

Early September 2017, I received an unexpected gift from my
Heavenly Father—the first peaceful day in Puerto Rico. It was so
peaceful that while I sat with Tony on the front porch, I thought
of all the negatives that my Heavenly Father had turned into positives.

The challenge of loud music in my neighborhood that kept me
up at night and caused me so much anxiety simmered down. It's
mostly played on holidays, weekends, and when the kids are on
vacation. I actually enjoy it sometimes. Thank God!

The challenge of having unfriendly neighbors is no longer a
challenge. I found out that the reason why the neighbors were not
friendly was that at one time, all the land around us, including
ours, was owned by one family. As years passed, the land was divided and sold. The original owners died, but their children and

grandchildren, who live around us, see us as strangers who invaded their property even though it was legally bought. When I learned this, I was able to understand their unfriendliness.

Paying my creditors every month was a challenge that filled me with so much stress. After much praying, I came up with a plan. So far, I've paid off two creditors, and at the end of the year, I will finish paying off the solar water heater and water tank that I bought on credit when I first moved to Puerto Rico—huge debt. This accomplishment motivated me to set a goal of paying off one creditor per year. It's going to be a slow process, but if I stick to it, I can be free of most of my debts within five years.

The relationship with my mother hasn't improved very much. The only way that I can deal with her without losing my mind is to stay away as much as possible. I still get anxiety when my mother is in one of her moods—but when I do, I try to remember that she is a fragile eighty-six-year-old woman who has struggled most of her life. I have a lot of bad memories of things my mother did during my childhood that I wish she hadn't—I'm sure my children also have some of me. How can I expect my children to forgive me for not being the mother they wish I had been—if I do not forgive my mother for her imperfections? How can I expect my Heavenly Father to forgive me—if I don't forgive?

Bambi and Fluffy have turned out to be a bitter-sweet experience and are part of the family. We love them, and even though Bambi still shows moments of aggression, we have not thought about giving him away for a long time.

Tony still feeds them, however for Bambi to trust me a little, I hand feed both dogs a few breakfast treats in the morning. It's become a ritual, and they love it. It also helps bring my anxiety level down. I'm not that afraid of Bambi anymore, but still cautious.

Sure, my life would be easier without them, but on the bright side, helping take care of them is a daily work-out that has helped me lose weight. Not to mention that they are really good guard dogs that alert us when they find snakes, insects, or bugs.

Bambi and Fluffy have turned out to be great therapy for Tony, even though they are not service dogs. He loves them, feeds them, takes care of them, and feels like they are his kids. It's very hard to get depressed when you have two little ones depending on you to take care of them. I doubt we would ever give them away.

As for Fernando, we spoke a few times when I first arrived in Puerto Rico, but when I realized that he still lived in his fantasy world of making promises he was not going to keep, I stopped communicating with him cold turkey. He is no longer part of my life. I can finally say that I found closure.

I see Fernando as someone my Heavenly Father sent so that I could experience the love that I had always prayed and searched for. Even though my relationship with him had some bad moments, he is part of a chapter of my life that I do not regret living.

I thank God for granting me the wish of feeling true passionate love with Fernando. I will always remember "our dance." I will always remember how good it felt to be in his arms. I will always remember how safe it felt when I walked by his side hand-in-hand.

I can say that I was loved by a real Prince Charming who made me feel like Cinderella, even if it was just for a decade of my life. Better a decade than never. I feel that even if we never see each other again, my love for him will always live till death and beyond.

Yes, many of the negatives that I've faced since arriving in Puerto Rico, my Heavenly Father turned into positives, but one

He used to turn into a huge miracle—my phobia of driving.

Driving in Puerto Rico is nothing like driving back in the states. The road to get to where we live is a narrow country road, on a hill, where you must pull over if a car is coming in the opposite direction. The main streets are very curvy and dangerous. And, most drivers don't use turn signals or follow traffic rules. With my lack of driving experience, and my anxiety and phobia issues, I really thought I would never be able to drive in Puerto Rico, and at first, I didn't want to.

After a lot of praying, three things motivated me to try. First, I trusted that my Heavenly Father was behind the wheel. Second, I just couldn't handle the stress of having my parents drive me everywhere I had to go—it was torture. Third, and the one that actually forced me to get behind the wheel—the fear that if I didn't drive Tony to his psychiatric appointments to pick up his prescriptions, he would end up hospitalized and back at square one.

God works in mysterious ways. He knew I needed something more than motivation—I needed confidence—so, He put a plan in motion.

When I went to change my driver's license from New Jersey to Puerto Rico, my Jersey license had expired. I was baffled because I had checked the expiration date many times to make sure I changed it before it expired, and every time I checked, I saw April 2016—not 2015.

It was shocking to be told that I had to start from scratch by taking a written test, getting a permit, taking driving lessons, and passing a road test because I had an expired license.

The whole process was frustrating, however after passing the road test, I realized that taking driving lessons had given me the confidence that I needed. What a miracle!

If someone had told me years ago that I would be driving in Puerto Rico, I would have told them they were crazy—yet, I'm driving, on country roads, and on the highway—and I owe it all to the mystery of an expired license, which I have no doubt was God's plan.

Speaking of miracles, Rebecca, and Simon, received an extraordinary miracle in August—the birth of their beautiful baby girl, Ariel Marie. And, when I say "miracle," I mean a huge miracle.

Rebecca had a miscarriage a year ago, and because of her health problems, the doctors considered her pregnancy to be high risk from the beginning. It was touch and go from the moment she became pregnant with Ariel until her birth.

I wanted so badly to be there for Rebecca during her pregnancy and labor, but I didn't have the money to cover the cost of airline tickets, hotel, car rental, and daily expenses—plus, I couldn't leave Tony alone.

It hurt so much not to be there for my daughter when she needed me the most—it hurt a lot—but I did keep in touch with her as much as possible. I also went internet shopping with her to look at baby clothes so that I could feel like I was there with her. I tried to give her as many tips as I could on taking care of a baby. I also sewed some baby blankets, which Rebecca received shortly before Ariel Marie was born.

I wasn't there with Rebecca physically, but I was there with her spiritually every single day. Tony and I prayed for her and the baby every night. I knew my Heavenly Father and His Son, Jesus Christ, were keeping them both protected.

God worked two miracles—Rebecca survived her pregnancy and labor, and Ariel Marie was born healthy. When Rebecca was born, she was one of my miracles, and now Ariel Marie is her miracle.

Alexander also received a huge miracle. While he was driving home from work in Tennessee, a pole came flying from a truck and plunged into his front window—missing him by inches. I have no doubt my Heavenly Father and Jesus saved his life that day.

I silently suffer being away from my children and grandchildren, but I thank God that I'm able to speak to them. I pray my Heavenly Father will grant me the miracle of hugging them once again, just like I pray that someday I can feel comfortable and happy in Puerto Rico.

Until then, I will try to find the good in every bad situation I face and enjoy the rare moments of peace that God blesses us with—like today where I sit next to Tony on the porch listening to a chorus of birds chirping as they fly from tree to tree, while Bambi and Fluffy sit by our feet waiting for birds or butterflies to drop in so that they can chase them away.

How I wish we could have more of these quiet, peaceful moments. I pray that one day soon, Tony and I can get a break from the chaos, unexpected events, and stress—so that we can enjoy our new life—something that we haven't been able to do in almost three years of living here.

While looking at the stretch of blue sky over the mountains, I thank my Heavenly Father and my Beloved Jesus for helping me find something good in our bad moments. I thank God for Rebecca and the baby being home, and both being healthy—for Alexander, Victoria, and my precious granddaughter Amber being ok in their new home in Florida—for the good moments that Tony has despite the voices he hears that torment him so much—and, I thank God for this rare moment of peace.

"Things seem so calm today," I thought. "Maybe now we can finally take a break from stress—and just breathe."

I turned to Tony and said, "I'm going to get all the wash and chores done this week so that next week I can take a break and just relax."

"I'm taking a break too," Tony answered.

"That's a plan. We'll work hard this week, and we'll rest next week. But, for now, let's go in and do the dishes," I said with a smile.

I had just finished putting away the dishes when I heard the weather report. Hurricane Harvey had caused devastation to parts of Texas. Thousands had lost their homes. Mexico was hit with an earthquake. Three storms were coming out of Africa, one behind the other, and all three were predicted to turn into hurricanes by the time they reach the Caribbean Islands.

"Ma, are we going to get hit with a hurricane?" Tony asked.

"Probably not," I answered.

"How do you know?" Tony asked.

"Well, as with any tropical island in the Caribbean, it is customary for Puerto Rico to get hurricane warnings—especially during hurricane season. However, Puerto Ricans say that the island is blessed because for many years, every time a hurricane formed in the Caribbean, it detoured, passing only as a strong tropical storm with rain, wind, and thunderstorms. We have faced and battled many challenges since we moved here, but thank God, bad weather has not been one of them. So, let's pray that these hurricanes detour and the island is blessed once again," I answered.

"But what if we do get hit?" Tony asked, concerned.

I sat by Tony's side and calmly said, "Many decades ago, when I lived in Puerto Rico, I experienced a few hurricanes. Except for one where the National Guard rescued us and took us to a shelter because of flooding, the others were scary but not dangerous. Don't worry. Remember, no matter what happens, God will always protect us."

Then, I sat with my calendar and began planning what I needed to get done before the holidays—outside and inside cleaning—Thanksgiving and Christmas food, decoration, and gift shopping lists.

By the time I finished my holiday lists, I was full of the holiday spirit and couldn't wait for Thanksgiving to begin my holiday baking. Worrying over weather predictions was the last thing on my mind.

I can DO
ALL THINGS *through* CHRIST
who strengthens ME.
PHILIPPIANS 4:13 KJV

CHAPTER ELEVEN
God Got This!

"Be strong and courageous. Do not be afraid or terrified because of them, for the Lord your God goes with you; he will never leave you nor forsake you."
(Deuteronomy 31:6 KJV)

The weather prediction was not wrong. The storms coming out of Africa did turn into hurricanes. The first was Hurricane Irma, which caused devastation to many small islands, including some parts of Puerto Rico, the Dominican Republic, Cuba, and Florida.

With Hurricane Irma, we lost internet service early Wednesday evening, on September 6th. Then, shortly before ten, we lost power and cell phone service.

Tony and I, and our dogs, camped out in the living room where the windows were boarded. We tried to sleep but couldn't.

Around midnight the wind was howling so loud that I thought the hurricane was passing over us—but it wasn't.

Two hours later, I began hearing the strangest pattern of sounds. The first, I can only describe as similar to a train about to arrive at a station. Once the train sound stopped, the sound of gusting wind took over for what seemed like minutes. Then, all went silent. This pattern of sounds continued until 4 am.

Normally, I would have been in a state of panic and high anxiety. Yet, I wasn't. Because when I started to feel anxiety built up, I could hear God say, "Do not fear."

The rest of the night, all we kept saying was, "God got this. Do not fear". And, I would add, "Please put a dome of security over our home, my mom's home, and all of Puerto Rico, and everyone that is in the path of this hurricane."

I believe that most Puerto Ricans were praying the same thing because when I turned on my solar radio, the first words I heard were, "The hand of God is over Puerto Rico."

We were blessed because although Irma's wind and rain were very powerful, and we lost electricity and water for three days, it did not affect the area where I live as much as other areas.

Hurricane Irma continued to Florida, causing destruction in many areas. By the time it reached the area where Alexander lives, it had weakened. My Heavenly Father protected them, just like He protected us.

While Hurricane Irma was causing devastation in Florida, the weather broadcaster announced that Hurricane Maria was right behind with the possibility of reaching category five by the time it reached Puerto Rico. They predicted that this time we would not be spared. It would pass over all Puerto Rico. Government officials warned that the hurricane would be catastrophic and to prepare.

I had prepared for Hurricane Irma with plenty of water, food, and supplies. But, for Hurricane Maria, I was not prepared. We were so busy dealing with car trouble that we didn't hear about the catastrophic predictions until a few days before we were supposed to get hit.

Our car was repaired the day before the hurricane. By then, we couldn't find bottled water anywhere, and the shelves at the supermarket were empty. The car only had a quarter tank of gas, and when we went to the gas station, the line was so long that we decided to go home to secure the windows and doors before it got dark instead of getting gas.

By bedtime, the rain and wind were mild, so instead of camping out in the living room, we went to sleep in our own bedrooms.

"Please, my Heavenly Father, let us sleep peacefully all night. Don't let it thunder, as it causes the dogs to wake up and start crying. Let Hurricane Maria detour away from us, just like Hurricane Irma did," I prayed. Then, I turned on my side and fell asleep.

The sound of howling wind woke me shortly after midnight. I tried to go back to sleep but couldn't. A few moments later, my night light and fan turned off. It was pitch dark. Except for the wind and rain, all was silent. Hurricane Maria was approaching.

Around five in the morning, Bambi and Fluffy woke us up crying. They must have been afraid of the sound of the wind and rain, which had gotten louder.

With lantern in hand, I let Bambi and Fluffy out of their sleeping area and went to the kitchen to boil water for coffee.

While drinking coffee, I could hear banging in the distance. The kitchen windows were boarded, so I couldn't see what was going on outside.

Despite the torrential sounds, I tried to do what I normally did every morning after drinking coffee—sit and read my morning devotionals and say my morning prayers.

By seven in the morning, the wind and rain were so strong and loud that it felt like the windows and doors were going to be ripped out of the wall. The house was literally vibrating.

This hurricane was not like the ones I had experienced. This one gave me a bad feeling and a strong sense that we needed to ride it out in the safest part of the house.

Back in the states, every time we had a tornado warning, we took shelter in a closet or bathroom. Our closets are big, but they have mirrored doors that could shatter; so, we chose the bathroom in my bedroom.

Quickly, we took a chair, quilts, food, water, solar radio, lanterns, and everything we thought we might need into the bathroom.

For five hours, Tony sat on a chair, and I sat on the toilet seat. Bambi and Fluffy lay quietly on quilts near our feet as if they felt something was wrong.

We listened to the only radio station available, trying not to focus on the deafening howling wind that sounded as if all souls had come up from their resting place, crying in sorrow and pain.

I prayed silently, trying not to worry Tony, even though I could tell he was.

At noon, the howling wind and rain suddenly stopped. The sun came out. Everything was calm. The eye of the Hurricane was over us.

I wasn't sure how long the calm of the eye would last before we started getting hit again, so I ran to my bedroom window to peek.

"Oh my God," I gasped.

What I saw was so horrible that I hardly can describe it. I put my hand over my mouth to stop myself from saying something that would scare Tony. It took a lot for me to hold back my tears.

The farmhouse down the road across from us was totally destroyed. The roof was gone. The walls looked like when you build a house with cards, and then it falls apart all lopsided.

"My God, please let that family be safe," I prayed.

The beautiful green countryside and hills that surrounded our home were not green anymore. Not one tree had leaves, and almost all of them were down as if a twister had hit them. The few trees that were still standing were bare and almost white, as if they had been shaved.

Fences were destroyed. I could see pieces of houses near my yard. It looked like a scene out of a scary movie.

I couldn't look anymore. I shut the window.

We had calm for an hour and twenty minutes. Enough time for my parents to check in on us to make sure we were ok. And to mop the flooded rooms that had not been boarded.

Suddenly, without warning, the wind, rain, and deafening sound started again, except that this time it was stronger, louder, and it lasted much longer.

The wind had shifted. It was hitting the opposite side of the house—the side we were in. Window panels banged so hard that it sounded like they were about to rip right off the window.

The bathroom did not feel safe anymore, but I couldn't think of any other part of the house that was safer, so we stayed.

Sitting, listening to the wind pounding on all the windows and doors, was never-ending torture. A few times, we thought we heard screams, but it could have been the wind.

We could feel the walls vibrating. I'm not kidding when I tell you that I really believed that the wind was going to lift the house, and we would be flying like in the Wizard of Oz movie.

I glanced over at Tony, who sat staring at the wall. I cannot imagine what was going through his mind or how much this would traumatize him.

I prayed and prayed, asking my Heavenly Father to keep us safe. I asked him to put a shield of protection over our house, my parent's house, and all of us.

I was scared. I prayed, asking God to take away the fear and strengthen my faith.

I reminded myself of all the times I had been in danger and how my Heavenly Father had kept me safe.

"I will not abandon you. I will not let you drown," my Heavenly Father and His Son, Jesus Christ, always told me.

I don't know how long it took for me to be able to get a grip; all I know is that I felt that I had to do something to distract us from the tormenting sound of Hurricane Maria.

"I'm hungry. Let's make sandwiches," I said, trying to sound as normal as possible.

Tony just nodded and smiled.

I slowly cut some Spam and spread cheese whiz on sliced bread. We silently ate sandwiches and drank warm cranberry juice. I must have been hungry because it tasted really good.

I turned on the solar radio but then turned it off because it was making us edgy. The radio was taking calls from people that were screaming and asking for help. It made me feel like it was the end of the world.

Tony and I made small talk. I really do not remember what we talked about, but it helped kill time during the agonizing hours in the bathroom.

Around 7 pm, the winds began to weaken, so we figured it was safe to peek and see what the rest of the house looked like. Things seemed ok in my bedroom, but when we opened my bedroom door, water started coming in from the hallway.

Tony's room had flooded. Everything was wet. The room where the dogs slept had also flooded. Water had come in through the front and side doors and windows, flooding the living room and some of the kitchen. We spent hours trying to mop as much water as we could.

Although the wind and rain was still strong, it was nothing like what we had heard in the past fourteen hours, so we decided to camp out in the living room instead of returning to the bathroom. We were so tired that before midnight Tony fell asleep on his recliner, and I fell asleep on the sofa with Bambi and Fluffy by my side.

Early the next morning, we stepped outdoors for the first time since the hurricane. I honestly thought we had been transported to another planet. Trees were down all around us. The ones that stood looked as if they had been shaved. There were no flowers, birds, butterflies, or bees. I wondered if the neighbor's horses, goats, rabbits, and chickens had survived.

Our back fence was gone. There were so many trees down in the back that I could not even see if there were any damages. The house was standing, thank God.

Since our land is surrounded by trees, I thought we only had a few houses around us. After the storm, I was shocked to see how many houses were on the bottom of the hill. We have a lot of neighbors; the huge trees just hid them.

I watched how the neighbors all walked around like zombies. It reminded me of how people walked after 9/11 in New York City. Everyone in shock.

Our small solar radio was the only means of hearing what was happening around us. Thank God for the one radio station that had been on before, during, and after the hurricane.

When I turned on the radio, I couldn't believe what I was hearing. The broadcaster kept asking people to call in and report their situations because there was no communication anywhere; and no way for help to get to anyone, except through their station.

The broadcaster reported, "The whole island is under a state of emergency. There is no electricity, cell phone service, cable, or internet. The gas stations ran out of gas before the hurricane, and there is no way for gas trucks to deliver gas. There is no bottled water. The supermarkets and stores are closed or destroyed. There is no way to get food. And no traffic lights are working. Puerto Ricans, we are in God's hands."

I had gone through a lot of hurricanes, but this one was different. Puerto Rico was totally isolated from the rest of the world. Help could only come by air or water, and who knew how long it would take.

How were we going to communicate with anyone if we did not have electricity, internet, house, or cell phone service, and the roads were blocked with fallen trees and debris?

After hearing the radio, I quickly did an inventory of how much bottled water and food we had left and how long it would last.

I looked at my list and wished I had gone food shopping before this hurricane. If we cut down, we might have enough bottled water, food, and dog food for six days.

I wanted so badly to communicate with Alexander and Rebecca to let them know we were alive and trying to survive with what little water, food, and supplies we had left, but I couldn't because there was no cell phone service anywhere on the whole island. Not hearing from us and not knowing how we were had to be torture for them. I prayed that their faith was strong enough to know that God was protecting us and keeping us safe.

The first couple of days after Hurricane Maria, the severity of the situation had not really hit us. We actually thought we were going to wake up the next day, and everything was going to be back to normal like it had with Hurricane Irma.

Since my generator did not work, my stepfather lent us his a few hours a day to keep the refrigerator slightly cold and to turn on the water tank.

I lined two big hampers with heavy-duty garbage bags filling them with water to use when the generator was not on. This idea had to come from my Heavenly Father, and it certainly helped a lot.

When my stepfather announced that he did not have any more gas for his generator, the news was a total wake-up call to the reality of our situation because it meant that we could not turn on the water tank or the refrigerator.

As I filled our cooler with ice still left in the freezer, I prayed, "My Beloved Jesus, what are we going to do when we no longer have water to drink, food, and water to wash ourselves? You know I freak out with germs. How are we going to wash and keep things clean—especially with the dogs not being able to go outside?"

On the third day after the hurricane, after the area where we live had been slightly cleared, my parents drove down very dangerous country roads, lined with tilted electrical poles that could fall at any moment, to try to find gas.

When they returned, they reported that almost everything was closed, there was no ATM service, no electricity, and water anywhere, and the gas station lines were so long that the average wait time was ten to twelve hours just to wait for the gas to be delivered to the station which didn't guarantee that you would be among the lucky ones that got gas before the gas pumps emptied.

For the next two weeks, my parents left their house at dawn to get gas for their generator and their car. There were times when they came back, after a ten-hour wait in a long line, empty-handed because the gas trucks did not arrive. A couple of times, they left at dawn and didn't return until almost midnight. I felt so bad for them. I couldn't do anything to help because our car was still in my stepfather's garage, blocked by a fallen tree, and with very little gas.

Could you imagine being in a line without a bathroom for ten to twelve hours, every day, for two weeks? I don't know how they did it. God bless them for venturing out when it was so dangerous, especially at their age. But, if they hadn't, we wouldn't have had the few hours of generator power that we were able to have to keep our refrigerator slightly cool.

When my water tank emptied, my stepfather attached a pipe to the drain that led from the roof to the side of the house, and then he put a five-gallon bucket under the pipe to collect rainwater. We couldn't drink this water, but we could use it to flush toilets and clean. God works in mysterious ways because the first two weeks after Hurricane Maria, it rained every day.

During one of their ventures, my parents found a water oasis a few towns away that gave out free water collected from a river that had not been contaminated with dead animals. Every couple of days, they would get in a line to bring water that we boiled to drink, cook, and take bucket baths.

My parents also traveled to the few stores that were open to buy canned food and whatever other supplies they could get to help us through this emergency.

I will never forget the day my parents brought home bread and donuts and another when they brought home pizza. I'm not lying when I say that Tony and I thought we had died and gone to heaven. It was the best bread, donuts, and pizza we had ever tasted.

One night while listening to our solar radio, the broadcaster announced that the electrical system in all Puerto Rico had been destroyed—my heart sank. The broadcaster also announced that the Military, Red Cross, and many other rescue organizations were on their way to Puerto Rico. The next day the skies were filled with dark green military helicopters. Help had finally arrived to the is-land—thank God.

Every night the radio broadcaster announced that food and water were being distributed throughout the island. I saw and heard helicopters, but no sign of help came to our area. "Where is all the help going? Do they even know we exist on this part of the island? How will we know where they are distributing food and water in our area if we don't have communication?" I wondered.

Hurricane Maria totally changed our way of life. It forced Puerto Rican women and men to live the life of pioneers from back in the early 1900's—or earlier.

Tasks that used to take less than an hour now took us most of the day. Thank God that when I was a little girl visiting my grandparents, they taught me country survival skills that I still remembered.

Rainwater was collected to wash clothes and dishes, flush toilets, and clean. If it didn't rain, we couldn't do any of these things.

Oasis water was boiled the night before, cooled overnight, and poured into empty bottles to drink and cook in the morning.

Thank God I have a gas stove, and Hurricane Maria did not destroy the full tank of gas we had bought before Hurricane Irma.

We cooked rice with whatever canned meat we were lucky enough to find at the supermarket. Spam became our steak. Canned tuna, chicken, turkey, and corn beef took the place of the meats I once cooked. They were all loaded with salt, which was not good for my high blood pressure. Would you believe canned meat tripled in price during this emergency?

I have a slight phobia of catching germs, so not being able to shower or clean and wash as thoroughly as I used to made me feel like I was dirty and everything around me was dirty. I imagined getting all kinds of bacteria. It got even worse when I started running out of cleaning supplies.

I worried about not being able to pay my bills due to the lack of internet and phone service. The stores were only accepting cash, but because my benefits were direct-deposited to a bank in the states, and the ATMs were not working, I could not get hold of my money.

Believe it or not, I had a bigger concern than getting water, food, or electricity. Tony's medication needed to be refilled by the end of September, but the pharmacy would not do so without his psychiatrist's authorization.

"Without a means of communication, how am I going to get the authorization for Tony's medication to be refilled?" I asked my Heavenly Father. The idea of asking my parents to drive to the psychiatrist's office came to me immediately after praying.

The day my parents left to go to Tony's psychiatrist's office, I prayed that they would come back with the medication refill authorization. I knew it would take them at least two hours to make the round trip to the doctor's office, but when five hours passed and they hadn't returned, I began to worry.

"If something happens to them for going on this venture, it will be my fault for asking them to go so far on dangerous roads," I thought.

Just then, I heard their car and was so relieved.

My heart sank when my stepfather said, "The area around the doctor's office is in very bad shape. There are no signs or anything that could tell us if the doctor was in another location.

We drove to the nearest clinic and asked if they had a psychiatrist on staff that could give us authorization for the medication. They said that because of the state of emergency, psychiatric medication could be authorized by any prescribing physician. Unfortunately, they didn't have one there at the moment.

So, we drove around and just happened to pass by a doctor we used to see many years ago. And guess what? It was open. There were no patients, but the doctor was in because he was checking out the damages. He gave us a prescription for all the medications and refills for four months.

We went to the pharmacy to pick up his medicine, which was

open and working with a generator. They refilled everything without a problem," my step-father said while handing me the medication.

I was so happy and so grateful. I thanked God over and over for this wonderful miracle. Again, He had used my parents to help us through a very difficult and possibly dangerous situation. Glory be to God.

Twelve days after Hurricane Maria, I saw the devastation for the first time when my parents drove me to a supermarket a few towns away.

Traffic lights and poles were torn in half. Some were dangerously dangling from cables and about to fall. Most of the houses we passed had no rooftops or were totally destroyed.

The line to get into the supermarket was almost as long as the gas station lines. Every pharmacy, store, and bank that we passed had long lines. When I entered the dark supermarket, most aisles were empty or blocked. I couldn't find the brands that I usually bought, so I had to buy whatever there was, even if it was loaded with salt, sugar, and all kinds of unhealthy ingredients. I even had to buy a dog food brand that I had never heard of.

"Please fill us with patience, love, faith, courage, energy, willpower, hope, and belief. Help me remember that we are blessed, compared to others that have lost everything and are going through worse," I prayed.

At home, the grass I wished the storm had destroyed was too tall for comfort. Tall grass brings bugs and dangerous insects. So far, I had killed three spiders inside the house. It freaked me out to imagine all types of insects crawling inside when it got dark.

Thousands of people were leaving the island. When I heard

that my stepfather's daughter-in-law was leaving for Florida the same week of Alexander's birthday, I took the opportunity to ask her to please call him as soon as she got there to tell him that we are all alive and doing as best as we could and not to worry about us.

On Alexander's birthday, I was sad, because it was the first time I hadn't spoken to him on his birthday. I prayed that my step-father's daughter-in-law had reached him and that he had called Rebecca to let her know we were ok. Not being able to speak to Alexander and Rebecca made me feel totally isolated and discon-nected from my loved ones.

By the time we were able to get our car out of my stepfather's garage, the lines at the gas station had gone back to normal. When we started the car, except for the front passenger window not clos-ing fully, everything else seemed fine; until my stepfather decided to take the car to the gas station to fill the tank.

As soon as Tony and my stepfather left for the gas station, it began to thunder and rain heavily. I prayed they would be ok.

When they returned, Tony was pale and shaking. He said it was raining so hard the roads flooded. He said he had never been so afraid. He also said that after filling the tank, all the warning lights lit up, and the gas meter fell to empty.

I thought that maybe because my stepfather's garage was open on one side, the car had taken in water during the hurricane. So, I left the car out in the sun for a few days to dry out. By the third day, all the warning lights were off, except for the "check engine" light. The gas meter kept switching from empty to full.

I prayed, "My Heavenly Father, you know our car is not a lux-ury—it's a necessity that takes us to places we need to go. Please fix it because there are no mechanics available."

When I heard the radio broadcaster announce that people were getting desperate, I could relate because no matter how much faith I had, I too, was feeling desperate at times.

I was worried about my health. Ailments I had under control were surfacing. My arthritic joints were hurting, especially the carpal tunnel and tendonitis in my wrist. My hand and wrists were swollen and in extreme pain due to washing and wringing clothes every day. The high salt content in the canned meats raised my blood pressure, causing dizziness, palpitations, and headaches. I also had discomfort and swelling on the right side of my face, neck, and head, which was worrying me. I needed to see a doctor, but I couldn't because the doctor's offices were damaged or closed. The wait time at an emergency room was over twenty-four hours long, and I couldn't leave Tony alone that long.

I was also worried about Tony. Ever since the hurricane, he had begun to hear voices again in his head and around him. He said they were torturing him more than ever. He desperately wanted to see his psychiatrist, but we didn't know when his office would open. The only thing that kept Tony strong and patient through all we were going through was a miracle that happened a few months before the hurricane. He had begun praying and reading the Bible every day. He was holding on to his faith.

The eighteenth day after the hurricane was a very blessed day. I finally had cell phone service and was able to speak to my two oldest children and pay my bills over the phone—some creditors actually extended my payments for three months due to the natural disaster—Glory be to God.

Alexander offered to send for me, Tony, my parents, and even the dogs. I told him I would keep it in mind just in case the situation did not improve. I really appreciated his offer but felt that with God's help, we would get through this.

One month after Hurricane Maria, the radio station played a message from the governor. He said most of Puerto Rico would not have electricity until the end of December. Then, contrary to what he said, the director of the power company said that what the governor announced was impossible—they predicted that it would take over six months. The news was disappointing and depressing.

One morning, after breakfast prayers, I thought about all the times that an entity had told me that something was impossible, yet the impossible became possible. I believed that God could do anything that humans said was impossible. I held on to this belief to keep strong and keep going. In the meantime, I took one day at a time and one challenge at a time.

One night, a great idea came to me on how to get money. All I had to do was write a check to myself and deposit it in the savings account I had opened in Puerto Rico, which I hadn't used. Then, once the check cleared, I could withdraw money. "Why didn't I think of this sooner? Thank you, Jesus!"

Speaking to Alexander, Rebecca and grandchildren brought me so much joy. When I heard my newborn granddaughter, my heart filled with happiness. I missed seeing pictures of my granddaughters. I hadn't seen a picture of my youngest granddaughter since she was born. It hurt not being a part of my grandchildren's world, but it was temporary. Someday, I would be able to hear them, see pictures of them—and spoil them with gifts.

By November, we still didn't have electricity; however, water was restored shortly before Thanksgiving. We showered and washed our hair for the first time in a long time, cleaned both bathrooms thoroughly, washed both dog's sleeping areas, carriers, and their sheets, mopped and bathed the dogs. It felt great—almost normal.

Shortly before Thanksgiving, the supermarkets started selling meat and bottled water; but I decided to continue with canned meat, even though it was not healthy because I had concerns over how meats were stored during the blackout.

On Thanksgiving, we went over to my parent's house. We did not have turkey with all the delicious trimmings and desserts I usually made; instead, we had rice and canned Spam. We thanked God for being alive and for our houses not being destroyed. We prayed for all those that had lost their homes and were suffering much more than we were.

After Thanksgiving, the Military and American Red Cross began distributing cases of drinking water and military food to our area. The military box had twelve pouches of daily meals, and in each pouch was enough food to last the day. The pouched meats included brisket, beef, shredded chicken, chili, and beef stew. Compared to the canned meat we had been eating, military food tasted like gourmet food. We were very grateful.

Christmas holidays came and went and still no electricity. We enjoyed listening to the solar radio every night where they played holiday music. We did our very best to enjoy the holidays, but I still missed all the holiday baking and decorating I used to do. I missed shopping for Christmas presents, especially for my granddaughters. "No biggie, when electricity and internet are restored, we'll celebrate all the holidays we missed, and I can shop and send everyone gifts," I said to myself, trying to cheer up.

By the middle of January, my patience was wearing very thin. Four months without electricity. How was it possible? Would any state of the United States be without electricity for this long? No!

Island residents were getting desperate. They continually went to their municipality, electric company, and government demanding answers. No one had a straight answer. No one was in charge. No one told the truth. The government blamed the electric company. The electric company blamed the government. The town mayors claimed that they had nothing to do with electricity issues.

Something just didn't seem right. The governor and mayors took an oath to take care of the needs of their citizens and country. During a disaster, they were supposed to come together despite their differences and work as a team. They were supposed to have a plan of action for each municipality and know when and where each section was going to be worked on and when they expected to energize it. Seriously, was that so hard?

How many people had to die because they did not have electricity for their oxygen or health equipment? How many people had to commit suicide because they were scared and traumatized by living in the dark? How many people had to die in traffic accidents because the traffic lights need electricity to work? How many people had to leave the island because they couldn't afford to pay for gas for their generators? Seriously, how many before someone took a stand?

Residents of the island understood that Hurricane Maria had caused vast devastation to the electrical system and that it would take a while to fix. But, for no one to give us an honest answer, as to when, so that we could prepare was torturous, disrespectful, unacceptable, and an act of human cruelty which was unjustifiable. Someone needed to be held accountable, but who that was, nobody seemed to know.

I knew that I should have been grateful for being alive, having shelter, food, a few hours of generator power a day to keep the refrigerator cool, and for having water, which in my book was the most precious of all necessities, but it wasn't easy to live in the dark with our health issues. Being without electricity for so long was really getting to us.

I stopped venting when I heard my inner voice say, "There is only one entity in this whole universe that has control over the electricity situation—our Heavenly Father."

Immediately, I prayed, "I believe that you know the exact day and time that our electricity will be restored. If it hasn't, it's because it isn't in your plan, and I know you have a good reason. I also believe that you understand how hard it is for us right now. I ask for patience so that I can stop stressing over it. You have given me so many miracles throughout my life. You have moved mountains that everyone said could not be moved. You made the impossible come true. I believe that we will have electricity soon because I believe in miracles!"

On January 26th, my stepfather's old generator started to make really loud noises. The next morning, he told us that he felt it was breaking down.

As I've said so many times throughout this story, "God works in mysterious ways. When things look like they couldn't get any worse, he sends us an amazing miracle."

January 29th was an incredible and blessed day. It all started early in the morning when I was opening my kitchen window after drinking coffee. I saw a red truck with flashing lights. My first thought was that someone was lost and about to make a U-turn, but when they honked and began moving away slowly, I felt something was up.

While I was doing my prayers, I heard my stepfather drive by. When he returned, Tony heard him talking to my mother excited about something, and then they went out before we had a chance to ask them why they were excited.

Tony and I wanted badly to believe that my stepfather's excitement had something to do with the electricity, but because in the past months, brigades had come and gone without doing anything, we didn't want to get our hopes high and then be disappointed.

It was garbage day, and Tony's turn to drive down to the garbage area. He had just driven away when I noticed that I had not put the garbage bags in the trunk of the car. Silly me!

I walked to the front gate with the garbage bags so that he wouldn't have to come inside the house to get them. When he returned, he was excited.

"No, Ma, I can't take the garbage now. There's a brigade of electricians blocking the road on the hill."

"Really? Oh my God, that's great," I said, "You can still take the garbage. All you have to do is park next to the house that was destroyed and walk the bags to the garbage area."

Tony drove away smiling, something I hadn't seen him do in a long time.

Do you know how they say that stress symptoms come from good and bad news? Well, I was so excited to know brigades were finally going to work on the electricity in our area that my stomach was in knots, and I had stomach cramps.

When Tony returned, he was over the moon with excitement.

"Ma, one of the brigade men spoke to me," he said excitedly,

"He walked up to me and said—English?"

"Really?" I asked.

"Yeah, then, he told me that if I wanted to pass, I had to do it now or else I wouldn't be able to pass again until they were done. I told him that I was only throwing out the garbage, and then I thanked him," Tony said.

All morning both Tony and I were excited and anxious. We kept looking out the window to see if we saw any trucks coming our way.

My nerves were so shot that when I was preparing lunch, I kept putting the wrong measurements and ingredients in the pot.

Shortly before lunch, my mother called. When Tony hung up, he was just as excited as earlier.

"Ma, Grandma, and Grandpa couldn't drive up the hill cause of the brigade trucks, so they parked near where the men are working and are watching them work while they eat take-out food. They said they'd be home when they are able to pass," Tony said while doing a happy dance.

Around three o'clock, I heard trucks coming, and when we looked out the window, two trucks were coming towards our house, and right between them was my stepfather's car.

I stood in awe while the workers from an American electric company from the states checked our electric poles.

"We'll be right back," one of the workers said, smiling. I just stood there speechless.

Fifteen minutes later, four of the workers returned. They did a final check. Then, one of the workers got on his walkie-talkie and said, "Ok, we're ready. It's a go."

"Madam," the worker said, turning to me, "Please turn on one of your light switches."

I had stomach jitters as I waited.

When the lights turned on, I felt faint—what a beautiful sight. I felt as excited as I used to feel when the Rockefeller Center Christmas Tree was lit in New York City.

One of the workers put his fist up in the air as a sign of, "Yes, we did it." The others cheered.

I felt so weak I couldn't cheer. My eyes were full of happy tears. I gave thanks to my Heavenly Father silently. And then, I walked up to the workers and said, "Thank you so very much."

Glory to God, we have electricity. Thank you, Jesus!

My heart was filled with gratitude and sadness. Gratitude for being blessed with water, electricity, food, and the basic necessities that the fury of Hurricane Maria had stolen from us four months ago. Sadness for the hundreds of thousands of people that were still suffering without these precious necessities. I prayed that they too, would be blessed just like we were—and that all Puerto Rico would be one hundred percent energized very soon.

I can DO
ALL THINGS *through* CHRIST
who strengthens ME.
PHILIPPIANS 4:13 KJV

CHAPTER TWELVE
Epilogue

On a beautiful sunny afternoon in March 2018, while taking a walk on my land, I stopped to admire the wonders of nature around me. Birds were chirping as they flew from tree to tree. Bees were buzzing, searching for nectar. Beautiful colored butterflies and dragonflies were dancing atop green grass. Surrounding our home were hills and mountains lined with trees majestically dressed in green leaves and ivy. It is hard to believe that all these wonders had disappeared six months ago—yet here they are—more beautiful than ever.

I glance towards my home with emotional gratitude. There's mold everywhere; it needs repairs, power washing, and paint due to minor damages from the hurricane; but it is a strong house. It shielded us from the storm. It is home, and I've learned to appreciate it—thanks to the Grace of God.

The back fence is gone. We still have piles of debris and fallen trees in the backyard. The washing machine broke down, the car needs a lot of repairs, and we still have to replace all the furniture and electronics that were ruined when the inside of the house flooded. God willing, I'm sure that with a little patience and money, it will all be repaired or replaced.

I look over at Bambi and Fluffy, who are barking and growling at a frog leaping as fast as it can away from them, and I can't help but laugh.

Walking around my land is always an adventure. I never know when I'm going to encounter a snake, mother spider, or weird bug, which still freaks me out—but I've learned to give them their space, because if Hurricane Maria didn't destroy them—unless they are dangerous—I don't think I will either.

I love my home. I love my land. I even love having our aggressive little Bambi and hunter Fluffy. What happened to change my mindset about these? Hurricane Maria happened.

Hurricane Maria was a traumatizing event. I pray that we never experience anything like it ever again. It was catastrophic for many, but for me, it was a hardship that my Heavenly Father, and His Son, Jesus Christ, used to take me away from modern civilization and bring me to a simpler way of life that forced me to reflect on my past hardships, where I am now, what type of person God wants me to be, and the many blessings, and miracles I've received.

The hurricane's aftermath forced me to live new experiences and learn lessons I would never have lived or learned if we had not been hit with the devastating storm. It tested my survival skills, my faith, my health, and my patience.

I survived a disaster that many had not, and the only reason I survived was that I held on to my faith. If I hadn't, my anxiety and phobia symptoms could have escalated to the point of no return.

The experience gave me a new perspective on life. It taught me that in the blink of an eye, a natural disaster could take away everything, forcing us to live a life that we never imagined we would live—a life without communication and basic necessities.

After the hurricane, I did not pray for the modern necessities that I couldn't live without, like television, cell phone, Kindle, laptop and computer, vacuum cleaner, microwave, washing machine, and coffee maker—I prayed for water, food, and electricity—basic necessities that I used to take for granted.

I used to leave the faucet water running while I brushed my teeth—now that I know how precious water is—I turn it off when I'm not using it.

I used to leave the television on all morning while I did chores around the house because I liked to hear it on, even if I wasn't in the room—now I turn it off when I'm not watching it.

I used to be on the computer or watching television most of the day—now I take time to listen to a radio station, read, write, have a conversation, play cards, and board games, walk around my land and stay in touch with nature.

I still don't have internet, cable, or home phone service. I can honestly say that not being on the internet has brought my anxiety and stress levels down. I'm not saying I don't need it because, in this day and age, we need the internet to do so many transactions and research—what I'm saying is that I don't miss social media— I'm happier without it. I do miss watching television, and if our cable company does not restore our service soon—I'm thinking of getting satellite service.

As for cell phone service, the hurricane experience taught me that I could not continue to rely on the old fashion flip phone I've been using for the past fifteen years that doesn't even have internet. If I had upgraded to a new model and plan, I would have been able to reach my children, search the web, and watch the news shortly after the hurricane. I'm clueless about using a modern cell phone, but I'm getting one very soon.

I used to worry about Tony surviving without me. I spent my days thinking of all the different situations he might not be able to deal with alone and asking God for more time to prepare him to live independently. After watching how resilient he was during and after Hurricane Maria, and how he helped me through it all, despite his mental illness symptoms and high anxiety, I strongly believe that if he keeps taking his medication and holding on to Jesus, he will survive without me because our Heavenly Father, and His Son, Jesus Christ, will always be by his side.

I used to feel guilty for not being there for Alexander, Victoria, and my beautiful granddaughter Amber. I felt I had let them down when they needed me the most. I don't feel like that anymore because I believe that it was in God's plan for us to be separated so that they could experience all they have and walk the path God planned for them without Tony and I holding them back.

I used to feel very guilty for not being there for Rebecca, Ariel, and Simon, when they needed me the most. It broke my heart knowing that Rebecca was facing so many challenges with not one member of her family there to help support and hug her. It took a lot on my part to realize that it was also in God's plans for Rebecca and me to be apart so that she could face and deal with the challenges that will make her a stronger woman and mother and walk the path God has planned for her.

I believe with all my heart that my Heavenly Father, His Son, Jesus Christ, the Holy Spirit, Mary Mother of Jesus, Saint Jude, Saint Anthony, all God's saints, and guardian angels will always protect, guide, and take care of all my children and grandchildren always, just like they took care of me.

I lived my days thinking that a relationship with my mother was hopeless. I kept waiting for her to change. It took a devastating storm to teach me that God used my mother and her husband to help us. Regardless of their faults, I had to show them gratitude and respect because that is what God taught me was the correct attitude to have.

As I check for fire ant mounds and pick up objects that could be hazardous to our pets, the first line of a passage from the Bible comes to mind—"To every thing there is a season, and a time to every purpose under the heaven:"(Ecclesiastes 3:1 KJV)."

I can relate to this passage, for I can honestly say that my life has been a journey full of people, adventures, joys, and hardships, which God placed or allowed in my path to fulfill His plan for me—everything and everyone had a purpose in my life.

The people that came into my life, whether for a moment, a season, or a lifetime, whether to bring me pain or joy—all, were meant to be part of my story—just like I was meant to be part of theirs.

The events and adventures I lived, whether good, bad, scary, painful, spiritual, wondrous, unexpected, romantic, passionate, miraculous, exciting, or joyful—all were part of God's plan.

Even the hardships that I faced had a reason. Some taught me lessons. Some made me stronger. Some God used to test my faith. Some brought me closer to my Heavenly Father and His Son, Jesus Christ—and some, like being sexually, physically, and mentally abused when I was a child, or my son's mental illness, I will probably die without ever knowing the reasons.

I can honestly say that not one of my hardships could compare to when my children were sick or going through a hardship of their own. No pain or sorrow is worse than when a child or a grandchild suffers.

343

Some hardships were actually consequences of bad choices I made, which caused me to detour from God's plan for me. But it was just a detour because eventually, my Heavenly Father guided me back on the right path.

Many of the hardships I faced, my Heavenly Father allowed, because no matter how painful or devastating they were, if they had not existed, He would not have been able to use them to bless me with so many miracles.

Yes, my life has been an incredible journey, and walking with my Heavenly Father and His Son, Jesus Christ, has been a blessed adventure. They are the best that has happened to me. Without them, I would never have been able to survive all the turbulence in my life.

I lift up my eyes to a beautiful clear blue sky and smile content, not because my life has become easier, because it hasn't, but because I have made peace with my past, and because I'm confident that even though I cannot avoid the fury of the storms that unexpectedly turn my life upside down, I do have the power to face them with the shield of faith, strength, wisdom, and courage, that my Heavenly Father, and His Son, Jesus Christ, have blessed me with. There is no doubt in my mind that I can face anything when I put on the armor of God. It says so in the Bible…

Put on the whole armour of God, that ye may be able to stand against the wiles of the devil. For we wrestle not against flesh and blood, but against principalities, against powers, against the rulers of the darkness of this world, against spiritual wickedness in high places.

Wherefore take unto you the whole armour of God, that ye may be able to withstand in the evil day, and having done all, to stand. Stand therefore, having your loins girt about with truth, and having on the breastplate of righteousness; And your feet shod with the preparation of the gospel of peace;

Above all, taking the shield of faith, wherewith ye shall be able to quench all the fiery darts of the wicked. And take the helmet of salvation, and the sword of the Spirit, which is the word of God:

(Ephesians 6:11-17 KJV)

Life is not easy. It is full of challenges, hardships, and unexpected events that can knock you right off your feet. But, if you ask God, His Son, Jesus Christ, and the Holy Spirit, to give you the strength, courage, and wisdom that you need to deal with every tribulation—I promise you—they will not forsake you, and they will never give you more than you can handle.

It doesn't matter who you are, where you come from, or what you look like. If you have a personal relationship with Jesus, faith in our Heavenly Father, and unconditional belief and trust in them, your life will be filled with wonderful and amazing blessings.

God is the most powerful being in this universe. His Son, Jesus Christ, is the King of Kings. That makes you, and me, and all His children royalty. We are the Prince and Princess Warriors of the most powerful army in the Universe—an army made up of our Heavenly Father, His Son, Jesus Christ, the Holy Spirt, Mary Mother of Jesus, their saints, and all their guardian angels.

On earth, we will always be hit with hardships, challenges, sorrow, and evil attacks—but no matter how horrible they seem—remember this, our Heavenly Father and His Son, Jesus Christ, will always have your back. All you need to do is confess your sins, turn your life over to them, believe, have faith, love, and trust them unconditionally—that's all they ask of you.

When you walk with our Heavenly Father and His Son, Jesus Christ, not only will they have your back, but they guarantee eternal life by their side in their Kingdom.

Let me explain.

When we're born, we don't have the slightest clue how long we will live. The average life expectancy is close to seventy years. Some live longer. Some die younger. But no matter how long we live here on earth—it is not eternal. Life on earth is—temporary.

When we're young, seventy years seems like a very long time. We live in the moment without giving growing old and dying a second thought.

As we get older, we get caught up in a busy world. We work our butts off trying to give ourselves and our family a better life. We're so busy that most of the time, we run around like a chicken without a head, wishing to have more than twenty-four hours in the day to accomplish everything on our to-do list.

Sound familiar?

When was the last time you turned off your cell phone and other electronics and just sat outdoors looking at the sky or listening to birds chirping? When was the last time you smelled a rose? When was the last time you took five minutes to sit and speak to God?

Just like I did, I'm sure you too will answer, "I'm too busy. I'll relax and enjoy all that when I retire."

I have news for you. Life is short.

You cannot predict your death. You can leave your home in the morning and get hit by a bus. You can fall in the shower and die from a skull fracture. You can be trapped in your house during a tornado, hurricane, flood, fire, or earthquake and die. Your heart could stop while you're sleeping. Although not probable, the world could be hit with a horrible spreading disease that could kill you. Even if you live a long life, in a blink of an eye—you will be old—and, before you know it—you will be on your deathbed.

You planned and prepared for all the events in your life, including retirement. Did you plan for the most important event of your life—your eternal life?

You see, life does not end after death, and once we die, there are only two destinations—Heaven or Hell—and you can only go to one. Neither is temporary—both are eternal.

So, don't you think it makes sense to educate yourself on both destinations and then plan and prepare for the one you choose for eternity?

I don't know about you, but I'm doing everything I can to walk through the Golden Gates of Heaven. Hell is not my destination, and I pray it isn't yours either.

So, how do we secure a place in Heaven?

Read the Holy Bible, and you will find the answer. I'm serious. The Bible teaches us all about Heaven and Hell and how we will end up in one or the other.

The Bible says that if we turn our life over to God and Jesus, they promise to prepare a place in their Heavenly Kingdom for us to live eternally after death—a place where there is no pain, sorrow, or hardships—a place where evil does not exist, and evil soul snatchers cannot touch us.

I believe in this promise with all my heart, which is why I am not afraid of death. Yes, my loved ones will grieve when I am no longer physically here, but if they believe in this promise, they will not grieve for long because they know that I am happy and safe in my final home—where someday we will meet again.

Of all the miracles my Heavenly Father and His Son, Jesus Christ, have blessed me with—the promise of eternal life in heaven is the most awesome miracle of them all.

May our Heavenly Father, His Son, Jesus Christ, and the Holy Spirit bless you with the many miracles waiting to be showered upon you—all you have to do is have Faith, Trust, and Believe.